Photoshop® Elements For Dummies®

Cheat Sheet

Toolbox Shortcuts

Note: To access the tools, press the key(s) listed. If you uncheck the option Use Shift key for Tool Switch in your Preferences, you can eliminate the need to press the Shift key to change tools.

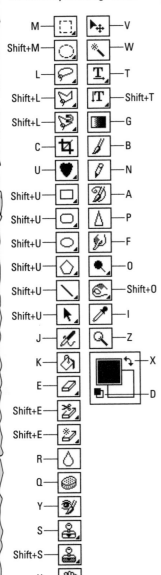

Fun with Selections

Selection	Windows	Mac
Fill selection with foreground color	Alt+Backspace	Option+Delete
Fill selection with background color	Ctrl+Backspace	⌘+Delete
Display Fill dialog box	Shift+Backspace	Shift+Delete
Cut selection	Ctrl+X	⌘+X
Copy selection	Ctrl+C	⌘+C
Paste image last cut or copied	Ctrl+V	⌘+V
Reapply last filter	Ctrl+F	⌘+F
Adjust levels	Ctrl+L	⌘+L
Free transform	Ctrl+T	⌘+T

Daily Activities

Selection	Windows	Mac
Cancel operation	Ctrl+period or Esc	⌘+period or Esc
Close image	Ctrl+W	⌘+W
General preferences	Ctrl+K	⌘+K
Display last preferences panel used	Ctrl+Alt+K	⌘+Option+K
Open image	Ctrl+O	⌘+O
Print image	Ctrl+P	⌘+P
Page setup	Ctrl+Shift+P	⌘+Shift+P
Quit Elements	Ctrl+Q	⌘+Q
Save image to disk	Ctrl+S	⌘+S
Save As	Ctrl+Shift+S	⌘+Shift+S
Save for Web	Ctrl+Alt+Shift+S	⌘+Option+Shift+S
Undo last operation	Ctrl+Alt+Z	⌘+Option+Z

Selection Tricks

Note: All selection tricks are performed with selection tools. (There's a shocker.)

Trick	Windows	Mac	Both Platforms
Draw straight lines	Alt+click with Lasso tool	Option+click with Lasso tool	
Add to selection outline			Shift+drag
Deselect specific area	Alt+drag		
Deselect all but intersected area	Shift+Alt+d		
Deselect entire image	Ctrl+D		
Reselect last selection	Ctrl+Shift+D	⌘+Shift+D	
Select everything	Ctrl+A	⌘+A	

Photoshop® Elements For Dummies®

Cheat Sheet

Navigation Tricks

Trick	Windows	Mac	Both
Scroll image			spacebar+drag
Zoom in	Ctrl+spacebar+click	⌘+spacebar+click	
Zoom in and change window size	Ctrl+plus	⌘+plus	
Zoom out	Alt+spacebar+click	Option+spacebar+click	
Zoom out and change window size	Ctrl+minus	⌘+minus	
Scroll up or down one screen			Page Up/Page Down
Scroll left or right	Ctrl+Page Up/Page Down	⌘+Page Up/Page Down	
Move to upper-left corner of image			Home
Move to lower-right corner of image			End
Zoom to 100%			Double-click on Zoom tool
Fit on Screen	Ctrl+0	⌘+0	

Layer Tricks

Selection	Windows	Mac
New layer	Ctrl+Shift+N	⌘+Shift+N
Clone selection to a new layer	Ctrl+J	⌘+J
Cut selection to a new layer	Ctrl+Shift+J	⌘+Shift+J
Change opacity of layer		1, . . . , 9, 0
Activate layer that contains specific image	Ctrl+click with Move tool	⌘+click with Move tool
Activate next layer up	Alt+]	Option+]
Activate next layer down	Alt+[	Option+[
Hide all layers but one	Alt+click on eyeball	Option+click on eyeball
Show all layers	Alt+click on eyeball	Option+click on eyeball
Select the contents of active layer	Ctrl+click on layer name in Layers palette	⌘+click on layer name in Layers palette

Copyright © 2002 Hungry Minds, Inc.
All rights reserved.

Cheat Sheet $2.95 value. Item 1636-1.

For more information about Hungry Minds,
call 1-800-762-2974.

Hungry Minds™

For Dummies: Bestselling Book Series for Beginners

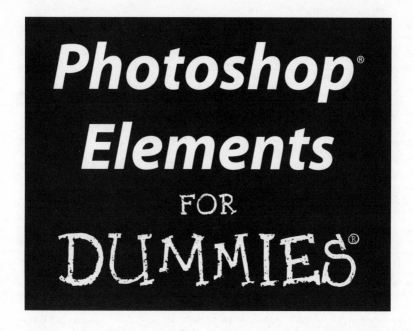

Photoshop® Elements FOR DUMMIES®

by Deke McClelland and Galen Fott

Hungry Minds™

Best-Selling Books • Digital Downloads • e-Books • Answer Networks • e-Newsletters • Branded Web Sites • e-Learning

New York, NY ◆ Cleveland, OH ◆ Indianapolis, IN

Photoshop® Elements For Dummies®

Published by
Hungry Minds, Inc.
909 Third Avenue
New York, NY 10022
www.hungryminds.com
www.dummies.com

Library of Congress Control Number: 2001097467

ISBN: 0-7645-1636-1

Printed in the United States of America

10 9 8 7 6 5 4 3 2 1

1B/QX/RS/QR/IN

Distributed in the United States by Hungry Minds, Inc.

Distributed by CDG Books Canada Inc. for Canada; by Transworld Publishers Limited in the United Kingdom; by IDG Norge Books for Norway; by IDG Sweden Books for Sweden; by IDG Books Australia Publishing Corporation Pty. Ltd. for Australia and New Zealand; by TransQuest Publishers Pte Ltd. for Singapore, Malaysia, Thailand, Indonesia, and Hong Kong; by Gotop Information Inc. for Taiwan; by ICG Muse, Inc. for Japan; by Intersoft for South Africa; by Eyrolles for France; by International Thomson Publishing for Germany, Austria and Switzerland; by Distribuidora Cuspide for Argentina; by LR International for Brazil; by Galileo Libros for Chile; by Ediciones ZETA S.C.R. Ltda. for Peru; by WS Computer Publishing Corporation, Inc., for the Philippines; by Contemporanea de Ediciones for Venezuela; by Express Computer Distributors for the Caribbean and West Indies; by Micronesia Media Distributor, Inc. for Micronesia; by Chips Computadoras S.A. de C.V. for Mexico; by Editorial Norma de Panama S.A. for Panama; by American Bookshops for Finland.

For general information on Hungry Minds' products and services, please contact our Customer Care Department within the U.S. at 800-762-2974, outside the U.S. at 317-572-3993 or fax 317-572-4002.

For sales inquiries and reseller information, including discounts, premium and bulk quantity sales, and foreign-language translations, please contact our Customer Care Department at 800-434-3422, fax 317-572-4002, or write to Hungry Minds, Inc., Attn: Customer Care Department, 10475 Crosspoint Boulevard, Indianapolis, IN 46256.

For information on licensing foreign or domestic rights, please contact our Sub-Rights Customer Care Department at 212-884-5000.

For information on using Hungry Minds' products and services in the classroom or for ordering examination copies, please contact our Educational Sales Department at 800-434-2086, or fax 317-572-4005.

For press review copies, author interviews, or other publicity information, please contact our Public Relations Department at 317-572-3168, or fax 317-572-4168.

For authorization to photocopy items for corporate, personal, or educational use, please contact Copyright Clearance Center, 222 Rosewood Drive, Danvers, MA 01923, or fax 978-750-4470.

Hungry Minds™ is a trademark of Hungry Minds, Inc.

About the Authors

Deke McClelland: Pioneering electronic publishing expert Deke is the author of *Macworld Photoshop 6 Bible* and *Photoshop 6 for Windows Bible* (both Hungry Minds, Inc.), which represent the best-selling guides of any kind on digital imaging. Having written more than 60 titles in 20 languages with 3 million copies in print, Deke is one of the most award-winning writers in the business, including a total of seven honors from the Computer Press Association. In addition to designing and editing a new visual learning series called *Look & Learn* (Hungry Minds, Inc.), Deke hosts the in-depth training videos *Total Photoshop, Total Illustrator,* and *Total GoLive* (all Total Training). He is a contributing editor for *Macworld* and *Photoshop User* magazines, and a member of the PhotoshopWorld Instructor Dream Team.

Galen Fott: Galen is Director of Online Training for Total Training Inc., makers of entertaining and enlightening video training for graphics software, and is an instructor in the *Total Premiere 6* series. Galen has presented over two hours of Photoshop training for the Apple Computer Web site, and he has also been a presenter for Adobe Systems. He is a regular reviewer for *Macworld* magazine and also wrote a feature for *Macworld* on digital video editing. In his theoretical spare time, Galen is involved in a number of other pursuits. As an animator, he has worked for clients such as AT&T and Paramount. As an actor, he has played leading roles in musicals across the country. And as a puppeteer, he has performed with the Jim Henson Company. Those with piqued interest can visit his somber Web site at www.grundoon.com.

Dedication

To Max and Burton: The future of digital imaging is in good (if grubby) hands.

And to Elizabeth and Laura: Whose good hands we're glad to be in.

Authors' Acknowledgments

The authors would like to thank Barbara Obermeier, Colleen Esterline, Brian Maffitt, Matt Wagner at Waterside Productions, Aya Taketomi at Adobe Systems, and the Corbis Corporation.

Publisher's Acknowledgments

We're proud of this book; please send us your comments through our Hungry Minds Online Registration Form located at www.dummies.com.

Some of the people who helped bring this book to market include the following:

Acquisitions, Editorial, and Media Development

Project Editor: Colleen Williams Esterline

Acquisitions Editor: Bob Woerner

Technical Editor: Geoff Schreiber

Editorial Manager, Freelance: Constance Carlisle

Senior Permissions Editor: Carmen Krikorian

Media Development Manager: Laura VanWinkle

Media Development Supervisor: Richard Graves

Editorial Assistant: Amanda Foxworth

Production

Project Coordinator: Regina Snyder

Layout and Graphics: Jill Piscitelli, Betty Schulte, Jacque Schneider, Julie Trippetti, Mary Virgin, Jeremey Unger, Erin Zeltner

Proofreaders: John Bitter, Linda Quigley, Susan Moritz, John Greenough

Indexer: TECHBOOKS Production Services

General and Administrative

Hungry Minds Technology Publishing Group: Richard Swadley, Senior Vice President and Publisher; Mary Bednarek, Vice President and Publisher, Networking; Walter R. Bruce III, Vice President and Publisher; Joseph Wikert, Vice President and Publisher, Web Development Group; Mary C. Corder, Editorial Director, Dummies Technology; Andy Cummings, Publishing Director, Dummies Technology; Barry Pruett, Publishing Director, Visual/Graphic Design

Hungry Minds Manufacturing: Ivor Parker, Vice President, Manufacturing

Hungry Minds Marketing: John Helmus, Assistant Vice President, Director of Marketing

Hungry Minds Production for Branded Press: Debbie Stailey, Production Director

Hungry Minds Sales: Michael Violano, Vice President, International Sales and Sub Rights

Contents at a Glance

Table of Contents

Introduction

• •

*H*ello, potential book-buying person. Please take this opportunity to make yourself comfortable. Have a seat on the little wooden stepstool there in the computer books section — or better yet, why not go plop yourself down in one of those comfy armchairs that are proliferating in bookstores these days. (Darn! That one was empty just a *second* ago!) Ah well, instead head over to the little bookstore café and have a beverage while you take a load off your feet. How about a nice tea? Lemon? Sure, why not. We want you to be perfectly comfortable while we tell you all about this book: *Photoshop For Dummies.*

Hey, wait a second . . .this is supposed to be *Photoshop **Elements** For Dummies!* What gives? (You quickly twirl the book around in your hands to check out the cover again, knocking over your tea, splashing it on the book, giving yourself a nasty paper cut, and getting lemon juice in it besides.) Ouch, that really smarts. But sure enough, that's what the cover says: *Photoshop Elements For Dummies.* Then why does it say *Photoshop For Dummies* in that last paragraph? A careless typo? A persistent hallucination? Or has there been a major foul-up in the Book Cover Wing of the Dummies Factories?

Okay, we'll come clean. (And hopefully this book will too, or you're buying it anyway.) Yes, this really is *Photoshop Elements For Dummies,* a book about Adobe's new program for correcting and modifying photographs on your computer screen. As you probably know, Adobe Photoshop Elements is an easier-to-use, scaled down version of Adobe Photoshop, a program legendary for its power and complexity. There are some distinct differences between the two applications; Photoshop Elements is missing some of Photoshop's high-end features, and it's got some exclusive tools of its own. But by and large, there's no escaping the fundamental truth in the following proclamation:

Photoshop Elements Is Photoshop

What exactly do we mean by that? Well, we don't mean that Elements isn't *any* easier to use than Photoshop; Elements has some truly helpful new features designed to lessen the learning curve. And we also don't mean that Elements doesn't need its own *For Dummies* book. (Perish the thought!) Here's what we mean: To get the most out of Photoshop Elements, you have to come to grips with the same complex concepts and tools that Photoshop uses. And if you've ever experimented with Photoshop, you know that isn't easy.

You want examples? We've got examples. First, take a gander at this Exceedingly Cute Cat photo:

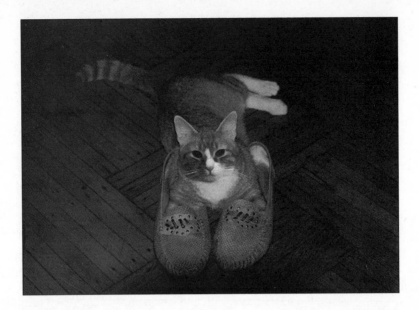

Exceedingly cute, huh? Maybe the photo's a little dark, but it can be fixed. Now, if you wanted to fix this somewhat dark photo with an image-editing application, and you saw a command called Brightness/Contrast, you'd be tempted to use it, wouldn't you? Heck, your TV's got brightness and contrast controls! And so do both Elements and Photoshop. Brightness/Contrast it is!

Terrible move. Brightness/Contrast is actually among the worst commands that either Photoshop or Elements has to offer. Sure, it's easy to use, but correcting photos on the computer is like many things in life: You get out of it what you put into it. Instead of Brightness/Contrast, what you should use to correct brightness — in either Photoshop or Photoshop Elements — is the Levels command. And here's the Levels dialog box when applied to the Exceedingly Cute Cat photo above:

Yikes! What the heck is that scary mountain range-looking thing? What do all those sliders and buttons do? And what does this monstrosity have to do with that Exceedingly Cute Cat?

Well, in truth Levels isn't really that difficult once you understand the concept it's based on, but we show it to you here to prove a point: Levels is a splendid tool for brightening up images, but it's hardly intuitive. And Levels is exactly the same in Elements as it is in Photoshop. If you think you would need help in learning Photoshop (and you would), you'll need help using Elements too.

And that's where this tea-stained book comes in.

About This Book

Before we tell you why you should buy this book, let's talk for a second about something you've already purchased: Photoshop Elements. (Incidentally, if by some twist of fate this book has ended up in your hands and you *don't* have Photoshop Elements, there's a free 30-day tryout version available for downloading from the Adobe Web site at `www.adobe.com/products/photoshopel/demoreg.html`.) When Adobe created Photoshop Elements, they started with Photoshop, took away some high-end professional features that you'd probably never use anyway, added some nifty new tools, and framed the whole thing in a user-friendly interface. The result is a program that boasts the majority of Photoshop's power — plus a couple of features that inspire Elements-envy in Photoshop users — for about one-sixth of Photoshop's price. Elements can give you professional results that are virtually identical to Photoshop — if you take the time to learn the fundamentals of how to use the program.

And since Elements' roots are in Photoshop, we hope you'll forgive us for feeling that we're particularly well suited to teach Elements to you. Deke has been using Photoshop since version 1.0 of the program was introduced and has gone on to become the best-selling author of *Photoshop For Dummies, Photoshop Bible,* and a bevy of other books on digital imaging. Galen, slacker that he is, didn't get with Photoshop until version 2.0 came out in 1991, but since then he's used it almost daily. It's the benchmark against which he's judged many other image-editing applications as a reviewer for *Macworld* magazine.

In this book, we set out to explain Photoshop Elements to you from the ground up, assuming that you know absolutely nothing about the program or even about image editing in general. (That, incidentally, is what's meant by the word "Dummies" in the title; we know you're not a Dummy about every topic. But the title *Photoshop Elements For Dummies About Photoshop Elements* was deemed to be lacking in elegance.) After a general introduction to image editing in Chapter 1, Chapter 2 digs in without much of an assumption that you've ever even used a computer before. Step by step, concept by concept, tool by tool, we gradually work through a thorough examination of Photoshop Elements and the incredible things it can do for your images.

Just as one CD contains both the Windows and Mac versions of Elements, so does this one book tell both Windows and Mac users everything they need to know to use Elements on their system of choice. You'll always find keyboard shortcuts given for both Windows and the Mac, the illustrations use both platforms, and where there are differences in system-level operations like printing, we deal with those individually.

As of this writing, Photoshop Elements doesn't run natively in the Mac's sleek new operating system, OS X. Until Adobe releases an OS X version, you can run Elements within OS X using Classic mode, or boot up in System 9.1 and go from there. If you're running Elements in Classic mode, note that the few portions of this book that deal specifically with the Mac operating system don't pertain to OS X.

What's in This Book

We've tried our best to organize the material in this book in logical order, with the lofty idea that you'd read it straight through from cover to cover. The first two parts in particular contain a whole lot of important stuff you ultimately need to know about how digital images on a computer "work" and how Elements works with them. But feel free to skip ahead or skip around if you get restless. All that info will still be there in the front of the book when you need it (and you will). The contents of this book are 100 percent guaranteed not to shift around from page to page or chapter to chapter for the lifetime of the book, or double your money back. There are even eight color pages stuck squarely in the middle of the book to show things about color that can't be explained in black and white.

To give you an overview of the kind of information you're likely to find in these pages, here's a quick rundown of the five parts.

Part 1: Element-ary School

We begin at the beginning, by answering the question "What exactly *is* image editing, anyway?" From there we get face-to-interface with Elements, exploring the array of tools and palettes it places on your screen. We talk about opening images, and then do a profile on the pixel, without which digital images wouldn't be. And while the last chapter is an examination of color, we hope it will be free of any purple prose.

Part 11: Be Prepared

This is the Part you'll skip because you're too eager to start cleaning up your photos, but you'll come back when you can't figure out what the heck is going on. It's perhaps not the most exciting stuff in the book, but it's vitally important. Chapter 6 tells you about how to save your files in the proper format. Chapter 7 tells you how to fix your mistakes and also how to print your images when there are no more mistakes to fix. Chapter 8 focuses on isolating parts of your pictures with selections, and Chapter 9 introduces the multi-leveled concept of layers.

Part 111: Realer than Life

This part of the book details how to take a bad image and make it better, or how to take a good image and make it great. In Chapter 10, we get down and dirty with the topic of cleaning up your images. In Chapter 11, we check out Elements' editing tools. Chapter 12 looks at Elements' powerful tools for brightening up your images — including that eagerly anticipated Levels command.

Part 1V: The Inspiration/Perspiration Equation

The last part was all about making images look better; this part begins with a chapter on how to make them look weirder, using Elements' many distorting capabilities. From there we start with a clean canvas and explore the subject of painting and coloring. From painting pictures, we move on to how to create a thousand words (or less) with Elements' Type tool. And we wrap up this part with a bang as we reveal some extraordinary tricks that Elements can do all on its own.

Part V: The Part of Tens

The Part of Tens is a Dummies tradition. You don't want to follow traditions? Don't read this part. But then you'll miss a few really neat Top Ten lists: Ten important techniques to remember that utilize the keyboard, ten ways to wreak havoc with people's faces, and finally, ten reasons you might possibly want to upgrade from Elements to Photoshop someday.

Icons Used in This Book

These *For Dummies* books have always gone out of their way to make learning easy for you. After the release of the very first *For Dummies* books, a scientific study revealed that while people were indeed learning great amounts from *For Dummies* books, others were distracted by a compulsive need to doodle in the margins. The publisher decided there was only one solution: Do the margin doodling themselves. And so the Dummies icon system was born. Over the years, the icons have taken on specific meanings, alerting you to the type of information the text might contain. Here are a few icons and their meanings:

You can pretty much bet there are going to be some eight- and nine-letter words in these sections. Technical Stuff is information that maybe isn't completely vital for you to know, but that can help enrich your understanding if you take a few minutes to wrap your brain around it.

This is the really good stuff. Generally, a Tip is a less-than-obvious technique for accomplishing the task at hand. Here's where you get to reap the benefits of our years of image-editing experience. Don't bother to thank us. It's our job. Oh, okay, you can go ahead and thank us.

Not that you should forget everything else, but these "Remember" sections contain particularly important points.

Okay, the worst thing that can happen to you when using Elements is that you'll lose a few hours of work. You're not going to find any warnings in this book that say "Clicking this command will make your laptop suddenly snap shut and break your fingers," or anything like that. But hey, lost work is no fun either.

Well, this is the stuff that's not really technical, or a tip, or particularly worth remembering, or a warning about anything. And yet it seemed somehow icon-worthy. So . . . it's gossip. So there.

Feedback, Please

Want to send us congratulations, compliments, or complaints? If so, you can visit Deke's Web site at www.dekemc.com and drop him a line, or stop by Galen's Web site at www.grundoon.com and e-mail him as well. We get a ton of e-mail, and unfortunately we can't respond to it all. But we do read it all, and especially appreciate suggestions for improving this book in its next edition.

You can also contact the publisher or authors of other *For Dummies* books by visiting the publisher's Web site at www.dummies.com, sending an e-mail to info@hungryminds.com, or sending paper mail to Hungry Minds, Inc., 10475 Crosspoint Boulevard, Indianapolis, IN 46256.

Part I
Element-ary
School

The 5th Wave By Rich Tennant

"Hey—let's put scanned photos of ourselves through a ripple filter and see if we can make ourselves look weird."

In this part . . .

*I*f just thinking about the name *Photoshop Elements* makes you feel as though you're about to drown in a sea of confusing concepts and terminology, consider this part of the book a life preserver thrown overboard with your name on it. (Yeah, life preservers usually have the name of the ship on them, but whatever.) Learning anything new can be intimidating, but we've set out to make the process just as painless as possible, starting with the very first chapter.

Speaking of that very first chapter, it seeks to answer the timeless question: "Just what exactly *is* Photoshop Elements, anyway?" We very slowly pick up steam in the next chapter; even if you're only vaguely acquainted with your own computer, you'll be fine. From there we look at the all-important topic of opening images and how to view them from different perspectives. Next, we take a penetrating look at that teeny tiny giant, the pixel. And finally, we teach you just enough about color theory to make you dangerous, yet to keep your colors Web-safe.

By the end of Chapter 5, you won't know everything there is to know about Elements — otherwise, we could have dispensed with the chapters that follow it — but you'll know enough to phrase a few intelligent questions. And please remember that as you read these chapters, there's no shame in being as yet uninformed. Millions of *For Dummies* readers would agree.

Chapter 1

Braving the Elements

• •

• •

As you know if you bothered to read the introduction to this book, Photoshop Elements is based on another Adobe application called simply "Photoshop." But you still might not be aware that Photoshop is (arguably) the most comprehensive and popular image editor around. In fact, there's probably not a single computer artist who doesn't use Photoshop almost daily, regardless of what other programs he or she may use. As an Elements user, you've got most of that professional power coiled up inside your computer, waiting for you to learn how to harness it.

You've probably at least seen, if not used, Elements and/or Photoshop, and it's likely you have a vague idea of what they're all about. But just so that we're all clear on the subject, the primary purpose of these applications is to make changes to photographic images that you've managed to get on disk, whether from a digital camera, a scanner, or a Photo CD.

If you've used Elements for only a week or so, you may have mistaken it for a fairly straightforward package. Certainly, on the surface of the program, Elements comes off as quite friendly. But lurking a few fathoms deep is another, darker program, one that is distinctly unfriendly for the uninitiated but wildly capable for the stout of heart. Sigmund Freud would no doubt declare Elements a classic case of a split personality. It's half man, half monster; half mild-mannered shoeshine boy, half blonde-grabbing, airplane-swatting King Kong; half kindly old gent with white whiskers chewing on a pipe, half green-gilled invader from another planet chewing on your . . . well, perhaps you don't want to know. In short, Elements has a Dr. Jekyll-and-Mr. Hyde thing going — only it's way scarier.

As you may recall from the last time you saw *Abbott and Costello Meet Dr. Jekyll and Mr. Hyde* — indisputably the foremost resource of information on this famous tale — this Jekyll character (not to be confused with the similarly named cartoon magpie) is normally your everyday, average, nice-guy scientist. Then one day, he drinks some potion or gets cut off in traffic or something and changes into his ornery alter ego, known at every dive bar in town by the surname Hyde. Elements behaves just the same way, except that no magical transformation is required to shift between the program's two halves. Both personalities — both "elements," if you will — coexist simultaneously in what you might call harmony.

This chapter explores in turn both sides of the Elements brain. (We'll leave the exploration of Abbott and Costello's brains for another book.) We'll also take a look at Elements' built-in Help features, which are the chief means of distinguishing Elements from its not-so-friendly big brother Photoshop.

The Bland but Benevolent Dr. Jekyll

To discover the benevolent Dr. Jekyll half of Photoshop Elements, you need look no further than the standard painting and editing tools. Shown in Figure 1-1, these tools are so simple, they're practically pastoral, like the kind of household appliances your great-grandmother would have been comfortable with. The Eraser erases, the Pencil draws hard-edged lines, the Airbrush sprays a fine mist of color, and so on. These incredibly straightforward tools attract new users just as surely as a light attracts miller moths.

Figure 1-1:
Many of
Elements'
tools have an
old-world,
rustic charm
that's sure to
warm the
cockles of the
most timid
technophobe.

But you quickly discover that, on their own, these tools aren't super-duper exciting, just like the boring Dr. Jekyll. They don't work much like their traditional counterparts — a line drawn with the Pencil tool, for example, doesn't look much like a line drawn with a real pencil — and they don't seem to be particularly applicable to the job of editing images. Generally speaking, you have to be blessed with pretty strong hand-eye coordination to achieve good results using these tools.

The Dynamic but Dastardly Mr. Hyde

When the standard paint and editing tools don't fit the bill, you try to adjust the performance of the tools and experiment with the other image controls of Elements. Unfortunately, that's when you discover the Mr. Hyde half of the program. You encounter options that have meaningless names such as Dissolve, Multiply, and Difference. Commands such as Image Size and Brightness/Contrast — both of which sound harmless enough — seem to damage your image. And clicking on icons frequently produces no result. It's enough to drive a reticent computer artist stark raving insane.

The net result is that many folks return broken and frustrated to the under-equipped and boring, but nonthreatening, painting and editing tools that they've come to know. It's sad, really. Especially when you consider all the wonderful things that the more complex Photoshop Elements' controls can do. Oh sure, the controls have weird names, and they may not respond as you think they should at first. But after you come to terms with these slick puppies, they perform in ways you wouldn't believe.

In fact, the dreaded Mr. Hyde side of Elements represents the core of this powerful program. Without its sinister half, Elements is just another rinky-dink piece of painting software whose most remarkable capability is keeping the kids out of mischief on a rainy day.

The Two Elements of Photoshop Elements

Generally speaking, the two halves of Photoshop Elements serve different purposes. The straightforward Jekyll tools concentrate mostly on *painting*, and the more complex Hyde capabilities are devoted to *image editing*. Therefore, to tackle this great program, you may find it helpful to understand the difference between the two terms.

Painting without the mess

Painting is just what it sounds like: You take a brush loaded with color and smear it all over your onscreen image. You can paint from scratch on a blank canvas, or you can paint directly on top of a photograph. The first option requires lots of talent, planning, and a few dashes of artistic genius; the second option requires an opposable thumb. Okay, that's a slight exaggeration — some lemurs have been known to have problems with the second option — but most people find painting on an existing image much easier than creating an image from scratch.

Notice in Figure 1-2 the rather drab fellow drinking a rather drab beverage. (Though you may guess this man to be Dr. Jekyll armed with the secret potion, most scholars consider it highly doubtful that Jekyll was this goofy. And in the recent Broadway musical, he certainly had way more hair.) We introduce this silly person solely to demonstrate the amazing functions of Elements.

Were you to paint on our unsuspecting saphead, you might arrive at something on the order of the image shown in Figure 1-3. All these changes were invoked using a single tool — the paintbrush — and just two colors — black and white. Suddenly, a singularly cool dude emerges. No planning or real talent was involved; it was just a matter of tracing over some existing details in the image. Better yet, the image isn't permanently damaged, as it would have been with a real-life paintbrush. Because the original image is saved to disk (as explained in Chapter 6), we can restore details from the original image at whim.

Figure 1-2: The unadorned "I Love My Libation" poster boy of 1948.

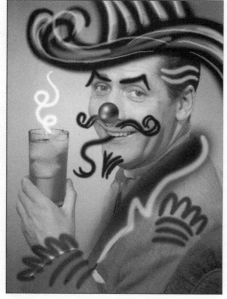

Figure 1-3:
A few
hundred
strokes
of the
paintbrush
result in a
party animal
to rival
Carmen
Miranda.

Editing existing image detail

The remade man in Figure 1-3 is the life of the party, but he's nothing compared to what he could be with the aid of some image editing. When you edit
an image, you distort and enhance its existing details. So rather than paint
with color, you paint with the image itself.

Figure 1-4 demonstrates what we mean. To achieve this grotesque turn of the
visual phrase, Deke indulged himself in a liberal amount of distortion. First,
he flipped the guy's head and stretched it a little bit. Well, actually, he
stretched it a lot. Then, he further exaggerated the eyes and mouth. He
rotated the arm and distorted the glass to make the glass meet the ear.
Finally, he cloned a background from a different image to cover up where the
head and arm used to be. The only thing he painted was the straw (the one
coming out of the guy's ear). Otherwise, he lifted every detail from one of two
photographs. (Meanwhile, Galen was drawing mustaches on pretty women in
magazines with a ballpoint pen.)

Mind you, you don't have to go quite so hog-wild with the image editing. If
you're a photographer, for example, you may not care to mess with your
work to the point that it becomes completely unrecognizable. Call you weird,
but you like reality the way you see it. Figure 1-5 shows a few subtle adjust-
ments that affect neither the form nor composition of the original image.
These changes merely accentuate details or downplay defects in the image.

Figure 1-4:
Image
editing has
no respect
for
composition,
form, or
underlying
skeletal
structure.

Figure 1-5:
You can
apply more
moderate
edits to your
image.

Just for the record, here are a few common ways to edit photographs in Elements:

- ✔ You can *sharpen* an image to make it appear in better focus, as in the first image in Figure 1-5. Generally, sharpening is used to account for focus problems in the scanning process, but you can sometimes sharpen a photograph that was shot out of focus.

- ✔ If you want to accentuate a foreground image, you can blur the focus of the background. The image on the right side of Figure 1-5 is an example.

- ✔ If a photograph is too light or too dark, you can fix it in a flash through the miracle of color correction. You can change the contrast, brighten or dim colors, and actually replace one color with another. Both of the images in Figure 1-5 have been color-corrected.

- ✔ Using Photoshop Elements' selection and move tools, you can grab a chunk of your image and physically move it around. You can also clone the selection, stretch it, rotate it, or copy it to a different image.

And that's only the tip of the iceberg. The book's remaining chapters explore Photoshop Elements as both a painting program and an image editor. Some chapters contain a little bit of information on both topics, with Part III pertaining to image editing in particular. But you'll find both aspects of Photoshop Elements' split personality flourishing inside this book, making it an ideal candidate for some big shot movie producer to come along and turn it into a fascinating psychological drama. Or maybe just a cheapie horror flick.

Psychiatric Help (The Doctor Is Built-in)

Poor Dr. Jekyll. He spent all his time trying in vain to mix together a drinkable antidote for that split personality problem of his, when all he needed was to seek help from another doctor — one of the *psychiatric* kind. Luckily, Photoshop Elements has seen the light, and the many built-in Help features that it puts at your disposal ensure that you'll never suffer by association with its split personality.

The Quick Start screen

Let's start with first things first — and the Quick Start screen is literally the very first thing you'll see once you've fired up Photoshop Elements. (Don't worry if you don't know how to start Photoshop Elements yet — we'll cover that thoroughly in the next chapter. If you feel lost, just smile and nod as you read, and come back to this section later. We'll understand.) As Figure 1-6 makes clear, the Quick Start screen gives you six options:

✔ **New:** Click here to start out with a pristine new canvas, just waiting for you to express yourself all over it. You'll be asked to specify some properties of the new canvas, but we'll get to those in the next few chapters.

✔ **Open:** Click here to work with an image already on your hard drive.

✔ **Paste:** If you've been working in another graphics application and have copied a selection to your computer's clipboard, this button creates a new document sized perfectly to fit your selection. This is the same thing as selecting File➪From Clipboard. Again, if this is all Greek to you (and you're not Greek), don't fret — we'll cover copying and pasting in Chapter 9.

✔ **Acquire:** Click here to start the process of bringing an image into your computer from a scanner or digital camera. Frankly, there are so many different scanners and cameras out there, each with its own quirks and oddities, that we can't possibly begin to explain this process for each and every device. But if you have a scanner or digital camera (and there's a good chance that your copy of Photoshop Elements came bundled with just such a device), then make sure you carefully read the manual that came with the device. The company's Web site can be another great place to turn to for help, as well as an easy source for downloading updated software for your device. And the Photoshop Elements manual that came with the program has a surprising amount of helpful information as well.

✔ **Tutorial:** Click here and Photoshop Elements will fire up a Web browser and direct you to three interactive tutorials for working with layers, using Photoshop Elements' Photomerge command, and creating animated GIFs to liven up your Web site. Another place to look for Photoshop Elements tips and tutorials is, naturally, on the Adobe Web site at www.adobe.com/products/tips/photoshopel.html. Tell them we sent you.

✔ **Help:** Just as with the Tutorial button, click here and Photoshop Elements will automatically launch a Web browser. But this time it will be filled with the Help documentation that came with Elements. This is very convenient if you don't have the printed manual around — and often this online Help contains last-minute changes that didn't make it into the printed manual. There's also a link to this documentation in the Shortcuts bar — it's the icon that looks like a question mark.

Okay, actually there are two more buttons in this window — the Close button (we trust you can figure that one out) and the "Show this screen at startup" button. Click on the checkmark for the latter to deactivate the feature and you'll receive a thoughtful reminder that this screen can be turned on again by choosing Show Quick Start under the Window menu. That's the great thing about Elements' Help features: They're there when you need them, but they happily stay just out of sight when you don't need them.

Figure 1-6:
The Quick
Start screen
helps get
your
Elements
work
session off
to a, well,
quick start.

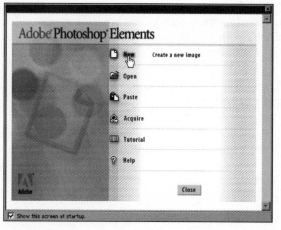

The Hints palette

So you launch Elements, click the Close button on the Quick Start screen, and leave your mouse cursor floating right in the middle of your desktop, hovering over nothing. One of the three windows already open by default is the Hints palette, captured in all its splendor in Figure 1-7. And what is this supposedly helpful Hints palette doing? It's giving hints about *itself,* bragging about how it can provide "helpful descriptions for using tools and palettes." Just what we needed — a self-referential tool. Next thing you know, the Pencil tool will start drawing little pencils, and the Hand tool will start making shadow puppets on your desktop.

Figure 1-7:
You can visit
the Hints
palette
anytime you
need a clue
about a tool
or palette.

But speaking of that Hand tool, move your cursor over to the left until it's hovering over the Hand tool. And now take a look at that Hints palette: It's telling you about the Hand tool! And that's the beauty of the Hints palette, folks. It gives you an instant and concise description of Elements' many tools and palettes.

But what if your thirst for knowledge isn't quenched, and you want to know more about the mighty Hand tool? Just click the tool to activate it, then move over to the Hints palette and click the More Help button. You'll be automatically linked to the Help documentation page for that tool.

The Recipes palette

If the thought of a Recipes palette makes you hungry, then put down this book, make yourself a sandwich, eat it, and then come back to us when you're finished (but please wipe your hands first). The Recipes palette can't help you remember how to make your Great Aunt Naomi's famous Porcupine Meatloaf, but it is a big help where Photoshop Elements is concerned.

In the Recipes palette, you'll find 31 image-editing recipes divided into 5 different categories. Say, for instance, you want to remove an ugly yellow cast from a cherished photo of your Great Aunt Naomi with a face full of porcupine quills. Click on the Recipes palette tab in the palette well at the upper-right corner of the screen. Under the Select a Recipe menu, choose Color Correction, and then click on Remove a Color Cast from the list. All you have to do now is follow along with the step-by-step instructions — but Elements makes it easier yet.

Any time you see a Play button like the one visible in Figure 1-8, you can click it and Elements will automatically bring up the appropriate command or tool for you. (You have to actually have an image open for this to work.) And to move back to the current category, just click the Home button.

Play

Figure 1-8: The Play button in the Recipes palette can save you precious time otherwise spent rooting around in menus.

But wait — there's more. At the bottom of the Select a Recipe menu, there's a lone command called Download New Recipes. Choose that command, and sure enough, Elements will go online (provided you have an Internet connection, of course) and fetch some new recipes from the Adobe Web site. At press time for this book, there were new recipes available for restoring faded photos, working with the Variations command, and several others. Check back frequently for updates. Those folks in the Adobe kitchens never rest.

Chapter 2

Dissecting Your Desktop

· ·

· ·

*I*f you're brand new to Photoshop Elements — or to computers in general — this is the chapter for you. You get the basic stuff you need to know before you can begin using the program to distort the faces of all your family members.

Even if you're already familiar with the basic interface of Elements, you might want to give this chapter a once-over to make sure we're all speaking the same language. Here, we can calibrate brains, so to speak.

Giving Elements the Electronic Breath of Life

Before you can use Elements, you have to start up — or launch — the program. Here's how:

1. **Start your computer.**

   Mac users: After you reach the Finder, proceed to Step 3.

2. **PC users: Click on the Windows Start button.**

3. PC users: Choose P̲rograms⇨Adobe in the Start menu.

A submenu appears, listing all your Adobe programs.

If you can't seem to locate Elements on your system, choose F̲ind⇨F̲iles or Folders in the Start menu. Type Photoshop Elements in the N̲amed field and select My Computer from the L̲ook-in pop-up menu. Click the F̲ind Now button. A list appears with all files and folders containing the words *Photoshop Elements.* Locate the program icon and double-click to launch the program directly from this list.

Mac users: Locate and activate the Adobe Photoshop Elements folder.

Use the mouse to move the arrow-shaped cursor over the icon and press the mouse button. Then choose FileOpen from the menu bar or press ⌘+O. A window labeled Adobe Photoshop Elements opens, containing an icon featuring an eye, and some other icons. You can open the Adobe Photoshop Elements folder by using a couple of shortcuts. Either double-click — press the mouse button twice in rapid-fire succession — on the folder icon or press ⌘+↓.

If you're not sure where Elements is located on your hard drive, choose File⇨Find from the menu bar (or press ⌘+F). Then type the words **Photoshop Elements** and press the Return key. A list appears with all files containing the words *Photoshop Elements.* Locate the program icon and double-click to launch the program directly from this list. If you still can't find the program, cry in anguish and beat your monitor with something soft and squishy.

4. PC users: Choose Photoshop Elements, and then Adobe Photoshop Elements.

Mac users: Double-click on the Adobe Photoshop Elements icon in the Adobe Photoshop Elements window.

Adobe Photoshop Elements is the greenish item that uses the eyeball and the colored circles as its icon.

5. Hope it works.

If you see the Elements splash screen — a kind of billboard that features a smiling lady peering through a Web browser with a digital camera at her side, along with some copyright information — you're in business. If your computer complains that it doesn't have enough memory to open Elements, check out the sidebar, "Why does Elements give your computer amnesia?" later in this chapter. If you see some equally discouraging message, scream loudly and hope that the resident computer expert is in close proximity. You need help. Check out the Elements manual or Adobe's Web site, or phone technical support.

Product Registration Locations

The labels on this sheet represent the worldwide locations designated to process Adobe product registration cards. Please choose the label nearest your location, place it on your registration card, affix the required postage, and then mail it.

Argentina
TNT Express Worldwide
JFK/SEA/781804
Casilla 64
1420 Sucursal 20
Buenos Aires
Argentina

Australia
TNT Mailfast
JFK/SEA/793150
Private Bag 5
Mascot
NSW 2020
Australia

Brasil
TNT Express Worldwide
JFK/SEA/781803
Caixa Postal 18 080
Aeroporto de Congonhas
São Paulo 04699-970
Brasil

Chile
TNT Express Worldwide
JFK/SEA/781792
Casilla 3797
Correo 21
Santiago
Chile

Colombia
Mailfast
JFK/SEA/781801
Apartado Aereo 95-444
Calle 64A No. 94-49, Alamos
Santa Fé de Bogota
Colombia

Europe
Product Registration
Adobe Systems Europe, Ltd.
P.O. Box 12354
Edinburgh EH11 0NR
Scotland, United Kingdom

Hong Kong, Peoples' Republic of China
TNT Express Worldwide
(H.K.) Ltd.
P.O. Box 98682
JFK/SEA/781794
Tsim Sha Tsui Post Office
Kowloon, Hong Kong

India
TNT Express Worldwide (India)
Limited
JFK/SEA/830048
P.O. Box No. 271
Bangalore, 560 052
India

Indonesia
Untuk Diserahkan Kepada
P.T. Skypak International
Summitmas Tower
JI, Jenderal Sudirman Kav. 61-62
P.O. Box 4019/JKT 10001
JFK/SEA/846360
Indonesia

Korea
TNT Express Worldwide
JFK/SEA/781800
P.O. Box 2
Yang Chun Post Office
Seoul
South Korea

Japan
Adobe Systems Co., Ltd.
User Registration Dept.
4F, Green Tower Bldg.
6-14-1 Nishi Shinjyuku
Shinjyuku-ku, Tokyo 160-0023
Japan

Malaysia
TNT Economy Courier
JFK/SEA/793152
Peti Surat No. 8087
Pejabat Pos Kelana Jaya
46781 Petaling Jaya
Malaysia

México
Skymex S.A. de C.V.
JFK/SEA/781795
P.O. Box 9-238
Administración de Correos Num. 9
15100 México, D.F.
México

New Zealand
TNT Mailfast
JFK/SEA/781797
P.O. Box 9111
Newmarket
Auckland
New Zealand

1	0	0	0	2	7

北京 100027 #10 信箱

TNT SKYPAK SINOTRANS
JFK/SEA/781793

Philippines
TNT Express Worldwide
P.O. Box 420
Pasay Central Post Office
JFK/SEA/846196
Pasay City 1300
Philippines

Singapore
TNT Express Worldwide
JFK/SEA/781798
Singapore Post Centre Post Office
P.O. Box 258
Singapore 914009

South Africa
TNT Mailfast
P.O. Box 39
JFK/SEA/865487
Isando
1600
Gauteng
South Africa

Taiwan
TNT Lite Docs
P.O. Box 87-801
JFK/SEA/781799
Taipei
Taiwan, R.O.C.

Thailand
TNT Express Worldwide
JFK/SEA/793151
MBE (Surawong) #245
167/1 Surawongse Road
Suriyawongse Bangrak
Bangkok 10500
Thailand

U.A.E.
JFK/SEA/865486

Mailfast
P.O. Box 15321
Dubai
U.A.E.

United States and Canada
Product Registration
Adobe Systems Incorporated
P.O. Box 34005
Seattle, WA 98124-9860
United States of America

Venezuela
TNT Express Worldwide
JFK/SEA/781805
Apartado Interno No. 10
Oficina Postal Telegráfica de
San Martin, Caracas
Venezuela

After your computer stops making little shicka-shicka noises and your screen settles down, you'll see the Elements Quick Start screen, which we covered in the last chapter. Go ahead and click the Close button for now, and you'll see the basic Elements interface, as shown in Figures 2-1 and 2-2. We cover the various elements of the interface later in this chapter.

Don't freak out and start running around the room in a frenzy if you're a little fuzzy on the meaning of *menu, dialog box,* and a few other terms. We cover all this stuff in fairly hefty detail in this very same chapter.

Note: As you read, you'll see that you can also use the keyboard and mouse in tandem. For example, in Elements, you can draw a perfectly horizontal line by pressing the Shift key while dragging with the Pencil tool. Or you can press Alt (Option on a Mac) and click on the Rectangular Marquee tool in the upper-left corner of the Toolbox to switch to the Elliptical Marquee tool. Such actions are so common that you often see key and mouse combinations joined into compound verbs, such as Shift+drag or Control-click.

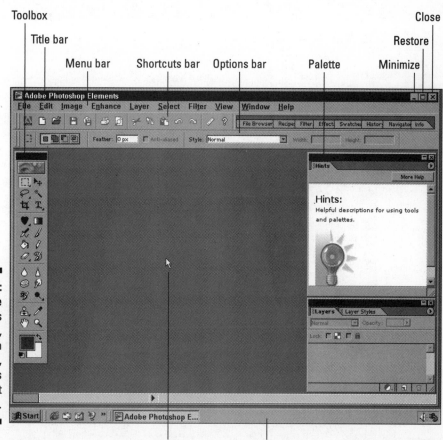

Figure 2-1: The Elements interface, shown in Windows, makes its first appearance.

Why does Elements give your computer amnesia?

If your computer says it's out of memory, it just means that a part of the machine is filled to capacity. Memory — known in computer dweeb circles as *RAM* (random-access memory, pronounced *ram,* like the sheep) — allows your computer to run programs. Elements needs lots of RAM — this version requires you to have a minimum of 64MB in your computer and prefers that you have even more. If you can't launch Elements because of a memory error, you have three options:

✔ Free up RAM by quitting all other programs that are currently running.

✔ PC users: Restart your computer by choosing the Shut Down command from the Windows Start menu and then choosing the Restart the Computer option. After your computer restarts, try to launch Elements again.

Mac users: Restart the computer by choosing Special⇨Restart at the Finder and try to launch Elements after the Finder reappears.

✔ Buy and install more RAM.

If you've never tried to upgrade the RAM in your machine, seek out expert advice from your local computer guru.

Menu bar   Cursor

Toolbox   Shortcuts bar   Options bar   Palette   Application menu

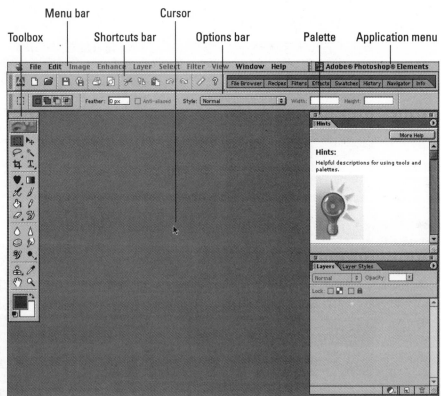

Figure 2-2:
The
Elements
interface,
shown on a
Mac.

Working with Windows

This section is relevant to PC users only. Mac people skip down to the "Switching between Elements and the Finder" section below. In Elements, as in most other Windows programs, you have two kinds of windows: the program window, which contains the main Elements work area, and image windows, which contain any images that you create or edit. To see the program window, refer to Figure 2-1; for a look at image windows, see Chapter 3.

Elements windows — both program and image — contain the same basic elements as those in other Windows programs. But just in case you need a refresher or you're new to this whole computing business, here's how the Elements program window works with Windows:

- Windows users can click on the Close button in the upper-right corner of the window to shut down Elements. If you have open images that haven't been saved, the program prompts you to save them. (For details on saving images, see Chapter 6.) The quickest way to close your program window (and Elements) is to press the keyboard shortcut for the Exit command, Ctrl+Q (as in Quit).

- Click on the Minimize button (refer to Figure 2-1) to reduce the program window to a button on the Windows taskbar. To redisplay the program window, just click on the taskbar button.

- You can also use the taskbar buttons to switch between Elements and other running programs. In the taskbar, just click on the button of the program you want to use.

- The appearance of the Restore/Maximize button changes depending on the current status of the window. If you see two boxes on the button, the button is the Restore button. Click on this button to shrink the window so that you can see other open program windows. You can then resize the window by placing your mouse cursor over a corner of the window until you see a double-headed arrow. When you see the arrow, drag the window to resize it. To move the window around, drag its title bar.

- After you click on the Restore button, it changes to the Maximize button, which looks like a single box. Click on the button to zoom the program window so that it consumes your entire screen. After the window zooms, the button changes back to the Restore button. Click on the button to restore your screen to its former size.

Switching between Elements and the Finder

In back of the myriad components of the Elements interface, you Mac users can probably see the icons and open windows from the Finder. (These are hidden in Figure 2-2 just to make the picture less confusing.) If you click on a Finder window or on the desktop, you're taken back to the Finder, and the Elements Toolbox and palettes disappear. If you have an image open, however, the image window remains visible. Here are some tips to help you manage working between the Finder and Elements:

- If you inadvertently click yourself out of Elements, choose Adobe Photoshop Elements from the list of running programs in the Applications menu, which is on the far-right side of the menu bar (refer to Figure 2-2), or just click on the Elements image window. The Toolbox and palettes return to the screen to show you that Elements is back in the game.

- You may be wondering why this program switching happens. The Finder is a piece of software, just like Elements. The only difference is that the Finder has to be running the entire time you use your Mac. This means that all the time you're using Elements, the Finder is working away in the background. When you click on the desktop or some other Finder element, the Finder comes to the foreground, and Elements goes to the background. But both programs continue to operate until you quit Elements or shut down your computer.

- If the clutter from the Finder gets too distracting when you're using Elements, choose the Hide Others command from the Applications menu to hide every Finder element except the icons.

- You can hide the icons by choosing Apple⇨Control Panels⇨General Controls. (If you don't know how to choose things from menus, see the section, "Maneuvering through Menus," later in this chapter.) Inside the General Controls dialog box, click on the Show Desktop When in Background check box to deselect it. Then close the dialog box. Bye-bye go the icons. (Note that you can't click on the background to switch to the Finder if you choose this option; you have to use the Applications menu to switch between programs.)

- Remember that you can always tell where you are just by looking at the Applications menu in the upper-right corner of your screen. It always shows a miniature version of the foreground program icon, if not also the name of the application. If you're at the Finder, the icon is a little smiley face. If the icon is an eyeball, you know you're in Elements. Other icons vary. A little W means Microsoft Word. A little X means Excel. A little Krusty the Clown means Bart Simpson has been using your computer (you lucky devil, you).

Maneuvering through Menus

As do all Windows and Macintosh programs, Elements sports a menu bar (refer to Figures 2-1 and 2-2) at the top of its window desktop. Beneath that menu bar, though, are two things many other programs don't have: a Shortcuts bar and an Options bar. The Shortcuts bar is a handy way to perform many common functions with just a single click of the mouse. It also features the palette well, a convenient place for placing palettes you don't need at the moment. The Options bar gives you additional control over the tool you currently have selected. Both of these bars can be repositioned by clicking the handle on the left side and dragging to another location. And if you ever want to reset the options in the Options bar, click the tool icon on the far left of the bar and choose Reset Tool to reset the options for that particular tool, or Reset All Tools to return them all to their default settings. We'll make frequent visits to both the Options bar and the Shortcuts bar when appropriate in the book; for now, let's belly up to that menu bar.

Each word in the menu bar — File, Edit, Image, and so on — represents a menu. A *menu* is simply a list of commands that you can use to open and close images, manipulate selected portions of a photograph, hide and display palettes, and initiate all kinds of mind-boggling, sophisticated procedures.

We explain the most essential Photoshop Elements commands throughout this book. But before we send you off to cope with a single one of them, here's a bit of background information on how to work with menus:

✔ To choose a command from a menu, click on the menu name and then click on the command name. Or you can press and hold the menu name, drag down to the command name, and release the mouse button at the desired command.

✔ Some commands bring up additional menus called *submenus.* For example, if you choose File⇨Automate, you display a submenu offering still more commands. If we ask you to choose File⇨Automate⇨Batch, you choose the Automate command under the File menu to display the submenu and then choose the Batch command from the submenu, all in one beautiful continuous movement. When you do it just right, it's like something out of Swan Lake.

✔ Did you notice those underlined letters in some of the commands in the preceding paragraph? Those letters are called *hot keys.* If you prefer using the keyboard rather than the mouse, and you're using a PC, you can press hot keys in combination with the Alt key to choose a command. For example, to display the File menu, press Alt+F. Then to choose the Automate command from the File menu, press U — no Alt key needed this time. You can also use hot keys to access options inside dialog boxes (we explain dialog boxes later in the section, "Talking Back to Dialog Boxes").

TIP

In addition to using hot keys, you can access some commands by pressing keyboard shortcuts. For example, to initiate the File⇨Open command, you can press the keyboard shortcut Ctrl+O (⌘+O on a Mac) — that is, press and hold the Ctrl key (⌘ key on a Mac), press the O key, and then release both keys.

✔ Some keyboard equivalents select tools, and some perform other functions. Either way, we keep you apprised of them throughout this book. If you take the time to memorize a few keyboard shortcuts here and there, you can save yourself a heck of a lot of time and effort. (For the most essential shortcuts, read Chapter 18. Also, tear out the Cheat Sheet at the front of this book, and tape it up somewhere within easy ogling distance.)

✔ Elements offers you yet another way to access some commands. If you right-click (Control-click on a Mac) inside an image window, you display a context-sensitive menu. In nongeek-speak, a context-sensitive menu, also known as a shortcut menu, is a mini-menu that contains commands that are related to the current tool, palette, or image, as shown in Figure 2-3.

Figure 2-3:
Right-click
(Control-
click on a
Mac) inside
the image
window to
access
context-
sensitive
menus.

Talking Back to Dialog Boxes

Elements reacts immediately to some menu commands. But for other commands, the program requires you to fill out a few forms before it processes your request. If you see an ellipsis (three dots, like so . . .) next to a command name, that's your clue that you're about to see such a form, known in computer clubs everywhere as a *dialog box*.

Figure 2-4 shows a sample dialog box. As the figure demonstrates, dialog boxes can contain several basic kinds of options. The options work as follows:

✔ A box in which you can enter numbers or text is called an *option box*. Double-click or click and drag in an option box to highlight its contents and then replace the contents by entering new stuff from the keyboard.

✔ Some option boxes come with *slider bars*. Drag the triangular slider to the left or right to lower or raise the associated numerical value. (All without hydraulics, mind you.)

Title bar   Drop-down menu   Close button

Slider bar   Option box   Button

Figure 2-4:
The
anatomy of
the dialog
box.

Check box

✔ You can select only one circular *radio button* (not shown in the figure) from any gang of radio buttons. To select a radio button, click on the button or on the option name that follows it. A black dot fills the selected radio button; all deselected radio buttons are hollow.

✔ Although you can select only one radio button at a time, you can usually select as many *check boxes* as you want. Really, go nuts. To select a check box, click on the box or on the option name that follows it. A check fills the box to show that it's selected. Clicking on a selected check box turns off the option.

✔ To conserve space, some multiple-choice options appear as *drop-down menus*. Click on the menu to display the option choices. Then click on the desired option in the menu to choose it, just as if you were choosing a command from a standard menu. As with radio buttons, you can select only one option at a time from a drop-down menu.

✔ Not to be confused with the radio button, the normal, everyday variety of *button* enables you to close the current dialog box or display others. For example, click on the Cancel button to close the dialog box and cancel the command. Click on OK to close the dialog box and execute the command according to the current settings. Clicking on a button with an ellipsis (such as Load. . . or Save. . .) displays yet another dialog box.

As you can with menus, you can select options and perform other feats of magic inside dialog boxes from the keyboard. The following shortcuts work in most dialog boxes:

- ✔ To advance from one option box to the next, press the Tab key. To back up, press Shift+Tab.

- ✔ PC users can also move from option to option by using the hot keys (those underlined letters in the option names). Press Alt+an option's hot key to move to that option.

- ✔ Press Enter (Return on a Mac) to select the button surrounded by a heavy outline (such as the OK button in Figure 2-4). Press Esc to select the Cancel button.

- ✔ Press ↑ to raise an option box value by one; press ↓ to decrease the value by one. Pressing Shift+↑ and Shift+↓ raise and lower the value by ten, respectively.

- ✔ If you change your mind about choices you make in a dialog box, you can quickly return things to the settings that were in force when you opened the dialog box. In most dialog boxes, pressing the Alt key (Option key on a Mac) magically changes the Cancel button to a Reset button. Click on the Reset button to bring back the original values.

If a dialog box gets in the way of your view of an image, you can reposition the box by dragging its title bar.

Playing Around with Palettes

Elements offers free-floating *palettes* that you can leave onscreen or put away at whim. The palettes, which are basically dialog boxes that can remain onscreen while you work, provide access to options that change the appearance of images and otherwise assist you in your editing adventures. We cover the specifics of using the palettes in chapters to come, but here's a brief introductory tour of how palettes work:

- ✔ What may look like just one palette can actually be a collection of palettes sharing the same palette window. For example, the Layers and Layer Styles palettes are housed in the same palette window (refer to Figure 2-5). To switch to a different palette in a palette window, click on its tab.

- ✔ When palettes are unwanted, they go hang out and sulk in the palette well, that dark gray area on the right side of the Shortcuts bar. You can always see their little tabbed heads sticking out of the well. If you find yourself wanting to see one of them again, just click on the tab. And if you think you'll need to keep the palette around for a while, drag it out of the well by the tab. You'll make its day.

✔ Click on the Close box to send the palette up to the palette well. In Windows, the Close box is on the far right of the palette's title bar; on the Mac, it's on the left side of the title bar. To hide and show palettes, you can also use the commands available under the Window menu.

✔ Press Tab to hide or display the currently open palettes, the Toolbox, the Shortcuts bar, the Options bar, and (in Windows only) the Status bar, which is covered in Chapter 3. Press Shift+Tab if you want to hide or display just the palettes, but leave the Toolbox, Shortcuts bar, Options bar, and Status bar as is. (Note that this trick doesn't work if the cursor is blinking inside the Layers palette's Opacity option box.)

Figure 2-5:
The many parts of a healthy palette.

✔ Some palettes have keyboard shortcuts you can use to hide and display them: F5 for the File Browser, F6 for the Recipes palette, F7 for the Filters palette, F8 for the Effects palette, F9 for the Layer Styles palette, F10 for the History palette, F11 for the Layers palette, and F12 for the Hints palette.

✔ Some palettes contain icons, just like the Toolbox does. Click on an icon to perform a function, such as adding or deleting a layer.

✔ Drag the title bar at the top of the palette to move the palette around onscreen.

✔ Shift+click on a title bar to snap the palette to the nearest corner of the screen. For example, if the palette is near the upper-right corner of the screen, Shift+clicking on its title bar moves it all the way into the corner, giving you more space to view your image onscreen.

✔ Every palette except the Info palette has a size box, as labeled in Figure 2-5. Drag the size box to resize the palette.

✔ Click on the collapse box (the zoom box on a Mac) to shrink the palette so that only the most essential options at the top of the palette are visible. It may take one or two clicks to get this to happen, depending on the palette. Click on the collapse box (zoom box on a Mac) again to bring all of the palette options into full view.

✔ Alt+click on the collapse box (Option+click on the zoom box on a Mac) to hide all but the title bar and the palette tabs. You can also double-click on a palette tab. The advantage is that you can access the palette again without having to drag it out of the palette well.

✔ You can combine multiple palettes into a single palette window by dragging a tab from one palette into another. You can also break any palette into its own window by dragging the palette tab out of the current window, as shown in Figure 2-6.

✔ You can also dock palettes vertically. Drop the tab at the bottom or top of another palette to stack two palettes.

✔ Press and hold on the right-pointing arrowhead on the right side of the palette, just below the title bar, to display the palette menu. Here's yet another hiding place for commands.

✔ If you get your palettes in an unbearable muddle, you can always restore things to the way they were when you first launched Elements by choosing <u>W</u>indow⇨Reset Palette Locations.

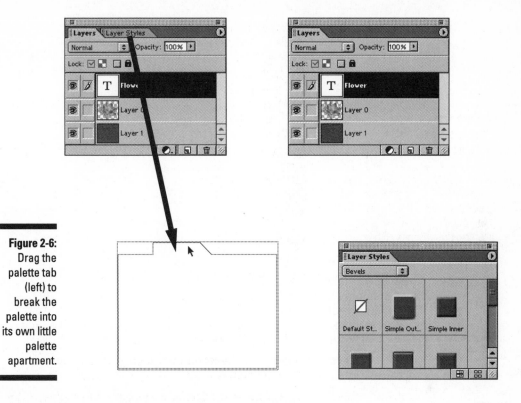

Figure 2-6:
Drag the
palette tab
(left) to
break the
palette into
its own little
palette
apartment.

Opening Up Your Toolbox

You're ready to move on to the tempestuous world of the Toolbox. As shown in Figure 2-7, the items in the Toolbox fall into two basic categories — tools and color controls. Future chapters explain in detail how to use the various gizmos in the Toolbox, but here's a basic overview of what's in store:

✔ The top four sections of the Toolbox (refer to Figure 2-7) are devoted to an assortment of tools that you can use to edit images, just as you might use an assortment of pencils and markers to draw a picture. To select one of these tools, click on its icon. Then use the tool by clicking or dragging it inside your image.

✔ A tiny, right-pointing triangle in the bottom-right corner of a tool icon indicates that more tools are hidden behind that icon on a flyout menu. To display the flyout menu and reveal the hidden tools, press and hold the mouse button on the icon. Drag over and down the column of tools until your cursor is hovering over the tool you want to use and then release the mouse button.

Figure 2-7:
Select a tool
or use a
color
control by
clicking on it
or by
pressing the
keys listed
here.

✔ You can also Alt+click (Option+click on a Mac) on a tool icon to cycle through all the tools hidden beneath it.

✔ The bottom section of the Toolbox contains color selection options. These icons respond immediately when you click on them.

✔ If you've been clicking away on the Toolbox icons and haven't seen any results, don't panic. Your copy of Elements isn't broken; the icons just don't do anything unless you have an image open. To find out how to open images, see Chapter 3.

✔ Actually, one of the icons in the Toolbox does do something with no image onscreen. If you click on the very top icon in the Toolbox — the one with the eyeball and colored circles — you bring up the Adobe Online dialog window. If you have access to the Internet, Adobe Online can give you access to tons of great info, such as new Recipes, tips, tech support, upgrades, and news on products and events.

✔ You can also access all the tools and two of the color controls from the keyboard. For example, to select the Dodge tool, you just press the letter O key. To select the Burn tool, which shares the flyout menu with the Dodge tool, you press Shift+O. Figure 2-7 shows other keyboard equivalents.

✔ If pressing the Shift key with the keyboard letter to access the tools on the flyout menu is just too strenuous, Elements gives you a solution. Choose Edit⇨Preferences⇨General and uncheck the option Use Shift Key for Tool Switch. You can now rotate through the tools by pressing the same letter repeatedly.

✔ If you can't remember the keyboard shortcut of a particular tool, pause your cursor over its icon for a second or two. A little label known as a *tool tip* appears, telling you the name of the tool and its keyboard equivalent. If this gets annoying, the feature can be turned off in the General panel of the Preferences dialog box under the Edit menu.

✔ One last tidbit: If you grab a tool and try to use it and all you see is the Cancel (the circle with a diagonal line) icon, simply click on the canvas. Elements prompts you with a reason why it can't perform the operation. For example, if you try to apply color on a text layer with the Paintbrush, Elements displays a message saying you couldn't use the Paintbrush because the type layer needs to be simplified first. This talk about type and layers will probably be fuzzy to you because you may not have peeked at Chapters 9 and 16. So go take a peek if you want — we'll catch up with you in the next chapter.

Chapter 3

"Open!" Says Me

. . . .

In This Chapter

▶ Opening and closing images

▶ Using the File Browser

▶ Creating a new, blank image

▶ Mastering your image windows

▶ Moving around your image

▶ Zooming in and out

▶ Working with precision in your images

. . . .

When you first start Photoshop Elements, you're presented with a plethora of tools, menus, and palettes (just check out Chapter 2 if you don't believe us!). However, until you have an image open, those contraptions are intriguing but ultimately worthless — it's like having an easel, a full set of brushes, and a whole paint box full of paints, but no canvas. And with Elements, you can't even climb up on billboards and paint mustaches on the faces in the ads. (Not that we've ever done anything like that.) No, if you want to become a digital Picasso (or Rembrandt, or Monet, or whatever artistic legend you choose), you need an open image.

This chapter explains how to open existing images and also how to create a new, blank canvas for an image you want to paint from scratch. Then we chart a course through the many ways you can navigate around the vast sea of your image. So strap a parrot on your shoulder and hop on board.

Don't Just Sit There, Open Something!

If you're a longtime computer buff, you may expect opening an image to be a relatively straightforward process. You just choose File⇨Open or press Ctrl+O (⌘+O on a Mac) and select the image file you want to display, right?

Well, in Elements "O" stands for "options" just as much as it stands for "Open." Scientific studies have shown that if you close your eyes and just click blindly around the Elements interface a dozen times, you'll hit at least three different file-opening features. Elements' main opening tool is the File Browser. As you can see in Figure 3-1, the File Browser is an excellent visual means of browsing through your computer and peeking at the graphics files contained therein.

Figure 3-1:
The File Browser is a visual reference that Elements' granddaddy Photoshop would do well to acquire.

Opening via the File Browser

How important is the File Browser? Just take a look at the stacking order of palettes in the palette well, and you'll notice that the File Browser is always the first palette on the left — a coveted place to be amongst those highly competitive Elements palettes. In truth, using the File Browser isn't so different from a standard Open command, except for the fact that the File Browser gives you a simultaneous preview of every image file in a folder or directory.

This is great if you have a batch of confusingly named files like "Wedding 1," "Wedding 2," "Wedding 3," and so on. The File Browser makes it easy to quickly see which of those photos shows the dog helping himself to the wedding cake. And digital cameras can dump a batch of pictures on your hard drive with long, meaningless strings of numbers for titles; the File Browser makes it a snap to sort through them.

To use the File Browser, you first have to activate it by clicking on its tab in the palette well; from there you can drag it out of the well and onto your desktop if you wish. The File Browser, by default, gives you an icon-by-icon view of your desktop, starting with your hard drive, then moving on to any drives or CDs you may have, then to folders, and then to individual graphics files. In short, the File Browser shows you any graphics files, as well as anything that might *contain* graphics files. You can navigate by double-clicking around the preview icons, digging deeper into drives and folders until you find the image you're looking for. If you find you've gone too far, click on the handy folder-with-the-arrow icon to go back one level, or use the drop-down menu to travel back all the way to the desktop if desired.

Opening the ordinary way

The File Browser aside, Elements has several other handy ways to open images. Chapter 1 looks at the Open command featured on the Quick Start screen. As Figure 3-2 shows, there's also a convenient one-click Open button on the Shortcuts bar; it's the third icon from the left, just past the Adobe.com link and the New file icon. But if you'd rather maneuver through menus, you're in luck. To open an image, walk this way:

1. **Choose File⇨Open.**

   If clicking icons or choosing menu commands is too much work, just press Ctrl+O (⌘+O on a Mac). The Open dialog box rears its useful head, as shown in Figure 3-3. (Your dialog box may not offer all the options in the figure, or the options may have different names, but the basic components work the same.)

Figure 3-2: If you're the point-and-click type, the Shortcuts bar was made for you.

New

Open

2. **PC users: Select the disk or folder that contains your image from the Look In drop-down menu.**

   After you select a disk or folder, the contents of that disk or folder appear in the box beneath the drop-down menu. Double-click on a folder in the box to display its contents, if necessary, until you find the file you want to open.

Favorites

Create new folder Details

Current folder Up one level List

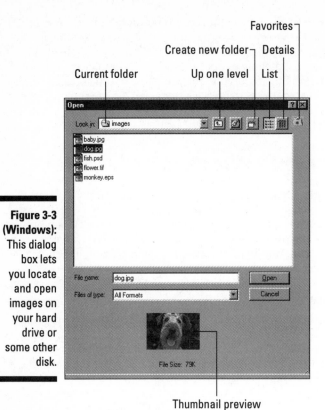

Figure 3-3 (Windows): This dialog box lets you locate and open images on your hard drive or some other disk.

Thumbnail preview

Favorites

Mounted Volumes

Recent documents

Current folder Thumbnail preview

Figure 3-3 (Mac): This dialog box lets you locate and open images on your hard drive or some other disk.

Mac users: Open the desired folder in the central list.

The scrolling list in the center of the dialog box shows you all the folders and images that are strewn loose on the disk.

You can click on the Mounted Volumes button to see the desktop, hard drives, external disks (such as floppies and zips), and networked items currently available to you. Assuming your image isn't lying about on the desktop, select the disk that contains the image you want to open.

It's also possible that the image is inside a folder on the desktop, in which case you want to select Desktop from the Mounted Volumes button.

Double-click on a folder name to open the folder. The list then displays all folders and images inside that folder. Double-click on another folder if you need to open it, and so on.

Elements also gives you access to Favorites and Recent documents sub-menus (second and third icons in the top right) in the Open dialog box, enabling you to grab your most popular images.

3. **Click on the image you want to open.**

   After you locate your image, click on its name in the list to select it. A preview of the image appears in the dialog box so you can see what your images look like one at a time.

   Mac users: Make sure the Show Preview button is activated. Be aware that previews may not be available in all circumstances.

   If you want to open multiple images in one fell swoop, press the Shift key and click on additional images. This applies to both platforms.

   PC users: Click on the Details button to display pertinent information about each image, including its size, type, and the date it was last edited.

4. **Click on the Open button.**

   You can also press Enter (Return on a Mac) or press Alt+O (⌘+O on a Mac). Alternatively, if you have a single image selected, you can simply double-click on the image to open it.

That's all there is to it. Your image is now open and ready to abuse — er, we mean use. But before you have a go at it in earnest, here are a few additional notes on opening images:

✔ To close a particular folder and view the contents of the folder that contains that particular folder, PC users click on the Up One Level button at the top of the Open dialog box (or click on the Backspace key).

✔ PC users should click on the Look In drop-down menu to display the list of folders that contains the current folder. For example, if the items in the drop-down menu read Elephant, Digestive Systems, and Food-Processing Enzymes, then the Food-Processing Enzymes folder resides inside the Digestive Systems folder, which is on the Elephant disk.

Mac users can press ⌘+↑ to advance up a folder. You can also press the current folder bar to display a drop-down menu of folders that contains the current folder.

✔ If you're having trouble opening a file and you know what the file type is, PC users have the option of choosing File⇨Open As or pressing Ctrl+Alt+O to specify the file format Elements should use.

✔ If you can't find a file in a certain folder, it may be because Elements doesn't think it can open the file. To see all files in a folder, whether Elements can open them or not, PC users select the All Formats option from the Files of Type drop-down menu. Mac users should select the All Documents option. If the file appears, go ahead and try to open it. It may not work, but it's worth a try.

✔ Mac users: In addition to double-clicking on a folder to open it, you can press ⌘+↓.

Creating a new image

To create a new image instead of opening an existing one, Elements gives you a typically wide range of options. You can use the Quick Start screen as mentioned in Chapter 1; use the New icon in the Shortcuts bar (refer to Figure 3-2); choose File⇨New; or press Ctrl+N (on a Mac, press ⌘+N). Whichever method you use, Elements displays the New dialog box. There, you can name your file; specify the width, height, and resolution (as discussed in Chapter 4); and set the color mode (as discussed in Chapter 5).

Behold the Image Window

After you open up an image, Elements displays the image onscreen inside a new image window. Several new items appear when you open an image, as labeled in Figure 3-4.

The following list explains all:

✔ The title bar lists the title of your image with the file extension (for more on file formats, see Chapter 6). The added bonus is that you can drag the title bar to move the window to a different location onscreen. Easy stuff.

✔ For Mac users: Every item labeled in the figure except the Status bar (and the odd-looking creature with the goggles, of course) is found in all windows across the board. Click on the Zoom box to collapse or expand the window to match the exact size of the image. If the image is too big for the screen, the window expands to include as much of the image as possible.

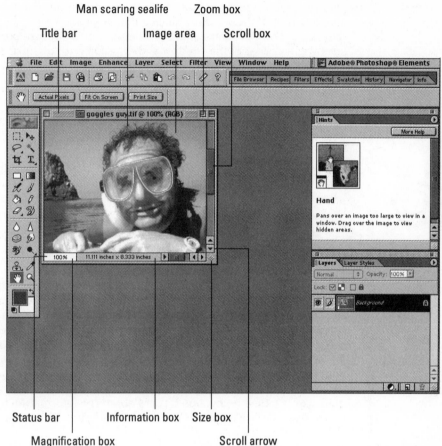

Figure 3-4:
An image
from Corbis'
"Active
Lifestyles 2"
collection.

- For PC users: Just like the main Elements program window, each image window has a Close button, Minimize button, and Maximize/Restore button. The buttons work just as they do for the program window (explained in Chapter 2) with one exception: The Minimize button reduces the image window so that only a small title bar is left onscreen. Click on the Restore button to bring the image back into view.

- Alternatively, you can choose File⇨Close or press Ctrl+W (⌘+W on a Mac) to close an image. You know, W as in *hasta la vista, window.* (If you've made some changes to the image, Elements asks you whether you want to save the new and improved image, a process explained in great detail in Chapter 6.)

✔ For PC users: To change the size of the image window, place your cursor over a corner of the window. When a double-headed arrow appears, drag the corner. For Mac users: Place your cursor over the size box in the lower-right corner of the window and drag. On both platforms, the image remains the same; you're just changing the size of the window that holds the image. Give it a try and see what we mean.

✔ On the PC, the Status bar is located at the bottom of the Elements window. On the Mac, it's located at the bottom of the image window. The Status bar gives you information about your image. On the PC, it also provides hints about the tool or command you're using.

PC users, don't see the Status bar on your screen? Choose Window⇨ Show Status Bar to display it. Remember that the Status bar disappears when you press Tab to hide the palettes and the Toolbox, as explained in Chapter 2.

✔ The Magnification box lets you zoom in and out on your image, as explained later in this chapter in the section "Zooming in and out on your work."

✔ Next to the Magnification box is the Information box, which shows you by default what the printed size of your document will be. Click on the right-pointing arrow, however, and you'll see that this box is a virtual factotum for image information, telling you more than you ever thought there was to know about such matters as image size, resolution, color mode, and so on. Clicking in the Information box itself will always tell you the image's pixel and print dimensions, channel information, and resolution. We cover the most important of these matters later in the book. For the time being, don't worry about the Information box too much. We just didn't want to leave you wondering, "What in the Sam Hill is this thingy here?"

✔ The scroll bars let you navigate around and display hidden portions of the image inside the window. Elements offers two scroll bars, one vertical bar along the right side of the image and one horizontal bar along the bottom.

If you click on a scroll arrow, you nudge your view of the image slightly in that direction. For example, if you click on the right-pointing scroll arrow, an item that was hidden on the right side of the photograph slides into view. Click in the gray area of a scroll bar to scroll the window more dramatically. Drag a scroll box to manually specify the distance scrolled.

Using the scroll arrows isn't the only way to move around your image; in fact, it's probably the least efficient method. For some better options, check out the techniques presented in the section, "The Screen Is Your Digital Oyster," coming up next.

✔ The area within the title bar and scroll bars is the image area. The image area is where you paint, edit, select details, and, otherwise, have at your image. Obviously, you look at the image area a lot throughout the many pages of this book.

You can open as many images onscreen as your computer's memory and screen size allow. But only one image is active at a time. To make a different window active, just click on it or choose its name from the bottom of the Window menu.

The Screen Is Your Digital Oyster

The Photoshop Elements Toolbox includes two navigation tools: the Hand tool, which lets you scroll the image inside the window with much more ease than the silly scroll bars afford, and the Zoom tool, which lets you move closer to or farther away from your image. The Hand tool and the Zoom tool are called navigation tools because they don't change the image; they merely alter your view of the image so that you can get a better look-see.

In addition to the above tools, there is another navigational aid, appropriately called the Navigator palette. The palette gives you a super-convenient way to zoom and scroll your image. In fact, after you're familiar with the palette, you may not use the Hand and Zoom tools at all. But in the interest of fair play, we present all the various options for moving around within your image in the upcoming sections.

Using the Hand tool

If you're familiar with other Windows and Macintosh programs, you need to know something about Elements: The scroll bars are relatively useless. Keep away from them. Promise that you'll always use the Hand tool or the Navigator palette (explained shortly) instead. Promise? Good. As for you new users, don't worry — you have no old habits to break.

Consider the following example: Figure 3-5 shows a Corbis image from the "Children and Teens" collection. The top view in the figure shows a young lad in obvious distress. The problem is that the picture is wider than the image window, so you can't see what's causing him such grief.

To view the rest of the scene, select the Hand tool by clicking on its icon in the Toolbox. Then position the Hand tool in the image window, as shown in the top example in Figure 3-5, click, and drag to the left. The image moves with the hand cursor, as shown in the bottom example, and reveals the source of the boy's torment.

Dragging with the Hand tool is like turning your head to view a new part of your surroundings, except you'll never get a crick in your neck. You can drag at any angle you please — up, down, sideways, or diagonally.

Hand cursor

Figure 3-5: Dragging with the Hand tool reveals that a bad haircut isn't the only thing a kid has to worry about.

You can also select the Hand tool by pressing the H key. To temporarily access the Hand tool when another tool is selected, press the spacebar. As long as the spacebar is down, the Hand tool is available. Releasing the spacebar returns you to the selected tool.

Using keyboard shortcuts

As in most other programs, you can also use keyboard shortcuts to move about your image. Press Page Up or Page Down to scroll up or down an entire screen. Press Shift+Page Up or Shift+Page Down to scroll in smaller increments. Press Home to go to the upper-left corner of the image, and press End to move to the lower-right corner.

And as if that wasn't enough, Elements offers keyboard shortcuts for moving right and left. Press Ctrl+Page Up or Ctrl+Page Down to scroll left or right an entire screen. Press Ctrl+Shift+Page Up or Ctrl+Shift+Page Down to scroll left and right in smaller increments. Mac users, substitute the ⌘ key for the Ctrl key here.

Zooming in and out on your work

When you first open an image, Photoshop Elements displays the entire image so that it fits onscreen. But you may not be seeing the details in the image as clearly as you want. If you want to inspect the image in more detail, you have to move closer. No, don't scoot your chair; read on.

Elements gives you several ways to zoom in and out on your work, as described in these next few sections.

Zooming doesn't change the size of your image in any way — not the size at which it would print, and not the size it would appear onscreen if you e-mailed it to somebody or posted it on the Web. It just temporarily adjusts the size at which you see the image onscreen. Zooming is like looking at some eensey-teensey life form under a microscope. The creature doesn't actually grow and shrink as you vary the degree of magnification, and neither does your image.

The Zoom tool

Using the Zoom tool is one avenue for changing your view of an image. Every time you click on your image with the tool, you magnify the image to a larger size. Here's an example of how it works:

1. **Select the Zoom tool.**

   Click on the Zoom tool in the Toolbox. It's the one that looks like a magnifying glass. You can also press the Z key to grab the Zoom tool.

2. **Click in the image area.**

   Elements magnifies the image to the next preset zoom size (the increments are set by Elements), as demonstrated in the second example of Figure 3-6. The program centers the magnified view about the point at which you click, as much as possible. In Figure 3-6, for example, the girl was zoom-clicked right between the eyes.

3. Repeat.

To zoom in farther still, click again with the Zoom tool, as demonstrated in the bottom example of Figure 3-6.

Figure 3-6: Clicking with the Zoom tool magnifies your image in preset increments.

A setting in the Options bar determines whether Elements resizes your image window to match the image when you zoom with the Zoom tool. If you want your image windows to be resized when you zoom, select the Resize Windows to Fit option.

The only hitch comes when the window bumps into a palette. When the window hits a palette that's anchored to the side of the screen (as opposed to floating in the middle of the screen), Elements thinks that it has hit some sort of wall and stops zooming. To get around the problem, simply select the Ignore Palettes option located in the Options bar.

Here's some other Zoom tool stuff to tuck away for future reference:

- ✔ To zoom out on your image, first switch to the Zoom Out icon in the Options bar (the magnifying glass with the minus sign in it). You can also Alt+click (Option+click on a Mac) with the Zoom tool to zoom out.

- ✔ As you zoom, Elements displays the *zoom factor* in the title bar and the Status bar. A zoom factor of 100 percent shows you one screen pixel for every pixel in your image. (Pixels are explained thoroughly in Chapter 4.)

  Keep in mind that a 100 percent zoom ratio more than likely doesn't correspond to the printed size of your image. If you want a rough idea of what the printed size will be, use the Print Size command, explained in the next section.

- ✔ To magnify just one section of an image, drag with the Zoom tool to surround the area with a dotted outline. Elements fills the image window with the area that you surrounded.

- ✔ To temporarily access the Zoom tool while another tool is selected, press Ctrl+spacebar (⌘+spacebar on a Mac). Press Ctrl+Alt+spacebar (⌘+Option+spacebar on a Mac) to get the zoom out cursor. In either case, releasing the keys returns you to the previously selected tool.

- ✔ You can also zoom in and out on your images from the keyboard. Ctrl++ (the plus sign) (⌘++ on the Mac) zooms in; Ctrl+– (the minus sign) (⌘+– on the Mac) zooms out. While this keyboard shortcut always resizes the window regardless of the settings in the Zoom tool's Options bar, the keyboard shortcut does obey the Zoom tool's Ignore Palettes option, whether you have the Zoom tool selected or not. Note that technically, the zoom in shortcut is actually Ctrl+= (⌘+= on the Mac); in other words, it's not necessary to also press the Shift key to access the plus sign.

The View commands

The View menu offers some more ways to change the magnification of your image. The first two zoom commands on the menu, Zoom In and Zoom Out, aren't of much interest; they do the same thing as clicking and Alt+clicking

(Option+clicking on a Mac) with the Zoom tool, except that you can't specify the center of the new view as you can with the Zoom tool. But you may find the other View commands helpful at times:

- Choose View⇨Fit on Screen or press Ctrl+0 (zero) (⌘+0 on a Mac) to display your image at the largest size that allows the entire image to fit onscreen.

- Choose View⇨Actual Pixels or press Ctrl+Alt+0 (zero) (⌘+Option+0 on a Mac) to return to the 100 percent zoom ratio. This view size shows you one pixel on your monitor for every pixel in the image, which is the most accurate way to view your image.

- You can also choose the Fit on Screen view by double-clicking on the Hand tool icon in the Toolbox. Double-click on the Zoom tool icon to change to the Actual Pixels view.

- Choose View⇨Print Size to display your image onscreen in a rough approximation of the size at which it will print.

- When you have either the Hand or Zoom tool selected, you can simply click the Actual Pixels, Fit on Screen, or Print Size buttons in the Options bar.

- You can choose View⇨New View to create a second view of your image. Don't confuse this with duplicating an image, which creates a new file. New View simply creates a second way of looking at the same file. New View can be useful when you are editing an image in a magnified view, yet want to see the overall results on your entire image without having to continuously zoom in and out.

The Magnification box

Clicking the Zoom tool and choosing the View commands are great when you want to zoom in or out to one of the preset Elements zoom ratios. But what if you want more control over your zooming? The answer awaits in the Magnification box (refer to Figure 3-4).

To enter a zoom ratio, just double-click or click and drag on the Magnification box and type the zoom ratio you want to use. If you know exactly what zoom ratio you want, press Enter (Return on a Mac) to make Elements do your bidding. But if you want to play around with different zoom ratios, press Shift+Enter (Shift+Return on a Mac) instead. That way, Elements zooms your image, but keeps the Magnification box active so that you can quickly enter a new ratio if the first one doesn't work out. When you're satisfied, press Enter (Return on a Mac).

When you use the Magnification box, the image window size doesn't change as you zoom, regardless of whether the Resize Windows to Fit option is selected in the Options bar.

Navigating by palette

The Navigator palette, shown in Figure 3-7, is the best navigational aid in Elements because it actually combines the functions of the Zoom and Hand tools in one location. The Navigator palette is usually lurking toward the right end of the palette well. Click on the tab to activate it, and drag it out onto the desktop if you wish. Or choose <u>W</u>indow⇨Show Na<u>v</u>igator. To make the palette smaller or larger, drag the size box in the palette's lower-right corner.

View box

Figure 3-7: The Navigator palette provides a nifty way to zoom and scroll your image.

Zoom slider

Zoom out   Zoom in

Magnification box   Size box

The palette provides a handy, all-in-one tool for scrolling and zooming. It's especially useful when you're working on a large image that doesn't fit entirely onscreen when you're zoomed in for detail work. Here are the how-to's for using the palette:

✔ In the center of the palette, you see a thumbnail view of your image, as in Figure 3-7. The palette shows your entire image, even if it's not all visible in the main image window.

✔ See the red box that surrounds a portion of the thumbnail? That's called the view box. The area within the box corresponds to the portion of your image that's visible in the main image window. As you drag the box, Elements scrolls your image in the main image window to display the area that's surrounded by the box. You can also click on an area in the thumbnail to move the view box over that portion of the image.

✔ Press and hold Ctrl (⌘ on a Mac), and the cursor in the palette changes to a zoom cursor. If you drag with the cursor while pressing Ctrl (⌘ on a Mac), you resize the view box, which, in turn, zooms the image in the image window.

✔ The palette also contains a Magnification box, as labeled in Figure 3-7. The box works just like the one in the Status bar; just enter a zoom factor and press Enter (Return on a Mac).

✔ To zoom in or out in the preset Elements increments (as with the Zoom tool), click on the Zoom In or Zoom Out buttons, labeled in Figure 3-7.

✔ You can also zoom by dragging the Zoom slider — drag left to zoom out, and drag right to zoom in.

If you're having trouble picking out the view box against the colors of your image, you can change the view box's color. Click on the right-pointing arrow in the upper-right corner of the palette and choose the Palette Options command. Then choose a new color from the Color drop-down menu.

Tools for the Terribly Precise

If you've ever used a page layout program such as PageMaker or QuarkXPress, you're no doubt familiar with the concept of *grids*. Shown in Figure 3-8, a grid is an onscreen device that helps you align items in your image. For example, in the figure the grid was used to keep the words spaced both horizontally and vertically in the image.

In addition to grids, Elements offers rulers that run across the top and left sides of the image window. Grids and rulers come in handy when you're feeling the urge to be especially precise with your work. And the Info palette helps you get a bead on exactly what's going on in your image.

Switching on the rulers

To display rulers, just click the Ruler icon in the Shortcuts bar — it's the icon that resembles a ruler (and we don't mean Queen Elizabeth). You can also choose View➪Show Rulers or press Ctrl+R (⌘+R on a Mac). To hide the rulers, click the Shortcuts bar's Ruler icon again, choose View➪Hide Rulers, or press Ctrl+R (⌘+R on a Mac) again.

By default, the rulers use inches as their unit of measurement. But if you want to use some other unit, say picas instead of inches, choose Edit➪Preferences➪ Units & Rulers or just double-click on a ruler. In the Units section of the dialog box that appears, select a new unit of measurement from the Rulers drop-down menu. You can also right-click (Control-click on a Mac) on either ruler to access a shortcut menu where you can select your desired unit of measurement.

Grid lines   Ruler

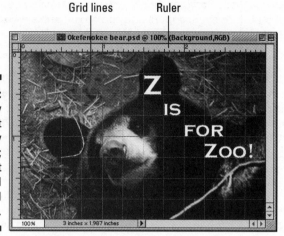

Figure 3-8:
Our furry
friend isn't
really
fenced in;
he's just
covered
with grid
lines.

Turning on the grid

The grid positions lines across your image at preset intervals. While you
can't move grid lines, you can turn them on and off, and change the spacing
and color of the lines.

To turn on the grid, choose View⇨Show Grid. To change the spacing and
appearance of the grid lines, choose Edit⇨Preferences⇨Grid. Elements presents you with a dialog box in which you can choose a color and line style for
the grid lines. Specify how far apart you want to space the lines, and choose
whether you want to subdivide the grid with secondary grid lines. You can
also choose a unit of measurement for the grid.

The lines of a grid have "snapping" capabilities — anything you drag near a
grid line automatically snaps into alignment with that line. You turn snapping
on and off by choosing View⇨Snap. A checkmark next to the command name
in the menu means that snapping is turned on.

Information, please

The Info palette can be a big help when you need to know precise values
related to your image. By default, the Info palette is divided into four parts:
The upper two sections give you the exact values for the color of the pixel
your cursor happens to be over, the bottom-left section tells you exactly
where in the image your cursor is located, and the bottom-right section tells
you the dimensions of an active selection.

The units of measurement are changeable in two ways. You can click on the tiny little arrows next to the eyedroppers and the crosshair, or you can use the Info palette menu (accessible by clicking the right-pointing arrow in the upper-right corner of the palette).

The bottom-left section works on an x and y coordinate system. Assuming you've set the units of measurement for this section to pixels (usually the most helpful setting, by the way), if you move your cursor into the upper-left corner of the image, you'll notice that the x and y coordinates are both at 0. Move your cursor to the right across the upper edge of the image — along the x-axis — and you'll see the x coordinate grow. Move your cursor down — along the y-axis — and you'll see the y coordinate grow.

The Info palette also gives you different kinds of feedback depending on which tool you're using. If your monitor is large enough — or if you have the luxury of working on a two-monitor system — you might want to keep it open at all times when you're working. In this information age, it's easy to get addicted to watching this palette.

Chapter 4

Pixels: It's Hip to Be Square

● ●

● ●

*I*mages that you create and edit in Photoshop Elements — or in any other image-editing application for that matter — are made up of tiny squares called *pixels*. Understanding how pixels work in an image can be enormously confusing to beginning image editors. Unfortunately, managing your pixel population correctly is essential to turning out professional-looking images, so you really do need to come to grips with how pixels work before you can be successful with Elements.

This chapter explains everything you need to know to put pixels in perspective, including how the number of pixels in an image affects its quality, printed size, size onscreen, and size on disk. You'll also see how to reduce or enlarge the size of the onscreen canvas on which all your pretty pixels perch. In other words, this chapter proffers pages of particularly provocative pixel paragraphs, partner.

Welcome to Pixeltown

Imagine that you're the victim of a terrifying scientific experiment that has left you 1 millimeter tall. After recovering from the initial shock that such terrifying scientific experiments tend to produce on one's equilibrium, you discover that you're sitting on a square tile that's colored with a uniform shade of blue. Beyond your tile are eight other blue tiles, one to your right and one to your left, one in front and one behind, and four others in diagonal directions. In other words, the tiles are aligned in a perfect grid, just like standard floor tiles but without the grout. You notice upon further inspection that each of the blue tiles differs slightly in shade and tone. As you slowly turn, it becomes evident that you're surrounded by these colored tiles for as far as your infinitesimally tiny, pinprick eyes can see.

You cry out in anguish and fling your dust-speck body about in the way that folks always do when plagued by these terrifying scientific experiments. As though in answer to your pitiful squeals, you start to grow. In a matter of moments, you increase in size to almost 5 centimeters tall. A bug that was considering devouring you has a change of mind and runs away. You can now see that you sit in the midst of a huge auditorium and that all the tiles on its vast and unending floor are colored differently, gradually changing from shades of blue to shades of green, red, and yellow. You continue to grow: 10 centimeters, 20, 50, a full meter tall. The tiles start to blend together to form some kind of pattern. Two meters, 5, 10. This must be how Alice felt in Wonderland. You've now grown several times beyond your normal height, reaching 20 meters tall. Your massive head bursts through the flimsy ceiling of the room.

When you reach the height of a 50-story building, your growth spurt comes to an end. You look down at the ruined auditorium, whose walls have been shredded to rubble by the great edges of your tremendous feet, and you notice a peculiar thing. You stand not on a floor, but on a picture, as rich in color and detail as any you've seen. The tiles, which now appear dot-sized to you, have merged together to create a seamless blend. You would expect the result to have the rough appearance of a mosaic — requiring a heavy dose of imagination to compensate for occasionally choppy transitions — but, in fact, it looks exactly like a continuous tone photograph.

The vision inspires you to claw at your temples, fling your arms about in circles, and shriek, "What's happening to me?!" The answer, of course, is nothing (other than a little overacting, that is). Well, okay, your body may be stretched out of shape, but your eyes are working fine. You see, when you get far enough away from a perfect grid of colored tiles — whether via a terrifying scientific experiment or more conventional means — the tiles disappear, and an overall image takes shape.

What does this little trip down sci-fi lane have to do with Elements? Well, a lot, actually. Like the image on the auditorium floor, your Elements image is made up of a grid of colored squares. In this case, the squares are called *pixels*.

By now, you're probably thinking, "Fine, images are made up of a bunch of itsy-bitsy square pixels. So what? Who cares? Quit wasting my time, darn it." The truth is, these tiniest of image particles are at the heart of what makes Elements and your electronic images tick.

Every single painting and image-editing function in Elements is devoted to changing the quantity, the arrangement, or the color of pixels. That's all Elements does. It sounds so simple that you figure it must be a joke, an exaggeration, or just a plain lie. But it's the absolute truth. Elements is merely an extremely sophisticated pixel counter, colorer, and arranger, nothing more.

Screen Pixels versus Image Pixels

Like the tiles in the preceding story, each pixel in a computer image is perfectly square, arranged on a perfect grid, and colored uniformly — that is, each pixel is one color and one color only. Put these pixels together, and your brain perceives them to be an everyday, average photograph.

The display on your computer's monitor is also made up of pixels. Like image pixels, screen pixels are square and arranged on a grid. For instance, a typical 13-inch monitor measures 640 screen pixels wide by 480 screen pixels tall. These screen pixels are kind of tiny, so you may not be able to make them out. Each one generally measures around $\frac{1}{72}$ inch across.

To understand the relationship between screen and image pixels, open an image. After the image comes up onscreen, double-click on the Zoom tool in the Toolbox, or choose View➪Actual Pixels. The Magnification box in the Status bar lists the zoom ratio as 100%, which means that you can see one pixel in your image for every pixel displayed by your monitor.

To view the image pixels more closely, enter a value of **200%** in the Magnification box. A 200% zoom factor magnifies the image pixels to twice their previous size so that one image pixel measures two screen pixels tall and two screen pixels wide. If you change the zoom factor to 400%, Elements displays four screen pixels for every image pixel, giving you a total of 16 screen pixels for every image pixel (4 screen pixels tall by 4 screen pixels wide). Figure 4-1 illustrates how different zoom factors affect the appearance of your image pixels onscreen.

Remember that the zoom factor has nothing to do with the size at which your image would print or display if e-mailed to a friend or posted on the Web — it only affects how your image looks onscreen at that moment. If you want to see onscreen a rough approximation of your image's print size, choose View➪Print Size.

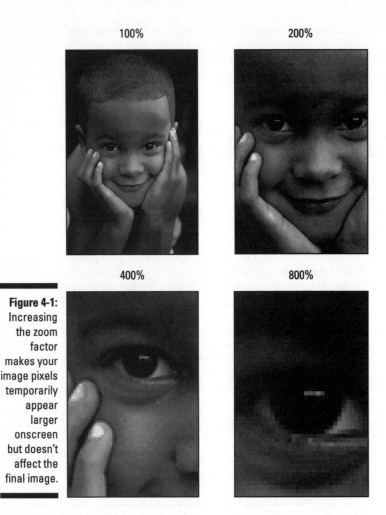

100%   200%

400%   800%

Figure 4-1:
Increasing
the zoom
factor
makes your
image pixels
temporarily
appear
larger
onscreen
but doesn't
affect the
final image.

Image Size, Resolution, and Other Tricky Pixel Stuff

An Elements image has three primary attributes related to pixels: *file size,* *resolution,* and *physical dimensions,* as explained in the following list. You control these attributes through the Image Size dialog box, shown in Figure 4-2. To display the dialog box, choose Image⇨Resize⇨Image Size.

Link icon

Figure 4-2:
You control
file size,
image
dimensions,
and
resolution
through the
Image Size
dialog box.

If you just want to get a quick look at the dimensions and resolution of an image, click on the Information box (next to the Magnification box). Elements displays a little box listing the dimensions, resolution, and other scary stuff.

✔ The *file size* of the image is a measure of how many pixels the image contains. (Elements refers to file size as *pixel dimensions*.) The image in Figure 4-1 is 256 pixels wide and 384 pixels tall, for a total of 98,304 pixels. Most of the images you create contain hundreds of thousands or even millions of pixels.

✔ The *resolution* of an image refers to the number of pixels that print per inch. For example, the resolution of the first image in Figure 4-1 is 180 pixels per inch *(ppi)*. That may sound like an awful lot of pixels squished into a small space, but it's about average.

✔ Not to be confused with pixel dimensions, the *physical dimensions* of an image are its physical width and height when printed, as measured in inches, centimeters, or your unit of choice. (Elements refers to physical dimensions as *document size*.) You can calculate the document size by dividing the number of pixels by the resolution. For example, the little boy in Figure 4-1 measures 256 pixels ÷ 180 pixels per inch = 1⅜ inches wide and 384 pixels ÷ 180 ppi = 2⅛ inches tall. Measure him with a ruler, and you see that this is indeed the case.

No problem, right? Sure, this stuff is a little technical, but it's not like it requires an advanced degree in cold fusion to figure out what's going on. And yet, the Image Size dialog box may well be the most confusing Elements dialog box. You can even damage your image if you're not careful. So be extremely careful before you make changes in the Image Size dialog box. (The upcoming sections tell you everything you need to know to stay out of trouble.)

Depending on your printer, on a PC you may be able to simply reduce or enlarge your image for printing via a scaling option in the printer's Properties dialog box, which you access by choosing File⇨Page Setup to display the Page Setup dialog box, then clicking on the Properties button, and then clicking on the Graphics tab. On a Mac, you may be able to reduce or enlarge your image for printing simply by entering a percentage value into the Scale or Scaling options box in the Page Setup dialog box. Choose File⇨Page Setup. On both platforms, Elements scales your image to the new size only during the print cycle. Your image isn't permanently altered, as it is when you use the Image Size dialog box. For more information, see Chapter 7.

Resolving resolution

Although the Resolution option box appears unceremoniously toward the bottom of the Image Size dialog box, it's one of the most critical values to consider if you want your images to look good.

The Resolution value determines how tightly the pixels are packed when printed. It's kind of like the population density of one of those ridiculously large urban areas cropping up all over the modern world. Take Lagos, Nigeria, for example, which is a city of approximately 13 million souls. The population density of Lagos is such that there are roughly 195,000 people packed into each square mile.

In order to increase the population density, you have to either increase the number of people in a city or decrease the physical boundaries of the city and scrunch everyone closer together. The same goes for resolution. If you want a higher resolution (more pixels per inch), you can either decrease the physical dimensions of the image or increase the file size (pixel dimensions) by adding pixels to the image. For example, the two images in Figure 4-3 have the same file size, but the smaller image has twice the resolution of the larger image — 180 ppi versus 90 ppi.

Conversely, population density goes down as people die or as the boundaries of the city grow. For example, if we were to mandate that Lagos spread out evenly over the entire 360,000 square miles of Nigeria, the population density would temporarily drop to 36 people per square mile (assuming, of course, that the other residents of Nigeria happened to be on vacation at the time). Likewise, when you increase the dimensions of an image or delete some of its pixels, the resolution goes down.

Before you get the mistaken idea that this analogy is completely airtight, we should in all fairness mention a few key differences between a typical image and Lagos:

> ✔ Lagos, as any city would, has its crowded spots and its relatively sparse areas. An image, by contrast, is equally dense at all points. Unlike population density, therefore, resolution is constant across the board.

✔ An image is always rectangular. Lagos could best be described as free form.

✔ Population density is measured in terms of area — you know, so many folks per square mile. Resolution, on the other hand, is measured in a line — pixels per linear inch. So an image with a resolution of 180 pixels per inch contains 32,400 pixels per square inch. (That's 180 squared, in case you're wondering.)

✔ The pixels in an image are absolutely square. The people in Lagos are shaped rather arbitrarily, with undulating arms and legs jutting out at irregular and unpredictable angles.

✔ You have total control over the size and resolution of an image. Like it or not, you could move to Lagos to increase the population by one, but otherwise Lagos is entirely out of your hands.

Figure 4-3:
Two images
with the
exact same
number of
pixels but
subject
to two
different
resolutions.

Changing pixel dimensions

The top two option boxes in the Image Size dialog box enable you to change an image's *pixel dimensions* — the number of pixels wide by the number of pixels tall. (The number of pixels in your image is also known as the *file size.*) Unless you really know what you're doing when it comes to pixels, avoid these option boxes.

Lowering the Pixel Dimensions values can be dangerous because what you're really doing is throwing away pixels. And when you delete pixels, you delete detail. Figure 4-4 shows what we mean. The physical size of all three images is the same, but the detail drops off from one image to the next. The first image contains 64,000 pixels and is printed at a resolution of 140 ppi; the second contains ¼ as many pixels and is printed at 70 ppi. The third contains only 4,000 pixels and has a resolution of 35 ppi. Notice how details such as the shadows from the girl's eyelashes and the distinction between individual hairs in her eyebrows become less pronounced and more generalized as the pixel population decreases.

Increasing the file size (by raising the Pixel Dimensions values) isn't such a hot idea, because Elements can't generate image detail out of thin air. When you raise the Pixel Dimensions values, Elements adds pixels by averaging the preexisting pixels (a process computer nerds call *interpolation*) in a way that may result in image softening and never results in the miraculous reconstruction of detail.

If changing the pixel dimensions is dangerous, you may wonder why Elements gives you the option to do so at all. Well, although we don't recommend ever adding pixels to an image, you may actually need to lower the pixel dimensions. If your file size is really large — that is, your image contains a ton of pixels — you may want to toss some of the pixels overboard.

In an ideal world, you'd want as many pixels as possible because more pixels means greater image detail. But if you're posting your image on the Internet, you may need to reduce your pixel dimensions so that the image will download more quickly and simply so that it can fit on your users' screens. Also, the more pixels you have, the more disk space the image consumes, which can be a problem if you're working with limited computing resources. Large file sizes can also slow down Elements substantially.

Even when you dump pixels from an image, you shouldn't attack the job from the Pixel Dimensions option boxes; you'll learn a better way in the steps in the section "Using the Image Size dialog box safely" later in this chapter.

Figure 4-4:
Three
images,
each
containing
fewer pixels
and printed
at a lower
resolution
than the
image
above it.

Changing the physical dimensions of the image

The Width and Height boxes in the Document Size portion of the Image Size dialog box reflect the actual printed size of your image. The drop-down menus next to the Width and Height options let you change the unit of measure displayed in the option boxes. For example, if you select picas from the Document Size Width drop-down menu, Elements converts the Width value from inches to picas. (A *pica* is an obscure typesetting measurement equal to ⅙ inch.) The percent option in the drop-down menu enables you to enter new width and height values as a percentage of the original values. Enter a value higher than 100% to increase the print size; enter a value lower than 100% to reduce the print size.

Yeah, okay, but what resolution should I use?

The Auto button in the Image Size dialog box is supposed to generate a perfect resolution value based on the line screen that your printer will use. The only problem is, no one knows what a line screen setting is. Rather than bother with trying to explain this arcane bit of printing technology to you at this point — what with your head already spinning with Lagos population data — here instead are some ideal and acceptable values for certain kinds of print jobs. See whether these work for you.

Type of Job	Ideal Resolution	Acceptable Setting
Full-color image for magazine or professional publication	300 ppi	225 ppi
Full-color slides	300 ppi	200 ppi
Color ink jet printers	300 ppi	200 ppi
Color image for laser printing or overhead projections	180 ppi	120 ppi
Color images for multimedia productions and World Wide Web pages	72 ppi	72 ppi
Black-and-white images for imageset newsletters, flyers, and so on	180 ppi	120 ppi
Black-and-white images for laser printing	120 ppi	90 ppi

Keep in mind that there are no hard-and-fast rules about resolution settings. You can specify virtually any resolution setting between the ideal and acceptable settings and achieve good results. Even if you go with a Resolution value that's lower than the suggested acceptable setting, the worst that can happen is that you'll get fuzzy or slightly jagged results. But there is no wrong setting.

When you change the document size of the image, either the resolution value or the number of pixels in the image automatically changes, too, which can affect the quality of your image. For more information, read the section "Resolving resolution" earlier in this chapter. And for details on how to change the print size without ruining your image, see the section "Using the Image Size dialog box safely" later in this chapter.

Keeping things proportionate

Both pairs of Width and Height option boxes in the Image Size dialog box list the dimensions of your image in the current unit of measure. If you enter a different value into either option box and click on the OK button, Elements resizes your image to the dimensions. Pretty obvious, eh?

But strangely, when you change either the width or height value, the other value changes, too. Are these twins that were separated at birth? Is there some new cosmic relationship between width and height that's known only to outer-space aliens and the checkout clerk at your local grocery store? No, it's nothing more than a function of the Constrain Proportions check box, which is turned on by default. Elements is simply maintaining the original proportions of the image.

If you click on the Constrain Proportions box and turn it off, Elements permits you to adjust the width and height values independently. Notice that the little link icon (labeled back in Figure 4-2) disappears, showing that the two options are now maverick independents with reckless disregard for one another. You can now create stretchy effects like the ones shown in Figure 4-5. The first example has the width value reduced by a factor of two, with the height value unchanged. In the second example, the height value was reduced, leaving the width value unaltered.

However, in order to deselect the Constrain Proportions check box, you have to select the Resample Image check box. As explained below, in the highly anticipated section "Using the Image Size dialog box safely," when the Resample Image check box is selected, Elements either adds or deletes pixels from your image to compensate for the changes to the width and height of the image. Because adding pixels can make your image look like mud, never increase the width or height value with Constrain Proportions deselected. Decreasing the width and height values is okay, as long as the Resolution value stays in the acceptable range (see the sidebar "Yeah, okay, but what resolution should I use?" earlier in this chapter for recommended resolution values).

Using the Image Size dialog box safely

As mentioned earlier in the section "Image Size, Resolution, and Other Tricky Pixel Stuff," you have three image attributes — size, resolution, and dimension — all vying for your attention and all affecting each other. These attributes, in fact, are like three points on a triangle. Change any one of the points, and at least one of the others has to change proportionately. If you decrease the file size (pixel dimensions), for example, either the physical dimensions (document size) or resolution (number of pixels per inch) must also decrease. If you want to increase the physical dimensions, you have to increase the file size — add pixels, in other words — or decrease the resolution.

Figure 4-5:
This little girl was allowed to use the Image Size dialog box without parental supervision, providing clear examples of what can happen when the Constrain Proportions check box falls into the wrong hands.

Thinking about all the possible permutations can drive you crazy, and besides, they aren't the least bit important. What is important is that you understand what you can accomplish with the Image Size dialog box and that you know how to avoid mistakes. So, now that you have all the background you need, it's finally time for a modicum of fatherly advice:

✔ Changing the Pixel Dimensions (file size) values can be dangerous, as explained in the section "Changing pixel dimensions." To avoid changes to file size, deselect the Resample Image check box at the bottom of the Image Size dialog box. When you deselect the option, the Image Size dialog box changes, and the Width and Height options in the Pixel Dimensions portion of the dialog box become unavailable to you. A link icon also connects the Document Size's Width, Height, and Resolution option boxes, showing that changes to one value affect the other two values as well.

✔ Remember that in order to turn off the Constrain Proportions check box, you have to turn on the Resample Image check box. If you make changes to the image's width and height values, Elements *resamples* (changes the number of pixels in) the image. If you lower the width and height values, you'll probably be okay. But if you try to raise the width and height values, you're likely to muck things up.

✔ Want a surefire way to tell whether you've changed the pixel dimensions? Your image looks different onscreen after you change the Resolution or Document Size values and exit the Image Size dialog box. As long as the pixel dimensions remain unchanged, you won't see any difference — none, zilch, zippo — onscreen. Onscreen, Elements just shows your image pixels with respect to screen pixels; resolution and document size enter into the equation only when you print the image.

✔ If you manage to mess up everything and change one or more settings in the Image Size dialog box to settings that you don't want to apply, you can return to the original settings by Alt+clicking (Option+clicking on a Mac) on the Cancel button. Pressing Alt (Option on a Mac) changes the word Cancel to Reset; clicking resets the options. Now you have your original settings back in place so that you can muck them up again. If you already pressed Enter (Return on a Mac) to exit the Image Size dialog box, click the Step Backward icon in the Shortcuts bar (the down-left pointing arrow) or press Ctrl+Z (⌘+Z on a Mac) to travel backward in time to before you dared to tamper with the image size.

✔ If you performed *another* action after you erroneously resized, you can keep clicking the Step Backward button or keep pressing Ctrl+Z (⌘+Z on a Mac) to keep moving backward in time until the unfortunate image sizing goes away. This does have its limits, which you'll learn more about when we look at the magnificent and powerful History palette in Chapter 7.

✔ Whatever you do, be sure to use the Bicubic setting in the Resample Image drop-down menu. We'd tell you what *bicubic* means, but you don't want to know. Suffice it to say that it keeps things running smoothly.

✔ If you want to change the unit of measure that displays by default in the Image Size dialog box drop-down menus, choose Edit⇨Preferences⇨ Units & Rulers and select a different option from the Rulers drop-down menu.

We may have scared you into thinking that changing the image size is something you never want to do. But you may, in fact, want to reduce the image size on some occasions — to get the image to print or display at a certain size, to enable your computer to handle the image, or to make the image download faster from the Internet. The following steps show you how to reduce your image size without turning your image into a worthless pile of goo.

Before you follow these steps, choose File➪Save As to save a backup copy of your image. The steps result in Elements tossing away pixels, and after you delete pixels, you can't get them back after you close your file. So always make a copy of the original in case things don't work out or you decide you want to use the original again at a later date.

1. **Open the image at the highest resolution possible.**

   For example, if you're opening a Photo CD image, select the 2048 by 3072 option from the Resolution drop-down menu. If that doesn't work — Elements may complain that you don't have enough memory to pull it off — try again and select the 1024 by 1536 option. Whatever works, go for it.

2. **Choose Image➪Resize➪Image Size to open the Image Size dialog box.**

3. **Note the values in the Pixel Dimensions Width and Height option boxes.**

   You may want to write 'em down — they're important.

4. **Make sure that the Resample Image check box is selected.**

5. **Enter your desired print width and height in the Document Size option boxes.**

   If you want Elements to retain the original proportions of your image, make sure that the Constrain Proportions option box is checked.

6. **Enter your desired resolution in the Resolution option box.**

   Check the sidebar, "Yeah, okay, but what resolution should I use?" earlier in this chapter for some suggestions on acceptable resolution values if you need help.

7. **Check the Pixel Dimensions values.**

   Did either of the values get bigger? If so, you need to reduce your Document Size Width and Height values or lower the resolution. Otherwise, Elements adds pixels to your image, and you may not be happy with the results.

   If the Pixel Dimensions values got smaller, on the other hand, proceed to Step 8.

8. **Make sure that you select the Bicubic option in the Resample Image drop-down menu.**

9. **Click on the OK button.**

   Elements resizes — or, if you prefer, *resamples* — your image in accordance with your perfect settings. If you don't like the results, click the Step Backward button or press Ctrl+Z (⌘+Z on a Mac) to put things back to the way they were.

What Does This Canvas Size Command Do?

There's another important command related to the topic of image sizing: Image⇨Resize⇨Canvas Size. Unlike the Image Size command, which stretches or shrinks the preexisting image, the Canvas Size command changes the size of the page — or canvas — on which the image sits. If you increase the size of the canvas, Elements fills the new area outside the image with the background color, which is white by default. If you make the canvas smaller, Elements crops the image.

When you choose Image⇨Resize⇨Canvas Size, the dialog box, shown in Figure 4-6, pops up from its virtual hole. You can play with the options found in the dialog box as follows:

✔ Enter new values into the Width and Height option boxes as desired. You can also change the unit of measurement by using the drop-down menus, just as in the Image Size dialog box.

✔ You can't constrain the proportions of the canvas the way you can in the Image Size dialog box. Therefore, the width and height values always operate independently.

✔ The Anchor section shows a graphic representation of how the current image sits inside the new canvas. By default, the image is centered in the canvas. But you can click inside any of the other eight squares to move the image to the upper-right corner, center it along the bottom edge, or place it where you like.

✔ If you reduce either the width or height value and press Enter (Return on a Mac), Elements asks you whether you really want to clip (or crop) the image. If you click on the Proceed button and decide you don't like the results, you can always click the Step Backward icon or press Ctrl+Z (⌘+Z on a Mac) to restore the original canvas size.

Figure 4-6:
Use the
Canvas Size
dialog box
to change
the size of
the virtual
page on
which the
image sits.

Canvas Size

┌ Current Size: 288K ─────────────┐
Width: 1.422 inches
Height: 2.133 inches

OK
Cancel
Help

┌ New Size: 1.05M ─────────────┐
Width: 2.5   inches ▲▼
Height: 4.5   inches ▲▼
Anchor:

Trimming Excess Gunk Off the Edges

While you can use the Canvas Size command to crop images, it's hardly the best tool at your disposal. Elements, the handy-dandy application that it is, has specialized tools for the job. The Image Size command can definitely turn an 8x10 wedding photograph into a nifty wallet-size snapshot without trimming off anyone's vital body parts. But suppose that your spouse up and runs off to Lagos with your next-door neighbor? What do you do then? Why, you crop the cretin out of the picture.

The sharp edges of the Crop tool

Novice photographers have a habit of worrying about getting too much imagery into their pictures. This can be a dangerous concern. In your effort to cut out background flack, you may overcompensate and cut off Grandma's head or the right half of little Joey's body. The fact is, it's better to have too much stuff in your photos than too little, for the simple reason that excess stuff can be cut away, but missing stuff has to be reshot. Since photography was invented, production artists have been taking knives and scissors to just about every image that passes over their light tables in an effort to clip away the extraneous gook around the edges and hone in on the real goods. Called *cropping,* this technique is so pervasive that professional photographers purposely shoot subjects from too far away knowing that someone, somewhere, will slice the image and make it right. Like the Canvas Size command, cropping changes the pixel dimensions and the document size of your image without changing the resolution. (Of course, the content of your image changes, too.)

Inside Elements, you can cut away the unpalatable parts of an image by using the Crop tool. To select the Crop tool without messing with the Toolbox, press C.

Here's how to use the Crop tool:

1. **Drag with the tool around the portion of the image you want to retain.**

   In Figure 4-7, that's the floating spaceman. A dotted rectangle called a *marquee* follows your drag to clearly show the crop boundaries. After you've drawn your marquee, Elements covers the area outside the marquee with a translucent *shield* to better frame the image. You can use the shield controls in the Options bar to specify the color and opacity of the shield or to turn it off entirely. Don't worry if you don't draw the perfect marquee; you get the chance to edit the boundary in the next step.

Handle   Resize cursor   ⌐Crop boundary

Figure 4-7:
Drag the square handles to change the crop boundary.

If you press the spacebar during your drag, Elements stops resizing the crop boundary and starts moving the entire boundary. This technique can be helpful when you're trying to position the boundary precisely. (You can also move the boundary after you create it without the spacebar.)

2. **Drag the crop boundaries as desired.**

   After you release your mouse button, Elements displays square handles around the edges of the marquee (refer to Figure 4-7). If the marquee isn't the right size, drag a handle to change the crop boundary. Your cursor changes to a double-headed arrow when you place it over a handle, indicating that you have the go-ahead to drag the handle. You can drag as many handles as you please — one at a time, of course — before cropping the image. Holding down the Shift key while dragging from one of the corner handles constrains the proportions of the crop. Holding down the Alt key (the Option key on the Mac) makes the resizing of the crop boundary occur around the visible center of the crop.

If you move the cursor outside the crop boundary, the cursor changes to a curved, double-headed arrow. Dragging then rotates the crop boundary. Once the crop boundary is rotated, dragging from one of the square handles with the Alt key pressed (the Option key on the Mac) enables you to create a nonrectangular crop. When you accept the crop (see Step 3 below), Elements does the necessary distortions to convert the nonrectangular crop back into a rectangular image.

3. **After you get the crop boundary the way you want it, double-click inside the boundary to crop the image or click the Commit button in the Options bar.**

   You can also just press Enter (Return on a Mac). Elements throws away all pixels outside the crop boundary. If you rotated the crop boundary in Step 2, Elements rights the rectangular area and thus rotates the image, as shown in Figure 4-8.

When you rotate an image in this way, Elements *resamples* your image — that is, it rearranges the pixels to come up with the rotated image. As discussed earlier, resampling can damage your image. For best results, don't rotate your image more than once. However, if you rotate your image only in 90-degree increments, Elements doesn't resample your image.

Figure 4-8: If the photograph isn't straight, you can rotate the crop boundary to match (top) while telling Elements to crop and straighten the image at the same time (bottom).

Rotate cursor

More good news about cropping

Do you think that's all a generous application like Elements has to offer in terms of cropping images? Ha! Elements has so many terrific cropping techniques that one would be tempted to refer to them as a "bumper crop," if one liked painfully bad puns.

✔ After you selected the Crop tool, but before you started dragging with it, you might have noticed some other choices in the Options bar. The Width, Height, and Resolution settings are useful for cropping an image to an exact dimension.

Another option that can be useful is the Front Image option. It enables you to crop one image so that it's the same size as another image. Suppose that you want to make image B the same size as image A. First, open both images. Crop image A to your desired size. Click on the Front Image button. Elements loads the size and resolution settings from image A to the Options bar. Select image B. Drag the Crop tool on the canvas and frame your image. When you press Enter (Return on a Mac) to execute the crop, Elements automatically resizes image B to match image A. Note that Elements resamples image B if necessary in order to match the size of image A. Click the Clear button to escape this cropping mode.

✔ If you've created an active crop boundary and you then change your mind about cropping the image, press Esc or Ctrl+period (⌘+period on a Mac) to get rid of the cropping boundary. Or you can also press the Cancel button in the Options bar.

✔ To move the cropping boundary in its entirety, just drag inside the boundary.

✔ In addition to using the Crop tool, you can crop a *selected area* (see Chapter 8) by choosing Image⇨Crop. The selection doesn't even have to be vaguely rectangular; it can be elliptical, polygonal, or even feathered. Elements won't really crop to that shape, but it gets as close to the boundary as it can.

✔ As mentioned earlier, you can also crop an image by using the Canvas Size command. You may want to consider this method if you need to trim your image on one or more sides by a precise number of pixels to get the image to a certain size. The Canvas Size command can also come in handy if you want to crop a very small area — say three pixels worth — along one or more edges of the image and you have trouble selecting the area with the Crop marquee. You can reduce the size of the canvas using Image⇨Resize⇨Canvas Size to eliminate the offensive pixels.

The Straighten and Crop commands

We interrupt this book for an Elements News Flash: A new command, known as Straighten Image, has arrived on the scene and has taken up residence inside the Image menu. This command, an Elements exclusive, is wanted by Photoshop users everywhere.

Actually, the Straighten Image command has a partner in crime — the Straighten and Crop Image command — and that's why we're dealing with it in this section on cropping. You've probably encountered the dreaded "crooked scan," as seen on the left in Figure 4-9. Sometimes — no matter how meticulous you are about placing a snapshot on the scanning bed of your flatbed scanner, no matter how slowly and gingerly you close the scanner cover — you get a crooked scan. You could raise the scanner cover and try to reposition it manually, or you could go ahead with the scan and attempt to fix it with the Crop tool as shown in Figure 4-9, eyeballing just the perfect angle to correct your crooked scan.

That's where the Straighten Image command comes in. Just go to Image➪ Rotate➪Straighten Image, and Elements will attempt to automatically correct the problem. The Straighten and Crop Image command (Image➪Rotate➪ Straighten and Crop Image) goes one step further: After it straightens the scan, it crops the background away, ideally resulting in something like the image on the right in Figure 4-9.

Figure 4-9:
The
Straighten
and Crop
Image
command
can
automatically
correct a
crooked
scan.

You'll find that these commands work much better if you leave a substantial amount of background around your image. In other words, if your scanning software gives you a preview of the image before you actually scan it, and you notice that the image is skewed in the scanner, go ahead and scan in a large chunk of background (usually the underside of your scanner's cover) surrounding the image. It can also sometimes help to lay a piece of paper between the back of the image and the scanner lid to give a more contrasting background. Of course you have to raise your scanner cover to do that, so you might as well take another crack at straightening the snapshot manually anyway.

In truth, Elements does a much better job with the automatic straightening than it does with the automatic cropping. Authorities speculate that may be why Straighten Image is available as a standalone command. Details at 11.

Image Gymnastics

If you checked out the Straighten and Crop Image command, you might have noticed your cursor breezing by a whole submenu of Rotate commands under the Image menu. Here's the lowdown on them:

- **Canvas 90° Left, Canvas 90° Right, and Canvas 180°:** These commands rotate the entire canvas. Left is counterclockwise; Right is clockwise. These commands can be useful if your image was scanned on its side or upside down, but it doesn't need cropping or straightening.

- **Canvas Custom:** Allows you to rotate your canvas a specific amount. If you rotate anything other than 90° or 180°, the canvas size will grow in order to accommodate the rotated image.

- **Flip Canvas Horizontal:** Creates a mirror image of your canvas.

- **Flip Canvas Vertical:** Creates a mirror image of your canvas and turns it upside down.

The commands at the top of the Rotate submenu perform identically to the commands listed here, but they only apply if your image has an active selection (see Chapter 8) or layers (see Chapter 9).

Chapter 5

Over (and Under) the Rainbow

As you might have guessed from the title, this chapter is all about color — the same kind of color that Dorothy encountered when she passed over the weather-beaten threshold of her old Kansas home onto a path of lemon-yellow bricks in that beloved classic, *Fight Club*. Or was it *The Wizard of Oz*? Maybe so. Anyway, when Dorothy was in Kansas — "under" the rainbow — everything was in black and white. But as soon as she went "over" the rainbow and stepped out of her ramshackle house into the Land of Oz, things were in color. (Okay, there is that one transitional shot when she's still in the house and she first opens the door that's *actually* shot in color, and they tried to make it *look* black and white inside the house, but you can tell it's really not. Hey, give 'em a break — it's the best they could do in 1939.)

So what's the lesson here? Kansas seemed pretty dreary and depressing next to Oz, with its helium-voiced midgets, combative trees, and bipedal jungle cats. Color must have it all over black and white, huh?

Well, little Dorothy Gale didn't ultimately think so. And, in truth, the absence of color can offer its own special attractions. It's the mysterious essence of a torch-lit castle on a stormy night. It's the refreshingly personal vision of a 16mm short-subject film you stumble across one evening on Bravo. It's the powerful chiaroscuro of an Ansel Adams photograph. In an age when every screen, page, and billboard screams with color that's more vivid than real life, black and white can beckon the eye like an old friend.

But on the off chance you think all that's a pretentious load of hooey, there's one specific area in which Kansas definitely kicks Oz's keister, and that's in the cost of professional printing. Despite the increasing influence of computers in print houses, color printing remains extremely expensive. Major four-color magazines spend more on ink than they do on their writers. The color medium costs more than the message, and that's a sad fact (especially for us magazine writers).

Though by no means free, black-and-white images are substantially less expensive to reproduce. Only one ink is involved — black. Other supplies, such as film and plates for the printing press, are kept to a minimum. Black-and-white printing is also incredibly versatile. You can print black-and-white images with any laser printer, you can photocopy black-and-white images using cheap equipment, and you can fax black-and-white images with relatively little loss in quality. And finally, black-and-white images require one-third of the overhead when you're working in Photoshop Elements, meaning that you can edit black-and-white images that contain three times as many pixels as color images without Elements complaining that it's out of memory. Kansas is starting to sound better and better, huh? No surprise, really. The Sunflower State is really as lovely as its nickname, while the Munchkins — to hear Judy Garland tell it — were a bunch of randy booze hounds.

Whether you choose black and white, color, or — like most folks — vacillate between the two, this chapter tells you how it all works. You find out how to use and create colors that you can apply with the painting tools. Not bad for a chapter based on an old MGM musical, eh?

Looking at Color in a Whole New Light

To understand color in Elements, you have to understand a little color theory. If you've had a color image open in Elements, you may have noticed the telltale initials RGB inside parentheses in the image title bar. These initials mean that all colors inside the image are created by blending red, green, and blue light.

Red, green, and blue? That doesn't sound particularly colorful, does it? But, in fact, these colors are the primary colors of light. The red is a vivid scarlet, the green is so bright and tinged with yellow that you may be tempted to call it chartreuse, and the blue is a brilliant Egyptian lapis. It just so happens that these colors correspond to the three kinds of cones inside your eyeball. So, in theory, your monitor projects color in the same way your eyes see color.

Go ahead and turn to Color Plate 5-1 in the middle of the book (but keep a finger here, of course). The colorful photo of the gentleman at the bottom of the plate looks very much like it would on your monitor. But lurking under the surface, as illustrated at the top of the plate, are three different color channels: red, green, and blue. When you see a color image like this on your

Color Plate 5-1: The red, green, and blue color channels in Photoshop Elements act like slides in separate projectors pointed at the same spot on a screen. You may find it hard to believe that three primary hues could mix together to produce so many colors, but it's true.

Color Plate 5-2: Pure white light from the sun (or a man-made light source) is made up of red, green, and blue light. When light passes through the cyan, magenta, or yellow printing ink, the ink filters out the red, green, or blue light and lets the other two pass through.

Color Plate 5-3: This figure shows the way light, dark, and medium pixels in the red, green, and blue channels mix to form various sample colors. Altogether, you can create more than 16 million color variations.

Background texture: Psychedelic Strings Effect

Color Plate 9-1: To create this composition, eight images were combined and blended together using various blend modes and Opacity settings from the Layers palette.

Background texture: Wood — Rosewood Effect

Color Plate 10-1: The Red Eye Brush tool was able to quickly remove that familiar eerie red glow (left) from the eyes of an innocent youth (right).

Color Plate 12-1: Don't be surprised if you open up a scanned image and find it looking like the one on the left. The image isn't beyond redemption; it just needs some color correction. In fact, the colors were corrected in about ten minutes using the Levels and Variations commands (right).

Background texture: Green Slime Effect

Color Plate 12-2: The results of adding blue (left) and yellow (right) to the image by using Enhance⇨Variations. Colors that have little or no blue or yellow in them — such as the reds in the bows and the greens in the packages and apples — remain virtually unaffected.

Color Plate 12-3: The colors of paradise lost (left) and found again (right) by selecting the Saturation radio button inside the Variations dialog box and increasing the saturation.

Background texture: Gold Sprinkles Effect

Color Plate 12-4: Here, the Levels command was used to correct the colors in a muted image. For reference, the histogram and Input Levels options from the Levels dialog box are inset with each step. Starting with the uncorrected scan (top left), the black slider triangle (top right), the white triangle (bottom left), and the gamma point (bottom right) were adjusted to create a sound image with excellent color depth.

Background texture: Wood — Pine Effect

Original   **More Blue**   **More Blue**

More Magenta   **More Magenta**   **More Blue**

Color Plate 12-5: This image had a preponderance of yellow and green (top left). It was fixed by clicking on the labeled previews in the Variations dialog box. For example, to produce the top middle image, the More Blue preview was clicked; to get the top right image, More Blue was clicked again.

Color Plate 14-1: When the Paintbrush tool was used to paint in the sun with yellow and the sky with blue, the paint obscured the sun's face and rays. Another try with the Opacity set to 40% resulted in weaker color (right).

Background texture: Rusted Metal Effect

Multiply

Screen

Overlay

Difference

Color Plate 14-2: The results of applying yellow and blue with the Paintbrush tool using each of four brush modes.

Color Plate 15-1: The area behind the jar was filled with custom gradients created by using the Gradient Editor.

Background texture: Bricks Effect

monitor, you're actually seeing the combination of these three channels. The red image on the left is the one being sent to the red cones in your eyes; the green image in the middle is hitting your green cones, and the blue image goes right to your blue cones.

Pretty nifty, huh? Here's another way to think about it: If you were to take the images you see in the red, green, and blue channels, print them to slides, put each of the slides in a different projector, and shine all three projectors at the same spot on a screen so that the images precisely overlapped, you would see the full-color image in all its splendor.

Yet another way to think about the color channels is as black-and-white images, as shown in Figure 5-1 below. Where areas in the red channel are very light, there will be a lot of red in the corresponding full color image. And where things are dark in the red channel, there won't be much red at all. Look at the plaid cloth in the image, and compare it between the red, green, and blue channels to get the idea.

Figure 5-1: The black-and-white channels combine to make a full-color image.

Every color channel contains light areas and dark areas, just like a black-and-white image. The light and dark pixels from each channel mix together to form other colors.

The following list explains how corresponding pixels from the different channels mix together to form a single full-color pixel:

✔ A white pixel from one channel mixed with black pixels from the other two channels produces the color from the first channel. For example, if the red is white, and green and blue are black, you get a red pixel.

✔ White pixels from the red and green channels plus a black pixel from the blue channel form yellow. This description may sound weird — two colors, red and green, mixing to form a lighter color — but that's exactly how things work in the upside-down world of RGB. Because you're mixing colors projected from a monitor, two colors projected together produce a still lighter color.

Do you follow? No? Well, suppose you had a flashlight with a red bulb and your friend had one with a green bulb. Maybe it's Christmas or something. At any rate, if you were to point your flashlight at a spot on the ground, the spot would turn red. No surprise there. But if you then said, "Look, Nancy, it's the missing key from the old Bigbee place," and Nancy pointed her green flashlight at the same spot, the spot wouldn't get darker, it would get lighter. In fact, it would turn bright yellow. "Gee wizikers, Ned, do you suppose this means Mrs. Welker is innocent after all?" (Unfortunately, we'll never know.)

✔ White pixels from the green and blue channels plus a black pixel from the red channel make a bright turquoise color called cyan. White red and blue pixels plus a black green pixel make magenta.

✔ By a strange coincidence, cyan, magenta, and yellow just happen to be the main ink colors used in the color printing process. Well, actually, it's not a coincidence at all. Color printing is the opposite of color screen display, so the two use complementary collections of primary hues to produce full-color images. The difference is that because cyan, magenta, and yellow are pigments, they become darker as you mix them. Yellow plus cyan, for example, make green.

Your monitor creates white by mixing the lightest amounts of red, green, and blue — the opposite of how things work on the printed page. Color printing exploits the fact that sunlight and man-made light (both referred to as "white light") contain the entire spectrum of visible light, including all shades of red, green, and blue. The primary printing inks — cyan, magenta, and yellow — are actually *color filters*. When white light hits cyan ink printed on a page, the cyan ink filters out all traces of red and reflects only green and blue, which mix to form cyan. Similarly, magenta is a green light filter, and yellow is a blue light filter, as illustrated in detail in Color Plate 5-2. This and other factors (such as purity of inks, variation of ink tints, whiteness of paper, and lighting conditions) result in the CMYK world.

✔ White pixels from all three channels mix to form white. Black pixels form black. Equally medium pixels make gray.

Although all of this is highly stimulating, it would probably make more sense if you could see it. If you're the visual type, take a look at Color Plate 5-3. The left side of the figure shows the RGB combinations just discussed. The right side shows RGB mixes that result in other colors, including orange, purple, and so on. Give it the once-over and see whether you can't feel your brain grow by leaps and bounds.

Managing Photoshop Elements Color

Now that you have some basic color theory, it's time for basic color management. People want to be able to have a true WYSIWYG (What You See Is What You Get) world. In other words, they want to be able to look at their monitor and see the exact colors they'll get coming out the other end. This "other end" can be in the form of printouts or an image on the Web viewed from another monitor.

Gimme good gamma

Getting exact color is next to impossible. However, devices can help — expensive hardware and software calibrators that come with high-end monitors — but most of us average Joes and Jos have to manage this dilemma on our own. Elements, however, (the friendly application that it is) comes with a little help in the form of the Adobe Gamma Control Panel.

1. **Choose Start⇨Settings⇨Control Panel and double-click on Adobe Gamma. (On a Mac, choose Apple⇨Control Panels⇨Adobe Gamma.)**

2. **If you want the deluxe guided tour of the Adobe Gamma Control Panel, choose Step By Step and let the Wizard (the Assistant on the Mac) show you the way. If you want the quick-and-dirty method, follow along as follows: Choose the Control Panel option and click on the Next button.**

   The Control Panel appears, as seen in Figure 5-2, giving you all the necessary setup options in one dialog box.

3. **In the middle of the dialog box, uncheck View Single Gamma Only. Then, using each of the sliders, make the inner colors match the outer colors for the red, green, and blue color swatches. Leave the other settings as they are.**

   If you aren't sure whether a setting is correct, check the documentation that came with your monitor or call the vendor. When you're done, Elements has the scoop on your monitor.

4. **Click OK.**

Choosing your color settings

Dealing with color space is without question the most complex and confusing aspect of working with digital images on the computer. In Elements' grand-daddy application, Photoshop, the Color Settings dialog box is an intimidating myriad of options and technical terms designed to make even seasoned pros curl up into a ball on the floor and whimper. Thank your lucky stars, then, that this has all been simplified quite eloquently for Elements.

Figure 5-2:
The Adobe
Gamma
Control
Panel
helps you
calibrate
your
monitor.

Don't forget that color management, at its core, is all about keeping colors consistent. Elements does its part by allowing you to embed profiles into images when you save them. A profile gives the next person to come along an idea of what an image looked like to the last person who worked on it. Elements can also read profiles from other systems and adjust the display of images accordingly. Clear as mud? Well, follow along now, and we promise this won't hurt a bit.

1. **Choose Edit➪Color Settings.**

   You should see a dialog box that bears an uncanny resemblance to the one in Figure 5-3. Only three options to choose from — this doesn't look so bad, does it?

2. **If you're happy with the status quo, leave things at the default setting of "No color management."**

   After all, things have worked pretty well so far, right? If you're happy with the colors you see when you use Elements and print from the application, there's no reason to change a thing.

3. **If you're going to be working with images for the World Wide Web, you can choose "Limited color management."**

   This setting takes into consideration what images look like when displayed on the average PC monitor, which after all is what most Web surfers are using.

4. **If you're working on images for print, you can choose "Full color management."**

   When we're talking about "print" here, we're talking about the world of professional printing — and if you're doing a lot of professional print work, it might behoove you to move up from Elements to the full version of Photoshop anyway. But this setting will help you get by in a pinch.

5. **Click OK.**

   There now, that wasn't so bad, was it?

Figure 5-3:
The Color
Settings
dialog box
makes color
management
a simple
affair.

Picking Color the Mix and Match Way

We have to say it: You've been very patient. After luring you into this chapter by comparing the subject matter to a beloved classic family movie, we've done nothing but bore you to tears with talk of color theory and color settings. You've really been quite tolerant during the presentation of all this dry, technical mumbo jumbo, and we'd like to take this opportunity to . . . hey — *wake up.*

All that sleep-inducing talk about color is important to understand if you're going to get the most out of Elements. But now it's time to turn to more practical color matters. Things like "How do I choose colors?" and "Where can I keep them once I've chosen them?" Read on, Mac- (or PC) duff.

Juggling foreground and background colors

In Elements' Toolbox, you can work with two colors at a time: a *foreground color* and a *background color*. Most tools and commands paint your image with the foreground color, but a few splash it with the background color.

The Toolbox displays two colors at the bottom. As shown in Figure 5-4, the foreground color is on top and the background color is on the bottom. To get some idea of how these colors work, read the following list:

- ✔ The foreground color is applied by the painting tools, such as the Airbrush, Paintbrush, and Pencil.

- ✔ When you use the Eraser tool, you're actually painting with the background color. (Unless you're on a layer, in which case you would erase to transparency. For more on layers see Chapter 9.)

- ✔ When you increase the size of the canvas using Image➪Resize➪Canvas Size (as explained in Chapter 4), Elements fills the new empty portion of the canvas with the background color.

- ✔ The Gradient tool, by default, creates a rainbow of colors between the foreground and background colors.

Figure 5-4:
The collection of color icons in the Toolbox.

Foreground color —— Swap 'em
Default colors —— Background color

The Toolbox includes icons that enable you to change the foreground and background colors, swap them around, and so on. Here are some guidelines to get you started:

- ✔ Click on the Foreground Color or Background Color icon to display the all-important Color Picker dialog box. Press Esc or click Cancel to leave that dialog box.

- ✔ Click the Default Colors icon (refer to Figure 5-4) to restore the foreground color to black and the background color to white.

- ✔ Click that little two-way arrow icon — childishly labeled Swap 'em in the figure — to swap the foreground and background colors with each other.

- ✔ You can also access the Default Colors and Swap 'em icons from the keyboard. Press D to restore the default colors, black and white. Press X to swap the foreground and background colors.

Defining colors

You can define the foreground and background colors in Elements in three ways:

- ✔ Click on the Foreground Color or Background Color icon in the Toolbox to summon the Color Picker.

- ✔ Use the Eyedropper tool to lift colors from your image.

- ✔ Use the Swatches palette.

Using the Color Picker

To access the Color Picker, shown in Figure 5-5, click on either the Foreground Color or Background Color icon. The first thing you should notice is the enormous square of color on the left of the dialog box; this is known to Elements cognoscenti as the color field. To its immediate right, you'll see a rainbow-colored bar commonly referred to as the color slider. The color rectangle in the upper-right corner of the controls is known, strangely enough, as the color rectangle. And below that you'll see a handful of option boxes and radio buttons. Introduce yourself to all the controls, and get to know their names, because you'll be spending a lot of time in the Color Picker.

Do you want to know the quick and dirty way to select a color using the Color Picker? Okay, here goes:

1. **Click on the Foreground Color or Background Color tool in the Toolbox, depending on which you want to set.**

2. **Drag in the color slider to set the specific hue you want.**
   (Make sure the radio button next to the H is checked first.)

Color rectangle

Color field   Color slider   Web safe color alert

Figure 5-5:
The Color
Picker
cordially
invites you
to pick a
color . . .
any color.

Hue, Saturation, and
Brightness values

Red, Green, and Blue values

Hexadecimal value

3. **Drag around in the color field to set the brightness and saturation for the hue.**

4. **Click OK.**

And that's it. Following these simple steps can reliably get you the color you want every time. There will be times, however, when you'll need to specify certain aspects of colors, and the preceding method won't suffice. It's for times such as these that we now present: The Rest of the Story.

The Color Picker also lets you choose colors numerically by entering values in the option boxes. You can work numerically with three different color modes. The option box at the very bottom is for specifying hexadecimal colors, which is very useful for Web design professionals, but generally classified as *too much information* for our purposes here. The top three option boxes (H, S, and B) let you specify colors according to their Hue, Saturation, and Brightness. We'll skip these for now, and instead turn our attention to the bottom three option boxes. Hopefully those three letters look vaguely familiar to you by now: R, G, and B stand, of course, for Reginald, Gertie, and Bert.

Okay, just seeing if you were paying attention. You can think of red, green, and blue as ingredients in baking the perfect color. You can add 256 levels of each of the primary hues, 0 being the darkest amount of the hue, 255 being the lightest, and 128 being smack dab in the middle. For example, if you set the R value to 255, the G value to 128, and the B value to 0, you get a vibrant orange, just like the one shown in the upper-right corner of Color Plate 5-3.

If you've never mixed colors using red, green, and blue, it can be a little perplexing at first. For example, folks often have a hard time initially accepting that all yellows and oranges are produced by mixing red and green. We encourage you to experiment. Better yet, we order you to experiment.

If you followed our little orange recipe above, you've probably noticed that the mysterious color rectangle now has a two-toned effect going on. While the top half is sporting that spiffy orange color, the bottom half is modeling the old foreground or background color you started with. That's what the color rectangle is all about: letting you compare your new color against the old one.

The HSB color mode is simply another way of describing color. Rather than breaking it down into three color channels, the HSB color mode breaks color down according to its Hue (which you can think of as the "color" of the color), Saturation (how rich the color is), and Brightness (how bright or dark the color is).

In truth, using the numeric values in the Color Picker is a very complicated, confusing affair. It works on the principle that the property with the checked radio button gets mapped to the color slider. The color slider then gives you the full range of options for that one property. The other properties are then mapped to the color field, and you can drag around inside the field to hone in on the color you want. Just experiment with this technique for a second, clicking on the various radio buttons and dragging around in the color slider and color field. How do you feel? Wait — don't smash your monitor with this book. Just click on the H radio button again. There now, isn't that better?

It can't be just sheer luck that the Color Picker defaults to having the Hues mapped to the color slider. The whole dad-gummed dialog box just seems to make sense that way. So keep it that way, we say.

If you're wondering about that almost-omnipresent little cube that pops up next to the color rectangle, it's there to warn you that the color you've chosen isn't Web-safe. The Web-safe palette consists of 216 colors that you can count on to display consistently across the entire World Wide Web, no matter the combination of platform, monitor, or browser. As more and more people upgrade from their old 8-bit, 256-color monitors, this becomes less and less of an issue. But if it concerns you, click on the colored square beneath the cube to change your chosen color to the nearest Web-safe color. You can also work in a purely Web-safe world by clicking the Only Web Colors check box beneath the color field.

Lifting colors with the Eyedropper tool

You can also change the foreground or background colors by lifting them from the image. Just select the Eyedropper tool — on the right side of the Toolbox just above the Zoom tool — and click inside the image on the color you want to use. If you have more than one image open, you can even click inside an image different from the one you're working on.

Here's some stuff to know about this incredibly easy-to-use tool:

✔ You can press I (for I-dropper) to select the Eyedropper tool instead of clicking on its Toolbox icon.

✔ The Eyedropper by default determines the foreground color. To set the background color, Alt+click (Option+click on a Mac) with the Eyedropper.

✔ You can temporarily access the Eyedropper tool when using some of the other tools by pressing the Alt key (Option key on a Mac). As long as the key is down, the Eyedropper is available. This trick works when you're using the Paint Bucket, Gradient, Pencil, Airbrush, Paintbrush, Background Eraser, Magic Eraser, Red Eye Brush, and Shape tools.

✔ If you use the preceding tip, you can change only the foreground color. You need the Alt key (Option on a Mac) to change the background color, so you can't use the key to temporarily access the Eyedropper. You have to select the Eyedropper for real (click on its icon or press I) and then Alt+click (Option+click on a Mac). If your keyboard offers two Alt keys (Option keys on a Mac), it doesn't help to press both of them!

✔ As you use the Eyedropper, you can keep tabs on the exact R, G, and B values for the colors in your image by looking in the Info palette.

✔ The Sample Size option in the Options bar determines precisely how the Eyedropper tool chooses a color. When set to Point Sample, it chooses the color of the precise pixel it's clicked on. When set to 3 by 3 Average, the Eyedropper looks not only at the pixel it's clicked on but in a 3-pixel by 3-pixel square all around the clicked pixel. It averages together the colors of those nine pixels, and that average color becomes the chosen color. Likewise for 5 by 5 Average, the Eyedropper looks in a 5-pixel by 5-pixel square and averages the color of those 25 pixels. This can be useful if, for example, you want to choose from a field of color in an image like the sky, and you're not as concerned with getting the color of any one pixel as you are with getting the general color of the sky.

Using the Swatches palette

At this point you may be thinking that only being able to keep two colors around — the foreground and the background color — is a trifle, shall we say, limiting. Enter the Swatches palette, as accurately depicted in Figure 5-6. No, it has nothing to do with stylish timepieces; the Swatches palette is nothing less than a repository for color.

Figure 5-6:
The
Swatches
palette.
Okay, it
loses a little
something
in black and
white.

To activate the Swatches palette, click on its tab in the palette well. You can grab it by the tab and drag it out onto the desktop if you wish. (It won't hurt it a bit.) As you can see, the Swatches palette already contains a pleasing assortment of colors. If you want a little more information about those colors, click the palette menu (the little arrow button in the upper-right corner of the palette) and choose Small List. You'll see the color swatches along with their descriptive names.

To set one of those colors as the foreground color, all you have to do is move your cursor onto a swatch — like magic, it turns into the Eyedropper tool. Just click, and there you go! If you want to set the background color instead, Alt+click (Option+click on the Mac) on a swatch. Simple, huh?

Elements comes with several preset swatch libraries located at the bottom of the palette menu, but the real power of the Swatches palette lies in its ability to let you create and save your own customized swatch libraries. To add the current foreground color to the Swatches palette, just move the cursor into the blank, gray area of the Swatches palette. The cursor automatically turns into the Paint Bucket tool. Just click, and Elements will ask you to enter a name for your swatch. If you want to dispense with the naming ceremony and just accept the default name, add the Alt key (the Option key on the Mac) as you click. You can also go to the Swatches palette menu and choose New Swatch, bypassing the Paint Bucket-clicking method altogether.

It's very important to learn how to organize the Swatches palette and to save libraries. If you're like most people, you'll be working along in Elements, mixing colors with the Color Picker, when you happen to come across the perfect color. "Ooh!" you say. "The perfect color! I know what to do: I'll add it to the Swatches palette!" So you hightail your mouse over to the Swatches palette, click to add the perfect color swatch to the default library, and resume work. Now, no matter what you do to the foreground and background colors, you can be sure that your perfect color is always waiting for you.

As your work continues, you discover many more perfect colors and add them to the Swatches palette as well. "Wow," you think. "I sure do love my Swatches palette. Perhaps I should get to know it better." So you decide to investigate it, clicking on the palette menu. "Hmmm . . . 'Reset Swatches' . . . I wonder what that does?" You select it . . . and BAM! All your perfect colors are gone forever. You sink to the ground, sobbing, "Why, oh why, didn't I read my *Photoshop Elements For Dummies* book thoroughly, from cover to cover? How completely foolhardy of me! I'm going to buy copies for all my friends to ensure that this tragedy never happens to them! In fact, I'm going to buy copies of the book by the truckload and pass them out to total strangers on the street!"

What you should have done (oh sure, *now* we tell you) is save your swatches. All you need to do is go to the palette menu, choose Save Swatches, and give your swatch library a distinctive name. By default, Elements will save your swatches in a folder called Color Swatches that contains all the other default swatch libraries that shipped with the program. That's a dandy place to save your libraries too.

As noted in the preceding tragic story, Reset Swatches takes you back to Elements' default swatch library, jettisoning any swatches you might have added to it. Load Swatches allows you to pick a swatch library and tack it on to the end of the current library. And Replace Swatches wipes the slate clean, replacing all the swatches in the palette with the library you select.

If you want to check out all the preset swatches, brushes, gradients, and patterns that Elements has to offer, you can always go to Edit➪Preset Manager. All of the various categories of presets are accessible via the Preset Type drop-down menu. To the right of each scrolling list of preset icons is also a drop-down menu that gives you reset and viewing options, as well as accessibility to the various libraries under each preset category. And, finally, you can also load, replace, save, rename, and delete libraries using the buttons on the right side of the dialog box.

Going Grayscale

Now that we've wasted most of the chapter in the colorful Land of Oz, you may be wondering when we're ever going to decide there's no place like home, click our heels, and head back to Kansas. Take heart: The heralded hour of black-and-white images has arrived.

The first thing to understand about black-and-white images is that the black-and-white world offers more colors than just black and white. It includes a total of 256 unique shades of gray and is therefore more properly termed *grayscale*. Each one of these shades is a color in its own right, which is why the term "black and white" can inspire fisticuffs among some grayscale devotees.

Second, all the stuff about creating colors in the preceding sections of this chapter holds true for grayscale image editing, as well. You have a foreground and background color. You can define colors in the Color Picker. (Click the B radio button, and adjust the levels of gray with the color slider.) And you can lift colors from a grayscale image using the Eyedropper tool.

But some aspects of grayscale editing are different than full-color editing, which leads us to the next two sections.

The road to grayscale

Most images that you'll come across will be in color. This means that working in grayscale generally requires a conversion inside Elements.

Unlike a three-channel RGB image, a grayscale image includes only one channel of imagery. If you plan to print in black and white, you should jettison all the extraneous color information, for two reasons. First, it's easier for Elements to keep track of one channel than three. In fact, given the same image size and resolution, Elements performs faster when editing a grayscale image than when editing in color. Second, you can better see what your printed image will look like. When you're designing an image to be printed in black and white, color just gets in the way.

To convert a color image to grayscale, just choose Image⇨Mode⇨Grayscale. Elements asks you whether you want it to discard color information. (The "Don't show again" check box is just Elements' way of asking you if you want it to ask you about this.) You can click on OK to convert to grayscale or chicken out and cancel. That's all there is to it. You now have a single-channel grayscale image. No matter what color you choose in the Color Picker, the color will appear as some shade of gray in the Foreground Color and Background Color icons. If you don't like the results of your conversion to grayscale, you can go back to the full-color original by clicking the Step Backward button in the Shortcuts bar or pressing Ctrl+Z (⌘+Z on a Mac).

Before you change a color image to grayscale, you may want to make a backup copy of the original image, just in case you ever want to have the image available in color in the future. For details on saving images, see Chapter 6.

If you have a layered file and only want to remove color from one layer, choose Enhance⇨Color⇨Remove Color or press Ctrl+Shift+U (⌘+Shift+U on the Mac). Elements drains the selected layer of all its color. Note that this doesn't convert the image to grayscale; even if the image consists of only one layer and you apply Remove Color, the image will still be RGB. Consequently, the size of the file on disk won't get any smaller either, so you lose the benefits of actually converting to grayscale. Remove Color is really most useful for layered files. For more information about layers, see Chapter 9.

A few more tips in black and white

Here are some final grayscale tidbits:

- ✔ To add color to a grayscale image, first convert back to RGB by choosing Image⇨Mode⇨RGB Color. Elements won't add a bunch of colors to the image, but it will let you add colors of your own.

- ✔ If you use the Image⇨Mode⇨Grayscale conversion method and your color image contains more than one layer (as explained in Chapter 9), Elements asks whether you want to flatten (merge) your image. If you want to keep your layers, click on the Don't Flatten button.

- ✔ If you're using an 8-bit monitor — that is, a monitor that can display only 256 colors — you're better off editing grayscale images. When you edit full-color RGB images, Elements shows only 256 of the 16 million possible colors at a time, resulting in *dithering,* an effect in which a random pattern of pixels is used to emulate lots more colors. When you edit a grayscale image, however, you can see every shade just right. Don't worry that Elements converts your entire screen, including Finder icons on the Mac, and all other background items to grays. This is a normal effect of editing in grayscale on an inexpensive computer system.

Part II
Be Prepared

The 5th Wave   By Rich Tennant

"Mary Jo, come here quick! Look at this special effect I learned with the new Photoshop Elements software."

In this part . . .

Yeah, we know. You want to start doing some image editing. You were very patient through the first part of this book: Jekyll and Hyde, dialog boxes, File Browser, Zoom tool, floor tiles, Image Size, Straighten and Crop, Wizard of Oz, Grayscale. All very nice, very interesting, and exceedingly well written (?), but now — if we don't mind too terribly much — you'd really like to get down to doing some image editing. Because you have this picture of yourself from your recent vacation to Maui that you want to e-mail to all your friends, but in the picture you have this unsettling disturbance on your chin that you'd really like to do something about . . .

Yeah, we know. But here's the cold, hard truth: There are really a few more things you need to know before you start image editing — things like saving files. Photoshop Elements has a truly bewildering array of options for saving files; there are well over a dozen different file formats to choose from. And what if you make a mistake as you're editing that vacation photo, and manage to give yourself a chin of Jay Leno–sized proportions? How can you go back and undo your work? Maybe you know about pressing Ctrl+Z on the PC or ⌘+Z on the Mac, but do you know about Elements' phenomenal time-traveling tool, the History palette? And how much do you really know about printing? For that matter, only when you come to grips with the power of making selections and using layers will you begin to realize the possibilities that Elements contains.

So patience, Gentle Reader. We'll get to the really exciting stuff, we promise. Just make it through this Part of the book with us, and it will be nothing but actual image editing from there to the end. Come on, that vacation photo can wait. Chin up.

Chapter 6

Saving with Grace

● ●

In This Chapter

▶ Understanding the basics of saving

▶ Saving with the correct file format

▶ Saving for the Web

▶ Quitting Elements

● ●

*I*f you've used a computer before, you may be wondering why we would devote an entire chapter to saving files. After all, you just press Ctrl+S (⌘+S on a Mac) and you're done, right? For that matter, Photoshop Elements lets you click a handy Save icon in the Shortcuts bar — the one that looks like the floppy disk. "What's to know about saving?" you ask. Well, if we were talking about any other program, you'd be right. If this book was about Microsoft Word, for example, we'd say, "Not to worry, Gentle Reader, saving a file is so simple, a newborn lemur could pull it off with the most cursory supervision from a parent or older sibling." If this book was about PageMaker, we'd add, "Saving makes tying your shoes look like a supreme feat of civil engineering."

But this book is about Photoshop Elements. And Elements, as you may or may not be aware, enables you to save images in more flavors than Willy Wonka manages to squeeze into an Everlasting Gobstopper. In the software world, these flavors are called *file formats,* and each one has a different purpose.

This chapter offers a thorough explanation of the saving process, including an exhaustive — well, okay, pretty decent — review of the various file formats you can use. With this chapter by your side, Ctrl+S (⌘+S on a Mac) can be a pretty easy command, after all.

Save an Image, Save a Life

Though we don't know you from Adam — or Eve for that matter — you're probably the kind of person who doesn't like to spend hours editing an image only to see your work vanish in a poof of onscreen smoke as the result of some inexplicable and unforeseen computer malfunction. If you are indeed that kind of person, finding out how to save your image is essential. By saving your image early and often, you improve your chances of weathering any digital storm that may come your way.

Saving for the very first time

If you're working on a photograph from a digital camera or scanner, after applying the first few edits to your image, save it under a new name and specify where you want to store it on disk. If you do this, the original image remains untouched so that you can return to it at a later date for inclusion in a different project. You can also select the Save As a Copy option, explained in Step 5 below. Here's how to save your customized image without harming the original:

1. **Choose File⇨Save As.**

   The dialog box shown in Figure 6-1 appears.

   You can also open the dialog box by pressing Ctrl+Shift+S (⌘+Shift+S on a Mac).

2. **Enter a name into the File name option box.**

   PC users: Filenames can include as many as 255 characters (although a 255-character filename is beyond excessive, don't you think?). The filename is followed by a period and a three-character file extension that indicates the file format (explained shortly). Don't use any spaces or special characters, such as ampersands or brackets, in your filenames. Stick with regular letters and numbers to be safe. You don't have to enter the extension because Elements does that for you.

   Elements lets you save a file with a lowercase extension. Note the check box at the bottom of the Save As dialog box. This option is also located in the Preferences dialog box in the Saving Files panel. Note that the lowercase extension option, whether checked or not, always overrides the Preferences setting.

   Mac users: You can enter any name up to 31 characters long. You may want to keep filenames below 20 characters so that you can see them in their entirety at the Finder level. Longer filenames become abbreviated when viewed by name. For example, FamilyReunionUnpleasantBrawl may appear as FamilyReunionUnpleasan... at the Finder. You also have the option of adding a three-character extension (such as tif) that indicates the file format (explained shortly in "The Elemental Guide to File Formats" section). The Append File Extension option is located in the Preferences command under the Saving Files panel. You can choose Never, Always, or Ask When Saving. You can also choose to save a file with a lowercase extension. If you select the Ask When Saving option, check boxes for Append and Use Lower Case appear in the Save As dialog box.

Figure 6-1:
Use this
dialog box
to name
your image
and decide
where you
want the
image to
hang out on
disk.

It's generally best to use the lowercase extension option. This option makes for fewer problems when creating images for the Web and for exchanging files between Macs and PCs.

3. Select a format from the Format drop-down menu.

This is the point at which you have to deal with the image flavors touched on in the introduction to this chapter. The drop-down menu provides all kinds of options, such as TIFF, JPEG, PICT, and others. We'll discuss the ramifications of the important formats later in this chapter.

Some formats are restricted to certain kinds of images. For example, you can only save images that contain layers (more about layers in Chapter 9) in the Photoshop (PSD), TIFF, or PDF formats. If a format is grayed out in the Format drop-down menu, that format isn't available for the kind of image you're trying to save.

4. **PC users: Use the Save in drop-down menu to select the folder in which you want to save the image.**

   Mac users: Use the Mounted Volumes button, folder bar, and any other controls to hunt down the folder in which to save the image.

   Chapter 3 explains all of the controls in these menus.

5. **Select one or more of the next options. Note that availability is based on the type of image, file format, and whether the image has layers (more about layers in Chapter 9).**

   • **As a Copy:** Instead of giving your image a different name, you can check the As a Copy option. This option automatically adds the word "copy" after your filename, thereby ensuring your original remains intact.

   • **Layers:** With this option checked, your image preserves all of its layers. If unchecked, your image is flattened into a background. (Repeat after us: More about layers in Chapter 9.)

   • **Color:** Checking this option embeds the color profiles you established in your Color Settings setup (see details in Chapter 5).

6. **Click the Save button or press Enter (Return on a Mac).**

7. **If another dialog box appears, fill out the options and press Enter (Return on a Mac).**

   Some formats present additional dialog boxes that enable you to modify the way the image is saved. We explain these later where appropriate.

Your image is now saved! Come heck or high water, you're protected.

The Thumbnail check box(es) at the bottom of the dialog box are visible (Mac) and accessible (PC) only if you've selected Ask When Saving in your Preferences under Saving. If you don't check the Thumbnail options when you save an image, you don't get a preview when you later try to open that image.

To make sure that Elements always saves previews, choose Edit⇨Preferences⇨ Saving Files. When the Preferences dialog box appears, select the Always Save option from the Image Previews drop-down menu. Click OK to exit the dialog box. Now a thumbnail will be saved by default and the thumbnail options in the Save As dialog box will not be visible. And you don't have to worry about it anymore.

The only times not to save a preview are when you're saving images for posting on the Web, or you're extremely limited on disk space; previews make the file size a little bigger, leading to longer download times, and it follows that they also require a bit more disk space than images without previews. The file-saving process also takes a teeny bit longer if you choose to save images with previews.

Joining the frequent-saver program

After you name your image and save it to disk for the first time, press Ctrl+S (⌘+S on a Mac) or choose File⇨Save every time you think of it. Think of it as a nervous twitch you actually want to develop. In either case, Elements updates your image on disk, without any dialog boxes or options popping up and demanding your attention. Then when something goes wrong — notice that we said *when*, not *if* — you won't lose hours of work. A few minutes, maybe, but that comes with the territory.

Creating a backup copy

If creating an image takes longer than a day, you'll want to make backup copies. The reasoning is that if you invest a lot of time in an image, you're that much worse off if you lose it. By creating backup copies — Dog1, Dog2, Dog3, and so on, one for each day that you work on the project — you're that much less likely to lose mass quantities of edits. If some disk error occurs or you accidentally delete one or two of the files, one of the backups will probably survive the disaster, further protecting you from developing an ulcer or having to seek therapy.

At the end of the day, choose File⇨Save As. The Save As dialog box appears, as when you first saved the image. Change the filename slightly and then click the Save button. Want to be doubly protected? More protection, you say? Save to another disk entirely. If the whole disk goes bad, you've got another.

The Elemental Guide to File Formats

Selecting a format is a critical decision. So, you need to pay attention to the sections to come, even if the subject is a rather dry one — which it is. Get a double espresso if you need one, but don't skip this information.

What is a file format, anyway?

Glad you asked. (But do you have to use that bold, italic tone of voice?) A *file format* is a way of saving the electronic bits and pieces that make up a computer file. Different formats structure those bits and pieces differently. In Elements, you can choose from about a zillion file formats when you save your image to disk, which makes things a tad bit confusing.

Luckily, you can ignore most of the file format options. The Raw format, for example, sacrifices colors and other image information, so avoid it. The Targa and Scitex CT formats are very sophisticated formats used by very sophisticated (and well-funded) creative types, so you can forget about those formats, too. Use the Pixar format if you want your toys to come to life and behave in vastly amusing ways, but only when you're not in the room. (Just kidding.)

Actually, you'll probably use only a handful of formats: TIFF, PDF, JPEG, GIF, and perhaps most importantly, Elements' native format, PSD, which is inherited from the application that gave it life: Photoshop. The following sections explain the most important file formats and when to use them.

TIFF: The great communicator

One of the best and most useful formats for saving Elements images is TIFF (pronounced *tiff*), which stands for Tagged Image File Format. TIFF was developed to serve as a platform-independent standard so that both Macintosh and Windows programs could take advantage of it. TIFF is an excellent file format to use for printed images. It can be imported into virtually every page layout and most drawing programs.

When you select the TIFF option from the Save As drop-down menu and click on the Save button, Elements displays another dialog box, shown in Figure 6-2. In the area labeled Byte Order, you can tell Elements whether to save the TIFF image for use on a Macintosh or Windows program. Unless you're going to be working exclusively on the Mac, it's a safer bet to select IBM PC. (Why are these options labeled Byte Order? Just to confuse you.)

In order to turn on TIFF's full range of compression options, first select "Enable advanced TIFF save options" in the Saving Files panel of the Preferences. The TIFF Options dialog box offers several compression methods. If you select one of the methods, Elements compresses your image file so that it takes up less room on disk. LZW compression doesn't sacrifice any data to make your file smaller and is great for compressing images with large sections of a single color. It's known as a *lossless* compression scheme. ZIP compression is also a lossless scheme and works well with images containing large areas of a single color. ZIP compression is common in the Windows world. The last compression method is JPEG, a *lossy* compression scheme. Lossy is the computer nerd's way of saying that stuff is lost during the compression process — namely, some of the data that makes up your image. The term is used with special frequency by Scottish nerds trying to impress women: "Och, ye've got a be-oo-tifully compr-r-ressed image ther-r-r-re, Lossy!" (Sorry, that's a terrible joke. We should be kilt.)

Figure 6-2:
The options that appear when you save a TIFF file.

Your best bet is to stick with LZW. Most programs that support TIFF also support LZW. For example, you can import a compressed TIFF image into either PageMaker or QuarkXPress. Only obscure programs don't support LZW, so there's really no reason not to select this option, unless your files are very large. In that case, LZW compression makes your files open and save a bit more slowly. It's a trade-off between saving space or saving time — take your pick.

TIFF also supports saving with layers. If the term *layers* is fuzzy to you, check out our upcoming book, *Layers For Dummies*. What the heck — on second thought, we'll just roll that stuff into Chapter 9 of this book. Lucky you.

You can use the Save Image Pyramid option to save multiple versions of an image. Each version has a lower resolution. The bottom of the pyramid is the full image. You can choose to open either the full image or one with a lower resolution. Not many programs support pyramid files right now, so it's best to leave this option unchecked.

And last, you have a Save Transparency option. This setting has no effect if you're opening your image back up in Elements; transparency will always be preserved. It only applies if you're opening the file in another program that supports PDF transparency (read on for more about PDF).

Photoshop PDF: The can-do kid

PDF is a very versatile, powerful format, and is another excellent choice for cross-platform work. Short for "Portable Document Format," PDF was created by Adobe, so it's little surprise that you'll find it heavily supported by Adobe applications like Illustrator, InDesign, and PageMaker. In fact, PDF has become an almost universally accepted format; all a person needs to view a PDF document is free Adobe Acrobat Reader software (which is included on your Elements CD). And if you want to save your Elements image with layers (more about layers in . . . oh, never mind), PDF is one of only three options.

After you choose Save As, pick Photoshop PDF from the Format drop-down menu, and click Save, another dialog box appears. Choose ZIP encoding if you want lossless compression; otherwise select JPEG and choose a Quality setting. As noted in the TIFF section, JPEG is a lossy compression format, but the upside is that the PDF file will be smaller. If your image contains Transparency, you'll have the option of keeping it within your PDF document. The Image Interpolation option means that low-resolution images in your PDF file will be smoothed out rather than appearing pixelated; it's probably best to turn this off, as the interpolation process can't really improve low-resolution images and usually just makes them appear fuzzy.

PICT File: The picture format for Mac users

Apple developed *PICT* as the primary format for Macintosh graphics. PICT is based on the QuickDraw screen language. Just about every Macintosh graphics program supports PICT, but support varies. PageMaker, for example, does a terrible job of printing imported PICT images.

One nice thing about PICT is that it offers JPEG compression. Say that you select the PICT File option from the Format drop-down menu in the Save dialog box and press Return. A dialog box with options appears (assuming you've got QuickTime running).

If you're saving a grayscale image, the Resolution options are 2, 4, and 8 bits per pixel. Color images offer Resolutions of 16 and 32 bits per pixel. But regardless of which Resolution options you see in the dialog box, don't change them! Doing so deletes colors from your image and prevents you from accessing the JPEG options. Remember that JPEG compression does degrade your image somewhat. If you're using JPEG compression, it's best to always select maximum quality in the PICT File Options dialog box.

Although PICT can use JPEG compression, that doesn't mean that the average Windows user will be able to open a JPEG-compressed PICT file. If you're worried about cross-platform compatibility, make sure you save your image in the actual JPEG format, not as a PICT with JPEG compression.

Chapter 6: Saving with Grace

BMP: The wallpaper glue for PC users

BMP is a popular PC format for saving graphics that you want to make part of your computer's systems resources, such as the wallpaper that you see behind your desktop. Programmers also use BMP to create images that appear in Help files.

When you save a file in the BMP format, the dialog box shown in Figure 6-3 appears. Don't worry about changing the radio button settings; use the defaults that Elements picks for you. If you're creating wallpaper, don't select the Compress (RLE) check box; Windows doesn't recognize files saved using this compression scheme. Otherwise, the compression scheme is a lossless (good) one, so select Compress (RLE) if you can.

Figure 6-3:
The BMP format is used mostly to create wallpaper for the Windows desktop.

What about Elements' native Photoshop format?

One strong bit of proof that Photoshop Elements is the offspring of Photoshop (a sterling lineage indeed) is that Elements' native file format is the Photoshop format. The three-letter extension for the Photoshop format is PSD.

PSD, TIFF, and PDF are the only formats that can save the layers in your image; all the others "flatten" (merge) the layers together.

Like TIFF and PDF, the Photoshop format offers a lossless compression scheme. And Elements can open and save images faster in its native format than in any other format. But some other programs don't support the Photoshop format. So, use it when you're sure the program you plan to import the image into supports it and you don't need compression.

Make sure, really sure, absolutely sure, that you do not check the option Maximize Backwards Compatibility in Photoshop Format in the Saving Files panel of the Preferences. Note that the option is checked on by default, so go uncheck it now. We'll wait right here.

Good job. Why the big deal about this option, you ask? It inserts a flattened (merged) version of the image in your file, which tremendously increases the file size. The option is supposed to ensure compatibility between Elements and programs that support the Photoshop file format but not layers. However, it's not worth the tremendous increase it creates in the file size. If you want to be able to use the image in other applications, save a copy of the image in another format.

What format to use when

Ooh, you cheated, didn't you? You skipped right over the sections on how formats work and why they were invented. Instead of reading all that juicy background information — information that would help you make your own decision about which format to use — you want easy answers.

Okay, fine. You plunked down good money so that understanding Elements would be easy for you, so we'll give you a break just this once. Think of the following list as your study guide to File Formats. But when you're standing around at a cocktail party and the discussion turns to JPEG compression versus LZW, and you don't have an intelligent word to offer, we don't want to hear about it.

- ✔ If you're just going to use the image in Elements, save the image in Elements' native Photoshop (PSD) format. 'Nuff said.

- ✔ If your image contains layers (. . . blah blah layers blah see Chapter 9 . . .) and you want to preserve those layers, you can choose the PSD (Photoshop), TIFF, or PDF formats.

- ✔ If you want to import your image into another program, TIFF is probably the most compatible choice.

- ✔ If you want to import your image into another program, saving disk space is a priority, and TIFF's LZW compression isn't doing the job, use JPEG compression.

✔ If you're a Windows user and want to create wallpaper to amuse your co-workers or just yourself, use BMP with RLE compression turned off.

✔ If you're creating a photograph to be sent by e-mail or posted on the Web, use the JPEG file format. For high-contrast graphics or partially transparent images, use CompuServe GIF. For more on these formats, read the following section.

Saving for the Web

Yes, JPEG and GIF are the two standard file formats to use when saving images for posting on the Web. Yes, you can choose File⇨Save As and save your image as a JPEG or GIF. But — even if you eat, sleep, and breathe the Web — we don't think you'll ever want to take your Elements image and use Save As a JPEG or GIF.

Why not? Because (fanfare, please) there is a better way! Using Elements' terrific Save for Web command is, for the most part, vastly superior to using the Save As command to create JPEGs and GIFs. Not only do you get a side-by-side preview of your original image versus the compressed version, but it's very easy to switch back and forth between JPEG and GIF to determine which is the better format to use in terms of image quality and download time. The Save for Web command gives you almost every option you have when you choose JPEG or GIF from the Save As command; we'll cover the few additional options that Save As provides in the sections to follow.

Hey — what about PNG?

In addition to saving JPEGs and GIFs, the Save for Web command also lets you save images in the PNG file format. PNG stands for *Portable Network Graphics* and was originally designed to replace the popular GIF format. PNG is much more sophisticated than GIF — it supports 24- and 48-bit images, allowing for a broader range of colors, while GIF supports only 8-bit images. PNG can support RGB, Grayscale, or Indexed color image modes. You can also have varying levels of transparency in a PNG image, something neither GIF nor JPEG can do. A downside to PNG files is that images are often larger than GIFs or JPEGs because they contain more colors than GIF and do not have the advantage of JPEG's great compression scheme. This makes the PNG file format good for small images, such as buttons and thumbnails with details. The biggest downside to PNG, however, is that it's still not yet widely supported. The major browsers on major platforms are coming around to PNG, but you can hardly count on your users to have the latest versions of those browsers. For this reason, you're still better off choosing between JPEG and GIF.

If you want to go ahead and give PNG a chance, you have two flavors to choose from: PNG-8 and PNG-24. The options for saving a PNG-8 file are virtually identical to saving a GIF, so refer to the GIF section in this chapter for details. Saving a PNG-24 file gives you precious few options, but again, you can refer to the GIF section for more information.

The Save for Web command

To open the Save for Web dialog box, click on the Save for Web icon in the Shortcuts bar (the floppy disk in front of the world), choose File⇨Save for Web, or press Ctrl+Shift+Alt+S (⌘+Shift+Option+S on a Mac). You'll see the large window in Figure 6-4. Elements shows the original image on the left along with a copy on the right with color indexing or JPEG compression applied, as it would appear when opened in a Web browser. You can modify the settings along the right side of the window.

To get a closer view, you can zoom and scroll the previews using the Zoom and Hand tools. You can also change the zoom ratio by changing the Zoom value at the bottom of the controls section. To preview a set of settings in your favorite Web browser, click on the button in the lower-right area of the controls. Your image appears in your selected browser window.

Figure 6-4:
The Save
for Web
command
lets you
compare
your original
image to
a Web-
compressed
version.

After that, it's just a matter of adjusting the various options along the right side of the window. The predefined settings appear under the Settings drop-down menu. Some of these might work perfectly for you, or perhaps you'll want to select one as a jumping-off point for creating your own settings with the options below. These options change according to the file format you choose. We'll look at JPEG and GIF in the sections below, and examine the options that the Save for Web dialog box gives you.

JPEG: The best choice for photos

JPEG stands for Joint Photographic Experts Group, but who cares? What's important to remember is that while JPEG can provide very good results with photographs, it does use lossy compression, meaning that some of your image data will be missing.

The good news, however, is that you'll probably never miss what's not around anymore — sort of like when you were a kid and you "lost" your little brother at the park. Depending on the level of compression used, you may notice a slight difference in your onscreen image after you save the file using JPEG. But if the image is saved at High or Maximum quality and then printed, the compression is usually undetectable. Like TIFF's LZW compression, JPEG compression saves you lots of disk space. In fact, a JPEG image takes up less space on disk than an LZW-compressed TIFF file — half as much space, maybe a tenth as much, depending on your settings.

Here are the settings:

- **Compression Quality (Low, Medium, High, or Maximum):** Select an option from the drop-down menu immediately below the word JPEG to set the image quality to one of Elements' predefined settings. The Maximum option is best because it preserves the most image data, but the High option usually produces very good results as well.

- **Progressive:** This option makes your image download from the Web in incremental stages. A rough "draft" version of the image will appear relatively quickly in your browser, and the image will become clearer in subsequent passes. While it's nice to quickly give users a hint of what the image will ultimately look like, this option can cause problems in some browsers. For fullest compatibility, leave it unchecked.

  Using the "Save As" JPEG Options box instead of the Save for Web command gives you the opportunity to specify the number of passes or "scans" it takes for your image to load fully.

- **ICC Profile:** This check box embeds a color profile with the JPEG image. The color profile adds about 3K to the file size, which means an extra second of download time at 28.8Kbps. And thanks to the fact that support for reading ICC Profiles in browsers is pretty sparse, the extra 3K goes wasted. Leave it off.

✔ **Optimized:** While this option can result in smaller files, it has so little impact on file size — often none whatsoever — it's best to turn it off. This option is unlikely to cause problems with Web browsers, but it may make the image incompatible with other image editors.

✔ **Quality:** This option gives you more incremental control over the quality of compression than the Compression Quality drop-down menu does. Higher values give better image quality but larger file sizes; lower settings give lesser quality but smaller file sizes. You can specify a setting by entering a value into the Quality option box or by using the slider. Where the "Save As" JPEG Options dialog box permits values between 0 and 12, the Save for Web value gives you a lot more incremental control, ranging from 0 to 100.

✔ **Matte:** This option applies only when you have transparency in your image. If your image has transparent or translucent pixels — maybe it has an oval, feathered outline that gradually fades to transparency — you must pick a background color to be matted into the image, since JPEG doesn't support transparency. For instance, if blue is selected, and the same shade of blue is used as the background for a Web page, then the edges of the image would appear to gradually fade into the Web page. Totally transparent pixels would be filled with the specified blue, and translucent pixels would be mixed with blue.

You can select a Matte color with the Eyedropper tool located in the upper-left corner of the dialog box. You can also click on the Matte color box to display the Color Picker with three Web-specific options, spotlighted in Figure 6-5. Select the Only Web Colors check box to select exclusively from the 216-color Web-safe palette. Click on the cube icon to the left of the Help button to replace a color with its nearest Web-safe equivalent. And if you're a hexadecimal geek (and proud of it!), you can enter the desired hexadecimal color value into the # option at the bottom of the dialog box.

Figure 6-5:
Elements'
Color Picker
has three
options
specifically
for Web
designers.

GIF: The choice of choosy Web designers

Computer hacks are divided on how you pronounce GIF. Some folks swear that the proper pronunciation is with a hard "G" — as in one *t* short of a *gift*. Other experts insist that you say it with a soft *g*, so that the word sounds just like that famous brand of peanut butter. (No, we don't mean Skippy.) Regardless of which camp you decide to join (we're in the peanut butter camp ourselves), GIF is best used for high-contrast images, illustrations created in Elements or imported from a drawing program, screen shots, and text. The biggest drawback to GIF is that it can save images with only 256 colors or less (8-bit color). However, it's the format you want to use for simple — no computer programming skills required — animations, called *animated GIFs*. We'll look at animated GIFs in Chapter 17.

Here are the GIF options:

- **Color Reduction Algorithm (Perceptual, Selective, Adaptive, Web, Custom):** This drop-down menu controls how the colors are reduced from 16 million to 256 or fewer. The color reduction algorithm creates a palette containing the colors used in the image.

   - Adaptive selects the most frequently used colors in your image. If an image contains relatively few colors and you want to keep the colors as exact as possible, apply this palette.

   - Perceptual is a variation on the Adaptive palette, which varies the reduced color palette to suit the image. But where Adaptive maintains the most popular colors, Perceptual is more intelligent, sampling colors that produce the best transitions. Use this palette with photographic images (if you don't want to use JPEG), where smooth transitions are more important than actual color values.

   - Selective is also a variation on the Adaptive palette, but better preserves Web colors. Use this palette when an image contains bright colors or sharp, graphic transitions.

   - Web is a palette of 216 colors and is usually used for graphics that display on ancient 8-bit monitors. There are better palettes to use than Web.

   - Custom enables you to load a color look-up table from your hard drive or disk. Not used that often for Web graphics.

- **Dithering Algorithm (No Dither, Diffusion, Noise, Pattern):** This option controls how Elements mimics the several million colors that you have asked it to remove from an image. The No Dither option makes no attempt to smooth out color transitions but results in smaller file sizes. Diffusion mixes pixels to soften the transitions between colors. The Noise option mixes pixels throughout the image, not merely in areas of transition. And the Pattern option just plain stinks. Stick with Diffusion.

✔ **Transparency:** If a layered image contains transparent areas, you can keep them transparent by turning on this check box. Bear in mind, however, that transparency in a GIF file is either on or off; there are no soft transitions as in an Elements layer.

✔ **Animate:** Only applies when you're creating animated GIFs, covered in Chapter 17.

✔ **Interlaced:** This option results in an interlaced GIF file, in which the image fades into view incrementally as it is downloaded by the Web browser. While this is a nice option when it works correctly, there can be problems with compatibility. Use with caution.

✔ **Colors:** Here's where you specify the number of colors in an image. You can also select predefined bit depths using the drop-down menu. Start with a low setting (such as 64), and see what happens to your image. Use the lowest number of colors that keeps your image reasonably intact. You may find that photographic images, especially those with a wide range of colors, require a higher setting than non-photographic images or photos with a limited color range. And JPEG might be a better option for photos anyway.

✔ **Dither:** This wonderful option controls the amount of dithering applied. When, and only when, Diffusion is active, you may modify the amount of dithering by raising or lowering this value. Lower values produce harsher color transitions but lower the file size. It's a trade-off. Keep an eye on the preview to see how low you can go.

✔ **Matte:** This is similar to the JPEG Matte setting. When Transparency is turned off, the Matte color is blended in with translucent pixels, and transparent pixels are completely filled with the Matte color. When Transparency is turned on, the Matte color still blends with translucent pixels, but transparent pixels remain transparent. This setting is useful for making an image blend in with the background color of a Web page.

Choosing GIF in the Save As dialog box brings up the Indexed Color dialog box (pictured in Figure 6-6), which gives you a few additional options:

✔ **Palette:** This is the same as the Color Reduction Algorithm option in the Save for Web dialog box. There are a few other choices here:

   • Exact: If an image already contains less than 256 colors, the Exact palette appears by default. If this happens, leave it as is.

   • System (Mac OS) and System (Windows): Use this palette only if you want to add a graphic to your system (like a desktop pattern or a file icon that will appear on your desktop).

   • Uniform: The worst palette of the lot. Consists of a uniform sample of colors of the spectrum. Don't use it.

- Previous: This palette uses the last look-up table created by the Indexed Color command. Usually used when creating a series of high-contrast graphics that need to maintain a consistent look.

Notice that you also have Master versions of the Perceptual, Selective, and Adaptive palettes. Local palettes are based on the colors in the open image, while master palettes take into account all currently open images.

✔ **Forced:** Sometimes an adaptive palette can very easily upset extremely important colors. For example, the white background of an image might turn a pale red or blue, even if white was a predominant color. With this option you can lock in important colors so that they don't change. Black and White locks in black and white. Primaries protects eight colors — white, red, green, blue, cyan, magenta, yellow, and black. And Web protects the 216 colors in the Web-safe palette. Very helpful indeed.

✔ **Preserve Exact Colors:** This option preserves areas of flat color when you select Diffusion. It's best to leave this check box turned on. By doing so, colors in your image that are also in the palette aren't dithered; therefore, lines, text, and other small details in your Web images have better onscreen quality.

Figure 6-6:
The Indexed Color dialog box controls the appearance of GIF images.

Any GIF file can store transparency information. After saving a GIF file with indexed color, you can make all occurrences of one of those colors transparent using the Color Table command. Choose Image➪Mode➪Color Table to display the dialog box shown in Figure 6-7 and then select the Eyedropper icon below the Preview check box. Now click on a color in the palette or in the image itself. Either way, that one color becomes transparent.

The Color Table command suffers one limitation: You can make just one color transparent at a time. To make a second color transparent, you must press Enter (Return on a Mac) to exit the dialog box and then choose Image➪ Mode➪Color Table again.

Figure 6-7:
Use the
Eyedropper
tool to
select a
color that
you want
to make
transparent.

The Preview menu

Before you exit the Save For Web window, there's one last set of options to explain. At the top of the window, to the right of the compressed image preview, you see an arrowhead in a circle. Click on it to reveal the Preview menu, shown in Figure 6-8. The commands in this menu control the appearance and feedback provided by the image previews.

Figure 6-8:
Choose a
command
from the
Preview
menu to
change the
appearance
of the
compressed
preview.

Browser Dither

✓ Uncompensated Color
   Standard Windows Color
   Standard Macintosh Color
   Photoshop Compensation

   14.4 Kbps Download Rate
✓ 28.8 Kbps Download Rate
   56.6 Kbps Download Rate
   128 Kbps Download Rate
   256 Kbps Download Rate

The commands are divided into three sections:

- **Browser Dither:** Select this option to see how a selected preview will look when displayed on an 8-bit monitor. This method is exceedingly useful for determining whether you need to go with a Web-safe palette.

- **Color Compensation:** Colors shift from one screen to the next and from the Mac to Windows. There's no way to predict exactly how an image will look on another screen, but you can use the four color commands to get a sense. By default, Uncompensated Color is active, so Elements makes no attempt at a prediction. Select Standard Windows Color or Standard Macintosh Color to see how the colors might look on another platform. The final color command, Photoshop Compensation, uses whatever color settings you've applied in Elements.

- **Download Rate:** The final five commands change the estimated download times listed below the preview.

Good Night, Image — and Don't Let the Programming Bugs Bite

To put Elements to bed for the night, choose File⇨Exit (File⇨Quit on a Mac) or press Ctrl+Q (⌘+Q on a Mac). Elements may display a message asking you whether you want to save the changes you made to your image. Unless you have some reason for doing otherwise, press Enter (Return on a Mac) to select the Yes button. The program then shuts down.

If you don't want to save your changes, press the N key for "No" (press D for "Don't Save" on the Mac). If you decide that you aren't ready to say good-bye to Elements after all, click the Cancel button or press the Esc key. Sweet dreams.

Chapter 7

It's Perfect. No, Wait! Okay, Print.

• •

• •

*H*ere's how you know that you're a consummate computer nerd: When you snag your favorite sweater, say something highly objectionable to your spouse, or spill a well-known staining agent on your newly installed carpeting, your first reaction is not one of panic or regret. You merely think, "Undo."

Unfortunately, the real world provides no Undo command. After a horrible deed is done, it takes an obscenely disproportionate amount of fussing, explaining, or scrubbing to fix the transgression.

Not so in the magical world of personal computing. Photoshop Elements, in fact, gives you access to *multiple undos*. Not only can you undo as many as 100 actions, but you can also actually *skip* previous steps. In other words, if you have performed five actions and want to return to the way your image looked after your second action, you aren't required to first undo steps five, four, and three. You merely select step two in the digital undo command headquarters — the History palette. Not only can you turn back the digital clock, you can also truly travel back in time.

And once you're done undoing, then what do you do? Chapter 6 looks at the Save for Web command, a great choice if your final destination is an image you can e-mail to friends or post on the Web. But if you want your image to have a life on the other side of the monitor, then the onscreen image is really just a figment of your computer's imagination. You won't be able to actually *feel* your work until the ink hits the paper. (Even so, try to wait until the ink dries.)

In this chapter you'll also learn how to go from an onscreen, imaginary image to hard copy. But it's hard to explain this process when there are so many unknown variables: what kind of printer you're using, what kind of cabling is installed, and even whether the printer is located in your home or your office. In other words, we're suffering from a terrific deficit of knowledge. So when we start talking about printing, your sympathy and understanding will be appreciated as we explain — very briefly — how to print from Elements using an everyday, generic printer. But first things first: Here's how Elements lets you do the Big Undo.

Time Traveling

The more you work with Elements, the more reflexive your actions become. Certainly, this means that you can work more quickly, but it also means that you are likely to make more mistakes. Reflexive, after all, is a close cousin to thoughtless. And when you don't think, you can wander into some pretty nasty situations.

Exploring the History palette in 11 easy steps

Elements ensures that you aren't punished for working reflexively. To get a sense of just how wonderful this flexibility can be, try out these steps:

1. **Open the History palette.**

2. **Create a new image.**

   The size is unimportant; just make it big enough so that you have room to paint a few brush strokes. Once you've created the image, notice that the History palette now has its first *state,* labeled New. A state is a record of exactly what an image looked like at a certain point in time — in this case, the New state shows you what the canvas looked like before you painted anything on it. You can't do anything with this first state; just affirm its existence. That'll make it feel good.

3. **Select the Paintbrush tool and drag across the image.**

   The Paintbrush is the fifth tool down from the right in the Toolbox. Make sure to draw a single brush stroke and no more. Now take a gander at the History palette. You've got a brand new highlighted state labeled Paintbrush under the New state. Again, for now, just notice this.

4. Take a break.

You've worked hard; you deserve it. Watch TV for your daily allowance of 16 hours. Take up macramé. Paint a wall and watch it dry. The point is, no matter how long you're away, Elements remembers the last operation you performed (as long as you don't have a power outage or some similar computing disaster).

5. Click the Step Backward icon (the curvy downward-left-pointing arrow) in the Shortcuts bar.

You should notice two things: Your brush stroke disappears from the image window, and the Paintbrush state becomes grayed out in the History palette.

6. Click the Step Forward icon (the curvy downward-right-pointing arrow) in the Shortcuts bar.

Your brush stroke reappears, and the Paintbrush state in the History palette becomes active again. Are you beginning to see how the Step icons and the History palette are interrelated?

7. Paint three more strokes.

Make sure each stroke is separate from the others. You should now have three more Paintbrush states in the History palette, for a total of four.

8. This time, rather than clicking the Step Backward icon, use the default keyboard shortcut of Ctrl+Z (⌘+Z on the Mac). Repeat twice.

Once you've traveled back to your very first brush stroke, try Ctrl+Y (⌘+Y on the Mac) to step forward in time, bypassing the Step Forward icon in the Shortcuts bar. Go ahead and step forward to the last Paintbrush state.

9. Click on the first Paintbrush state in the History palette.

This is yet another way to time travel in Elements: By clicking directly on states in the History palette, you can travel backward or forward in leaps without revisiting every state.

10. Go up to the Edit menu and choose the first command, Undo State Change.

The default keyboard shortcut for this command is Ctrl+Alt+Z (⌘+Option+Z on the Mac). You'll notice that this command automatically takes you to the bottom of the History palette.

11. Choose the command again — but notice that now it's labeled Redo State Change.

You're taken back to where you were at the end of Step 9: The first Paintbrush state is active. The Undo/Redo command toggles between the History palette's final state and the state that was active when you chose the command.

Granted, this is all a bit confusing, and in truth there's a measure of redundancy in having both Undo/Redo and Step Forward/Step Backward at your disposal. But remember that Undo/Redo (Ctrl+Alt+Z on the PC, ⌘+Option+Z on the Mac) is a toggling command. It's useful for quickly switching back and forth using the same keyboard shortcut to see whether you like the effect of the last edit you made to your image. Undo/Redo gives you a quick before/after comparison.

Step Backward (Ctrl+Z on the PC, ⌘+Z on the Mac) lets you keep Undoing until you run out of History states. Step Forward (Ctrl+Y on the PC, ⌘+Y on the Mac) lets you do just the opposite, allowing you to keep Redoing until you reach the last action you performed.

If you simply want to reverse the last edit you made to your image, either undoing or stepping backward will do the trick. Step Backward has the easier keyboard shortcut, so it's probably your best choice.

Stepping backward, stepping forward, undoing, and redoing all work whether you have the History palette open or not.

Travel restrictions

Stepping backward, stepping forward, using the History palette, and the using the Undo/Redo command all combine to give you a great deal of flexibility as you work. However, here are some important things to keep in mind about these tools:

- ✔ The only actions you can undo or step through are ones that could actually change the image. Using the Zoom or Hand tools isn't reversible because they affect only temporarily what part of the image you're seeing onscreen.

- ✔ The Save, Save As, and Save for Web commands render the Undo command null and void. After the save operation completes, the Undo command appears dimmed, meaning that you can't choose it. You can, however, Step Backward to a state of the image before it was saved, provided that you've kept the image open.

- ✔ You can't Step Backward from the Exit command (Quit command on a Mac). There's a surprise. Also, when you relaunch Elements, it has no idea what you did during the previous session, so you can't reverse the last changes you made before quitting.

✔ You also can't reverse changing a foreground or background color, adjusting a setting using one of the commands under the Edit⇨Preferences submenu, hiding or displaying palettes, changing a palette setting, changing a setting in the Options bar, or selecting a tool.

The History palette

Let's take a closer look at this powerful palette, as depicted in Figure 7-1. The History palette records all your operations and creates a running list of the steps — in other words, the state of your image at that point in history. As you perform each operation, Elements names each state and displays a corresponding icon according to the tool or command used. It doesn't record operations such as palette and tool settings or color and preferences changes.

Here's a list of the History palette's features and functions and how to take advantage of them:

✔ To return to a previous state, click on the desired state. Notice that Elements temporarily undoes all steps after that state and that they appear grayed out. Click the Step Forward button in the Shortcuts bar, press Ctrl+Z (⌘+Z on a Mac), or choose Edit⇨Step Forward to return to your last state; you can also simply click on your last state.

✔ The grayed out states are referred to as *undone states.* You can redo an undone state by clicking on it. If you perform a new operation, the undone states disappear. Choose Edit⇨Undo or Ctrl+Alt+Z (⌘+Option+Z on a Mac) *immediately* to get the undone states back. After you move on to other commands, they're gone for good.

✔ To step backward through the palette one state at a time, press Ctrl+Z (⌘ +Z on a Mac). To move forward, press Ctrl+Y (⌘+Y on a Mac). These commands are also accessible via the History palette menu.

✔ The keyboard equivalents for Stepping Backward and Forward through the History palette and also for Undo/Redo can be customized via the Preferences⇨General command.

✔ Drag the History state slider (refer to Figure 7-1) forward and backward to scroll through and see each state rapidly disappear and reappear in order.

✔ You can establish the number of maximum history states (from 1 through 100) you want to retain in the Preferences⇨General command. If your computer is low on RAM, you may want to set this value to a lower number. Remember that after you exceed your maximum, the oldest step disappears, then the next oldest, and so on.

- ✔ If you're absolutely sure you're happy with your image, and your computer is slowing down or running out of memory, you can delete the history states by choosing the Clear History command from the palette pop-up menu. If you change your mind, immediately select Edit⇨Undo or press Ctrl+Alt+Z (⌘+Option+Z on a Mac). If you have multiple files open, you can clear all their histories at once by choosing Edit⇨Purge⇨Histories.

- ✔ You can delete a single state by selecting it and choosing Delete from the palette pop-up menu. You can also simply select the state and click on the trash can icon at the bottom of the palette (refer to Figure 7-1). Alternatively, you can drag and drop the state onto the trash can icon.

- ✔ Every file has its own history; therefore, you can work on multiple images simultaneously and independently of each other.

- ✔ After you close your image, its history disappears forever. The states in the History palette aren't saved with the file.

Figure 7-1:
The History palette records every step you take. The Police recorded "Every Breath You Take."

Abandoning Edits en Masse

Sometimes you make small mistakes, and sometimes you make big ones. If, after several minutes of messing about, you decide that you hate all your edits and want to return the entire image to its last saved appearance so that you can just start over again, you can possibly do one of two things. First, you might be able to select the top state in the History palette. Selecting the top step theoretically restores the image back to the way it appeared when you first opened it. However, if you've already exceeded your maximum number of History states as set in the General Preferences dialog box, then the first state has been bumped off the top of the History palette. If this happens, you can choose File➪Revert. The program reloads the image from disk and throws away all your changes.

You have an advantage in using the History palette rather than the File➪ Revert command. The History palette restores the *original* image regardless of whether you saved along the way, whereas File➪Revert reloads the last saved version, which may include some undesirable changes.

Just in case you change your mind or your fingers slipped, you can reverse File➪Revert, so breathe easier. The History palette records the Revert command.

The Command Still Known as Print

If you've ever wasted an expensive sheet of photo paper on a terrible print, you'll agree that someone really needs to work on being able to undo the act of printing. Imagine if Print appeared as a state in your History palette; clicking the Step Backward icon would feed the paper back into your printer; the ink would be sucked off the paper and back into the cartridges, and then the printer would spit out a pristine white sheet of paper into the feeder tray. Alas, this is not to be. So let's take a close look at printing, and see if we can figure out how to get it right the first time.

For starters, we're going to be totally rash and assume the following:

- ✔ You have a printer.
- ✔ Your printer is plugged in, it's turned on, and it doesn't have a 16-ton weight sitting on top of it. In other words, your printer works.
- ✔ The printer is properly connected to your computer. A cable running out of your computer and into your printer is a good sign.

✔ The proper printer software is installed on your computer.

✔ Your printer is stocked with ribbon, ink, toner, paper, film, pacifiers, little bits of felt, spring-like gizmos that go "ba-zoing," or whatever else is required in the way of raw materials.

If you've used your printer before, everything is probably ready to go. But if something goes wrong, call your local printer wizard and ask for assistance.

This May Be All You Need to Know about Printing

When things are in working order, printing isn't a difficult process. Though it involves slightly more than picking up your mouse and saying "print" into it, printing doesn't require a whole lot of preparation. In fact, a quick perusal of the following steps may be all you need to get up to speed:

1. **Turn on your printer.**

   And don't forget to remove that printer cozy your uncle knitted for you.

2. **Choose File⇨Save or press Ctrl+S (⌘+S on a Mac).**

   Although this step is only a precaution, it's always a good idea to save your image immediately before you print it because the print process is one of those ideal opportunities for your computer to crash. Your computer derives a unique kind of satisfaction by delivering works of art from the printer and then locking up at the last minute, all the while knowing that the image saved on disk is several hours behind the times. If you weren't the brunt of the joke, you'd probably think that it was amusing, too.

3. **Check that the image fits on the page.**

   Click the Print Preview icon in the Shortcuts bar (the one with the piece of paper and the magnifying glass). You can also choose File⇨Print Preview, or press Ctrl+Alt+P (⌘+Option+P on the Mac). Elements displays a preview of how your image fits on your chosen paper size. The white area in the Print Preview represents the size of the page. If your image fits entirely inside the white area, it will fit on the printed page. If it exceeds the boundaries of the white area, the image is too big for the page and needs to be reduced. Turn on the Scale to Fit Media check box in the Scaled Print Size section of the dialog box. This should result in your image shrinking in the Print Preview, but it doesn't affect the actual image.

4. **Select a printer, paper size, and page orientation.**

   You accomplish all this inside the Page Setup dialog box, which you can display by clicking the Page Setup button in the Print Preview dialog box. When you've verified your settings, click OK to leave the Page Setup dialog box.

5. **Click the Print button in the Print Preview dialog box.**

   Elements displays the Print dialog box. Here you can specify how many copies of the image you want to print.

6. **Press Enter (Return on a Mac).**

   Experts say that this is the easiest step. Well, one guy got a blister on the end of his finger, but otherwise the vote was unanimous.

Congratulations! You've got hard copy. But on the off chance that you're unclear on how a couple of the preceding steps work or you're simply interested in excavating every possible nugget of information from this book, go forward to probe the depths of the rest of this chapter.

Choosing a Printer in Windows

If you have only one printer hooked up to your computer, you can skip this section entirely. But if you're part of a network or you have more than one printer available to you, you need to tell Elements which printer you want to use.

To select a printer, open the Page Setup dialog box. You can do this in several ways: Choose File➪Page Setup, press Ctrl+Shift+P, or click on the Setup button inside the Print dialog box (choose File➪Print or press Ctrl+P to open the dialog box). However you go about it, a dialog box similar to the one shown in Figure 7-2 appears. (Your dialog box may look slightly different depending on your printer and which version of the operating system you're using.)

To select a printer, just choose the printer name from the Name drop-down menu. Choose the paper size and printer tray from the two drop-down menus in the middle of the dialog box. (We discuss other options in this dialog box in other sections in this chapter.) Click on OK or press Enter to exit the dialog box.

Choosing a Printer on a Mac

If you use the same printer day in and day out to produce pages of text and numbers, you probably don't need to worry about the Chooser. Provided with every Mac, this little program is designed to let you confirm the connection to your printer and select a different printer over a network. So, unless you just want to make sure that everything's okay or you want to specify the exact printer you intend to use, skip to the next section.

To access the Chooser dialog box, select the Chooser command from the Apple menu. The left side of the dialog box, as shown in Figure 7-3, contains a bunch of icons that represent the kinds of printer drivers that are available to your system. Not to be confused with the drivers you use to knock golf balls into uncooperative printers, these drivers serve as a liaison between your computer and your printer.

✔ If you use a PostScript device — meaning a printer that supports the PostScript printer language — select the LaserWriter Driver icon. Nearly every printer over $1,000 supports PostScript, which is, without a doubt, the professional printing standard.

✔ If you see a driver icon that matches your specific model of printer, select it. For example, if you own a Hewlett-Packard DeskJet 970 and you installed the software that came with it, you should see an icon labeled DeskJet 900 Series, which happens to look like your printer. You'd be plum crazy not to select it.

✔ Some fax/modems enable you to print to remote fax machines over the phone lines. If you own a fax/modem, you may be able to select a driver icon for the modem.

✔ If you're on a network, you see a list of networked printers on the right side of the dialog box. Select the printer you want to use by clicking on it.

After you finish doing all that stuff, click on the close box on the left side of the Chooser title bar. A message may appear, telling you to confirm your settings using the Page Setup command. Don't worry; the next section explains how to do exactly that.

If any other message appears — one announcing that the printer is not available or has taken leave of its senses, for example — you very likely have a cabling problem or your printer is not turned on. Otherwise, you're in business.

Figure 7-3:
You can
select the
printer you
want to use
from the
Chooser.

Getting Image and Paper in Sync

The Print Preview dialog box, immortalized in Figure 7-4, offers much more than a preview of your printed image. Here are some of its other wonders:

✔ **Center Image:** Check the Center Image option to position your image. To enter new position values, either deselect the option or turn on Show Bounding Box and simply drag your image preview thumbnail to the desired location on the page.

✔ **Scaled Print Size:** This setting enables you to reduce or enlarge the image for printing only. Enter any percentage below 100% to reduce the dimensions of the printed image. The printer still prints all the pixels in the image, but the pixels are just smaller. You can also enter a value in the height or width boxes, or turn on Show Bounding Box and resize the image in the preview by dragging from the sides or corners. You'll notice that scale, width, and height are linked, meaning that changing any one affects the other two.

✔ **Scale to Fit Media:** This option makes the image fit exactly on the size of the paper. This is generally only a good option if your image is too large to fit on the page.

✔ **Show Bounding Box:** This option places a box with handles around your image, showing the precise image boundaries.

✔ **Print Selected Area:** If you select a portion of your image using one of the tools we discuss in Chapter 8, you can print only the selected area by selecting the option that says, surprise, Print Selected Area. If you just want to take a quick look at an isolated area, you can use this option to save time and ink.

✔ **Show More Options:** This brings up the Output and Color Management options (a drop-down menu below Show More Options lets you toggle between the two).

✔ **Output:** This option allows you to add certain items to your print.

- Clicking Background brings up the Color Picker to let you choose a colored background to print behind your image.

- Border places a black border around your image and allows you to specify the thickness.

- Caption allows you to print a caption under your image. To enter this caption, you first have to Cancel out of the Print Preview box and choose File➪File Info. Type your desired caption in the Caption Section, and click OK. When you return to the Print Preview dialog box, you will be able to see where your caption will print under the image preview.

- Enabling Corner Crop Marks will create printed guides that can help if you plan to cut out your image from the printer paper.

- The final Output option, Encoding, only applies when printing to a PostScript printer. Check your printer's specifications to determine the appropriate setting.

✔ **Color Management:** This option is based on the idea of *color spaces*. Different devices operate in different color spaces. Monitors, desktop color printers, and high-end offset printers all have their own unique color space. The Color Management options enable you to convert the color space of your image while printing. For example, if you created an RGB Elements document with Full color management turned on in the Color Settings, then your Document Source Profile is Adobe RGB (1998), and you can choose to have your image's color converted to the color space of your Epson printer upon printing. (For more on color management, see Chapter 5.)

In the Print Space section, under Profile, choose Same As Source to print using your Source Space. Your Source Space is determined by the color management (if any) you activated in the Color Settings. If you want to print using the color profile of another device, for example, a Hewlett-Packard or Epson printer, choose that profile from the list.

Choose PostScript Color Management to print to a PostScript printer (PS level 2 or higher). With this option, Elements enables the *printer* to manage all the color conversion instead of Elements. Leave Intent set at the default, Relative Colorimetric.

If all you want to do is print in color from your desktop printer, first choose Same As Source for your Print Space. Then print another copy using your printer's color profile for your Print Space, if you can find the profile in that monstrous list. Compare both copies to see which one looks better. If you have a late model printer, you may also want to check the documentation for the manufacturer's recommendations.

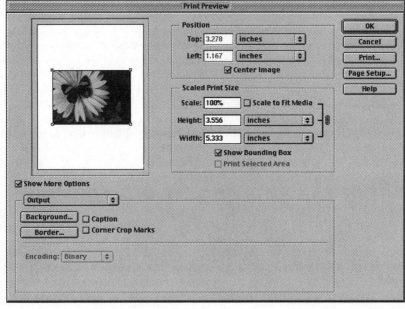

Figure 7-4:
You can preview how the image fits on the page by using the Print Preview dialog box.

The Page Setup dialog box lets you make additional choices that will affect your final printed output. To open Page Setup, choose File➪Page Setup, press Ctrl+Shift+P (⌘+Shift+P on the Mac), or simply click the Page Setup button in the Print Preview dialog box.

✔ In addition to scaling and positioning your printed image using the Print Preview, another possibility is to rotate the image on the page. For example, if the image is wider than it is tall, you can print it horizontally by rotating the page 90 degrees. Though your Page Setup dialog box may not look exactly like the one shown in Figure 7-2, you should find two Orientation radio buttons: Portrait and Landscape. (It may be necessary to click the Properties button to access the Orientation options.) If you choose Portrait, your image prints upright on the page; if you choose Landscape, Elements rotates the image so that it prints sideways on the paper.

✔ The specific options found inside the Page Setup dialog box vary depending on the kind of printer you're using. Note that the Page Setup dialog box also offers a scaling option. Scaling options let you reduce or enlarge the image for printing only. Mac users will probably find a Scale option box somewhere within the Page Setup dialog box. Windows users should click on the Properties button to hunt down this option. When the Properties dialog box appears, click on the Graphics tab. If you see a Scaling option, you're in business. As you'll notice, however, you don't have as much flexibility as you do with the Print Preview scaling feature.

✔ The Scaling value remains in effect until you open up the Page Setup dialog box and change it. So, if you don't want to scale future print jobs, be sure to change the setting back to 100% after you print the current image.

Keep in mind that changes made inside the Print Preview and Page Setup dialog box have absolutely no effect on anything except how your image prints. You can't do any permanent damage via this particular dialog box, so feel free to change settings recklessly and without regard to personal safety.

Changes made inside the Image Size dialog box (Image⇨Resize⇨Image Size) are another story. As we explain in Chapter 4, you can easily do permanent damage to your image by making unwise decisions pertaining to image size.

Sending the Image to the Printer

After you've made it past the obstacle course of options provided by the Print Preview and Page Setup dialog boxes, you're almost home free. All you need to do is make a few last-minute calls, like how many copies you want to print. Click the Print button in the Print Preview dialog box to display the Print dialog box, shown in Figure 7-5. You can also click the handy Print icon in the Shortcuts bar (it looks like a printer), choose File⇨Print, or press Ctrl+P (⌘+P on a Mac). Like the Page Setup dialog box, the options available in the Print dialog box may vary depending on your printer.

If the image is still too large for the page, Elements displays an error message to warn you that a portion of your image will be cut off of the page and asks whether you want to proceed. If you say no, the error message disappears, and you can then resize the image to fit the page, as discussed earlier in this chapter. If you say that you want to go ahead and print anyway, the Print dialog box appears.

If you're absolutely confident that your image should fit on your selected paper size, but Elements still barks at you that it won't fit, check the page orientation (portrait or landscape) in your Page Setup dialog box. Even if your image fits on the paper, if it isn't oriented correctly Elements sometimes thinks it's too large.

Figure 7-5:
The Print
dialog box.

That's it. Just click on the OK button (Print on the Mac) or press Enter (Return on a Mac), and you're off. Depending on the size of the image, you should have hard copy in a matter of a few minutes.

Chapter 8

Herd Them Pixels

● ●

In This Chapter

▶ Selecting with the lasso, marquee, and Magic Wand tools

▶ Editing selections

▶ Working with selections

▶ Hiding selections

● ●

*I*f you're an old ranch hand, you may find it helpful to think of the pixels in your image as a bunch of cows. A pixel may not have any horns, and you don't have to watch where you step when you're around it, but it's a cow all the same. Consider these amazing similarities: Both pixels and cows travel in herds. Come on, when's the last time you saw one pixel out on its own? They're both dumb as dirt. And obstinate to boot. And — here's the absolute clincher — you round them both up by using a lasso.

The only difference between pixels and cows is in the vernacular. When you lasso a cow or two on the lone prairie, it's called ropin'. When you lasso a mess of pixels, it's called selectin'. And after you select the desired pixels, you can do things to them. You can move them, duplicate them, and apply all kinds of alterations as described in future chapters. Selecting lets you grab hold of some detail or other and edit it independently of other portions of your image. It's a way of isolating pixels to manipulate them.

This chapter discusses methods for selecting portions of an image. With a little practice, you can rustle pixels better than most hands rope dogies, and that's no bull.

Learning the Ropes of Selecting

Photoshop Elements provides several selection tools, all labeled in Figure 8-1. These tools include the Lasso, the Polygonal Lasso, the Magnetic Lasso, two so-called marquee tools, and an automatic color selector known as the Magic Wand (phoenix feather not included). Here's how they work:

✔ Drag inside the image with the Lasso tool to select free-form areas. The shape of the selection conforms to the shape of your drag.

✔ Use the Polygonal Lasso tool, which shares a flyout menu with the regular Lasso tool, to select pixels that are married to more than one pixel. Oops, sorry — that's the Polygamal Lasso. The Polygonal Lasso draws selections made up of straight sides. You can also hold down the Alt (Option on a Mac) key and click with the regular Lasso, but you have the option of using the dedicated Polygonal Lasso tool.

✔ Sharing the flyout with the other two lasso tools is the Magnetic Lasso tool (which sounds like the perfect tool for ropin' a mechanical bull). Click the Magnetic Lasso on the edge of your object and then move the lasso around that edge. Keep reading this chapter for further details!

✔ The Rectangular Marquee tool lets you select a rectangular area. Just drag from one corner of the area you want to select to the other. The outline drawn with the tool looks like a border of moving dots — which is how "marquee" managed its way into the tool's name.

✔ The Elliptical Marquee draws oval selections. The word ellipse, incidentally, is what mathematicians say when they're talking about ovals. In fact, we could just call it the ovoid marquee tool, but you might forget and think we were talking about some home pregnancy test.

✔ The Magic Wand selects areas of continuous color. For example, if you want to select the sky without selecting the clouds, you just click in the sky. At least, that's the way it's supposed to work, but you never know. The Magic Wand isn't always as magical as you may think.

Figure 8-1:
Use these selection tools to select the portion of your image that you want to edit.

Now that you know how the tools work, let's see how to get to the tools. The arrow in the lower-right corner of the Marquee and Lasso tool icons in the Toolbox indicates that a flyout menu of hidden tools lurks beneath each icon (see Chapter 2 for more information).

To switch between the tools on the flyout menus, you can Alt+click (Option+click on a Mac) on whichever tool icon happens to be visible in the Toolbox at the time. You can also select tools using these keyboard shortcuts:

- ✔ Press the M key to access the active marquee tool. Whichever marquee tool is active, press Shift+M to get the other one.

- ✔ Press L to get the lasso tools. As with the marquee tools, a common shortcut switches you between the three lasso tools: If the regular Lasso tool is active, pressing Shift+L brings up the Polygonal and the Magnetic Lassos alternately.

- ✔ Press W to get the Magic Wand. The tool is more unpredictable than magical, making W — for Wacky Wand — a logical keyboard equivalent.

Throwing lassos

Both the regular Lasso tool and the Polygonal Lasso tool are so easy to use, your newborn can master them. If you don't have a newborn, you'll have to muddle through on your own. The Magnetic Lasso is trickier, however, but nothing you couldn't pick up with a little guidance from a toddler.

Using the regular Lasso tool

Here's a complete set of instructions for using the regular Lasso tool:

1. **Trace around the portion of the image that you want to select with the tool.**

   That's it. In Figure 8-2, for example, the mushroom was dragged around to select it independently of its surroundings. As the figure shows, Elements displays a dotted outline around the selected area after you release the mouse button. This outline represents the exact path of your drag. (If you release before completing the shape — that is, before meeting up with the point at which you began dragging — Elements simply connects the beginning and ending points with a straight line. So you won't hurt anything if you release too early.)

Granted it's not easy to draw the outline just right, as in Figure 8-2. There's no trick to it; just get plenty of practice. If your outlines aren't quite so accurate, however, don't sweat it. There are plenty of ways to modify the outline after you draw it.

Lasso cursor ⌐   ⌐Selection outline

Figure 8-2:
Select the
mushroom
by dragging
around it
with the
Lasso.

Drawing straight-sided selections

Suppose that you want to select a cube sitting in the center of an image.
You can drag around it with the Lasso tool, but a better option is to use the
Polygonal Lasso, which makes it easy to create selections with straight sides.

To select an object in this manner, click with the Polygonal lasso to set the
beginning of the first line in the selection. Then move the mouse cursor to
the point where you want the line to end and click again. Keep clicking to
create new line segments. To complete the selection, you have two options.
If you double-click, Elements draws a segment between the spot you double-
click and the first point in your selection. You can also move the cursor over
the first point in your selection until you see a little circle next to the
Polygonal Lasso cursor. Then click to close the selection.

The Polygonal Lasso can also be used for images with both curved and
straight segments. You can switch to the regular Lasso in mid-selection to
create a curved segment. Just press and hold down the Alt (Option on a Mac)
key and drag to draw your curved line. When you release the Alt (Option on a
Mac) key, the tool reverts back to the Polygonal Lasso.

You can also press Alt (Option on a Mac) while drawing a selection with the
regular Lasso to access the Polygonal Lasso. Press Alt (Option on a Mac) and
click to set the endpoints of your straight-sided segments, as you normally
do with the Polygonal Lasso. To start another curved segment, just drag. You
can keep the Alt key (Option key on a Mac) down or not — it doesn't matter.

But be sure that the mouse button is down any time you press or release the Alt (Option on a Mac) key, or Elements completes the selection outline.

Selecting with the Magnetic Lasso

This lasso tool takes a little getting used to and may not produce a great selection in all cases. But it's easy to use, and if you take some time to understand the method behind its madness, it can be a quick remedy for your selection needs.

The Magnetic Lasso works best with high-contrast images — that is, the object you want to select is a different color than the background. Using the settings in the Options bar, the Magnetic Lasso analyzes the difference in the color of the pixels between the object you want to select and the background, and snaps to your object's edge. Here's how to use this quirky tool:

1. **Select the Magnetic Lasso tool.**

2. **Click on the edge of the object you want to select.**

3. **Move the cursor around the edge of the object.**

   Don't press the mouse and drag — just move the mouse. Simple! The Magnetic Lasso creates an outline with square anchor points around the edge of the object. If the line is off the mark, back up your mouse and try again. If you need to delete an anchor point as you are moving around the edge, press the Backspace (Delete on a Mac) key. To create your own anchor points, click with the mouse. Adding your own anchor points can be helpful if the Magnetic Lasso seems reluctant to stick to the edge you select.

4. **Continue around the object and click on your starting anchor point to close the outline.**

   You'll see a small circle next to your cursor indicating closure of the outline.

5. **As soon as the outline is closed and you release the mouse, a selection marquee appears.**

6. **Press Esc or Ctrl+period (@cmd+period on a Mac) to cancel the Magnetic Lasso in mid-selection.**

To create a straight segment while using the Magnetic Lasso, press Alt (Option on a Mac) and click with the mouse. You can see that the tool icon of your cursor temporarily changes to the Polygonal Lasso. Release the Alt (Option on a Mac) key and drag for a second to reset the tool back to the Magnetic Lasso. From then on, just move the cursor without clicking or dragging.

Exploring your lasso options

Whether you use the regular Lasso, the Polygonal Lasso, or the Magnetic Lasso, you can modify the performance of the tool via the options common to all three tools in the Options bar (see the next section for options specific to the Magnetic Lasso). Though small in number, the options for the lasso tools are some tough little hombres:

- ✔ Both Feather and Anti-aliased affect future selection outlines drawn with the lasso tools. In short, Feather makes the outline fuzzy, and Anti-aliased slightly softens the edge of the outline. If you want to modify an outline that you've already drawn, you have to choose a command under the Select menu (more on this in the section "Automatic Selection Discombobulators").

- ✔ Normally, selections drawn with the lasso tools have soft, natural-looking edges. This softening is called *anti-aliasing*. To turn off the softening, click on the Anti-aliased check box in the bar to get rid of the check mark. From now on, outlines drawn with the tool will have sharply defined and sometimes jagged edges.

- ✔ Figure 8-3 shows two lassoed selections moved to reveal the white background in the image. In the left example, the Anti-aliased check box was turned off; in the right example, the option was turned on. The edges of the left example are jagged; the edges of the right example are soft. (Chapter 9 explains all the ways to move selections. But if you want to try moving a selection now, just drag it with the Move tool, which is the top-right tool in the Toolbox.)

- ✔ Most of the time, you want to leave the Anti-aliased check box turned on. Just turn it off when you want to select precise, hard-edged areas. (Which may be never. Who knows?)

- ✔ Enter a value into the Feather option box to make the outline fuzzy. The value determines the radius of the fuzziness in pixels. If you enter a value of 3, for example, Elements extends the fuzzy region 3 pixels up, 3 pixels to the left, 3 pixels down, and 3 pixels to the right. As shown in the first example of Figure 8-4, that's a lot of fuzz. A higher value results in a more fuzzy selection outline, as witnessed in the right example, which sports a Feather value of 10.

- ✔ In case you're wondering, the four square buttons on the left of the Options bar enable you to add or subtract to selections you've already drawn. We'll get to those later in this chapter.

Looking at the unique Magnetic Lasso options

The Magnetic Lasso has unique options in the bar that are related to the sensitivity of the tool's operation. They are the following:

- ✔ **Width:** This option determines how close to an edge you have to move the mouse for Elements to "see" the object. You can set it to a higher number for smooth, high contrast objects, and it will still hug the edge of the object. Set it to a lower value if the image has a lot of nooks and crannies or the contrast isn't that high. The range of the width option is 1 to 40 pixels. To change it while you are actually using the tool, press the [key to lower the number and the] key to raise the number.

✓ **Edge Contrast:** This option tells the Magnetic Lasso how much contrast is required between the object and the background before the lasso can be "attracted to" or can hug that edge. The range for the Edge Contrast option is 1% to 100%. If you find a good deal of contrast between the object and the background, put in a higher value in order to get a cleaner selection. If the image is low contrast, lower the value for this option.

✓ **Frequency:** The number in the Frequency option tells the Magnetic Lasso when to automatically insert anchor points. The range for Frequency is from 0 to 100. If you want more points, insert a higher number; for less points, use a lower value. High values are better for rough, jagged edges, and low values are better for smooth edges. As you move around the edge of your object and create the outline, Elements pins it down with an anchor point.

Start with default settings for the preceding Magnetic Lasso options, carefully make your selection, and see how it works. If your image is low contrast, you may want to lower the Edge Contrast to 5% or so. If edges are jagged or rough, try raising the Frequency to around 70 and lowering the Width to 5 pixels. If all else fails, and the Magnetic Lasso just isn't behaving, you can always go back to the regular Lasso and the Polygonal Lasso. They may not be as high tech, but they're reliable.

Anti-aliasing off   Anti-aliasing on

Figure 8-3:
The difference between dragging a jagged (left) and anti-aliased (right) selection.

Jagged edges   Soft edges

Feather 3 pixels   Feather 10 pixels

Figure 8-4:
A bigger
Feather
value
means
fuzzier
fungus.

Using the Marquee tools

If you want to create a selection that's rectangular or elliptical, you use —
guess what — the Rectangular and Elliptical Marquee tools. The Rectangular
and Elliptical Marquee tools are so easy to use that they make the Lasso look
complicated. You just drag from one corner to the opposite corner and release
the mouse button. (Okay, ovals don't have corners, so you have to use your
imagination a little bit.) The dotted marquee follows the movements of your
cursor onscreen, keeping you apprised of the selection outline in progress.

But Elements has never been one to provide you with only one way to use a
tool — or, in this case, two tools. For example, you can also use these tools to
select perfect squares or circles. The program's cup of flexibility forever run-
neth over, and the marquee tools are no exception.

Grabbing a square or circle

Every so often, you may feel the urge to apply some puritanical constraints to
your selection outlines. Enough of this random width and height business —
you want perfect squares and circles. Lucky for you, Elements obliges these
fussbudget impulses by letting you constrain shapes drawn with the marquee
tools:

✔ To draw a perfect square, press the Shift key after you begin dragging with the Rectangular Marquee tool. To draw a perfect circle, press Shift after you begin dragging with the Elliptical Marquee tool.

✔ Drawing squares and circles is a little trickier than you might expect. For the best results, you should first begin dragging, press and hold Shift, drag to the desired location and release the mouse button, and finally release Shift. In other words, press Shift after you start the drag and hold it until after you complete the drag.

✔ If you press Shift before dragging, you run the risk of adding to the previously selected area, as explained later. Here's the deal: If you selected a portion of your image before you started Shift+dragging, Elements sees to it that the area remains selected and selects the marqueed area as well. Meanwhile, the shape of the marquee isn't constrained to a square or a circle. Befuddling, huh? If this happens to you, undo the selection and try again, taking care to press Shift during — not before — your drag.

The marquee tools can come in handy not only for selecting part of your image but for creating geometric shapes as well. For example, if you want to draw a hollow rectangle, create a marquee with the Rectangular Marquee tool. Then choose Edit⇨Stroke to stroke the marquee with a color — in other words, to paint a line along the marquee.

Getting even more control over selections

Are you crazed for control? Do your tyrannical desires know no bounds? If so, you probably aren't appeased by drawing a square or a circle. What you want is to apply even more stringent constraints.

For example, suppose that you're the sort of pixel-oppressor who wants to select a rectangular or oval area that's exactly twice as wide as it is tall. With your marquee tool selected, choose Constrained Aspect Ratio from the Style drop-down menu in the Options bar. The Width and Height option boxes come to life, letting you specify an *aspect ratio,* which is a precise proportion between the width and height of a marquee. To make the marquee twice as wide as it is tall, enter **2** as the Width value. Then press Tab to highlight the Height value and enter **1**. The deed is done.

To constrain the marquee to an exact size, select Fixed Size from the Style drop-down menu, and then enter the exact pixel dimensions of your desired marquee into the Width and Height option boxes.

One last item submitted for your approval: Like the lasso options discussed earlier in this chapter, the marquee options sport Anti-aliased and Feather options, which respectively soften the selection outline and make it blurry. However, the Anti-aliased check box is dimmed when you use the Rectangular Marquee tool. Perpendicular edges never need softening because they can't be jagged. Anti-aliasing, therefore, would be a waste of time.

Drawing from the center out

As mentioned earlier, you draw a rectangle or oval from corner to opposite corner. But you can also draw a marquee from the center outward. To do this, begin dragging with either marquee tool and then press Alt (Option on a Mac).

If you decide midway into your drag that you don't want to draw the shape from the center outward, just release the Alt (Option on a Mac) key and continue dragging. What was once the center of the marquee now goes back to being a corner.

To draw a square or circle from the center outward, press both Shift and Alt (Option on a Mac) after you begin dragging with the appropriate marquee tool. (If you press Shift and Alt — Option on a Mac — before you begin dragging, you select the intersection of two selections, as explained later.)

Wielding the Wand

The Magic Wand is even easier to use than the marquee tools. (Pretty soon, things get so easy you won't need us at all.) But it's also the most difficult selection tool to understand and predict. To use the tool, you just click inside an image. Elements then selects the area of continuous color that surrounds the cursor.

'Scuze me while I click the sky

Figure 8-5 shows how the Magic Wand works. In the first image, the Magic Wand tool was clicked in the sky above the fake dinosaur. Elements automatically selected the entire continuous area of sky. In the second example, the selection was made more apparent by pressing Ctrl+Backspace (⌘+Delete on a Mac), which filled the selection with the white background color. The selection outline is gone because the area was deselected. (Don't worry, deselecting is explained in full, rich detail in the section "The wonders of deselection.")

Notice that the wand selects only uninterrupted areas of color. The patch of sky below the creature's tail, for example, remains intact. Also, the selection bit slightly into the edges of the dinosaur. Pressing Ctrl+Backspace (⌘+Delete on the Mac) removed very small pieces along the top of the plastic behemoth.

Teaching the wand tolerance

You can modify the performance of the Magic Wand by accessing the ever-popular Options bar, which offers four basic options — Anti-aliased, Contiguous, Use All Layers, and Tolerance.

Figure 8-5:
Here's what
happens
when you
click in the
sky above
the T-Rex
with the
Magic
Wand (top)
and fill the
selection
with white.

We cover Anti-aliased earlier in this chapter, in the section "Exploring your lasso options," so we're not going to beat that poor horse anymore. The Use All Layers option comes into play only when your image contains more than one layer (see Chapter 9). When Use All Layers is turned off, the Magic Wand selects colors only on the active layer. If you want the Magic Wand to select colors from all visible layers, turn the option on.

When Contiguous is checked on, the Magic Wand selects only pixels that are adjacent to each other. If it is not checked on, the Magic Wand looks throughout the image for any pixels that fall within the Tolerance range.

This brings us to Tolerance, which has the most sway over the performance of the Magic Wand. It tells Elements which colors to select and which not to select. A lower Tolerance value instructs the wand to select fewer colors; a higher value instructs it to select more colors.

Figure 8-6 shows what we mean. Each row of images demonstrates the effect of a different Tolerance value, starting with the default value of 32 at the top and working up to 180 at the bottom. In each case, the Magic Wand was clicked at the same location, just to the right of the big giraffe's schnoz. The left image in each row shows the selection outline created when we clicked the Magic Wand; the right image shows the selection filled with white and then deselected.

The problem is that finding the best Tolerance setting is a completely random exercise in the futile art of trial and error. Like changes to any tool setting, changes to the Tolerance value have no effect on the current selection. You have to click with the Magic Wand to try out each and every new value. In fact, here's the typical approach:

1. **Click with the Magic Wand tool.**

   The point at which you click marks the base color — the one Elements uses to judge which other colors it should select.

2. **Express displeasure with the results.**

   Gnash your teeth for good measure.

3. **Enter a new Tolerance value in the Options bar.**

   Enter a higher value to select more colors next time around; enter a lower value to select fewer colors.

4. **Choose Select⇨Deselect or press Ctrl+D (⌘+D on a Mac).**

   Elements deselects the previous selection.

5. **Repeat Steps 1 through 4 until you get it right.**

   There's no foolproof approach or magic formula here; just a whole lotta clickin' and tweakin'. Doesn't really sound so magical, huh?

Tolerance: 32

Tolerance: 90

Figure 8-6:
A Tolerance
value of 32
selected too
little sky; a
value of 180
selected all
the sky but
also got
some huge
chunks of
giraffe face
and rolling
foothill. A
value of 90
appears to
be just right.

Tolerance: 180

There's one more option that affects the performance of the Magic Wand, but it isn't located in the Magic Wand's Options bar. Guess what it is. Come on, give it a try. Give up? We don't blame you, as it's truly weird and very out of place. The missing Magic Wand option is actually located in the Eyedropper tool's Options bar. Click on the Eyedropper tool and check it out. The Sample Size setting determines how many pixels the Eyedropper looks at when it samples a color. The default setting, Point Sample, means that the Eyedropper will sample only the precise pixel it's clicked upon — just that one single pixel and no others. The color of that pixel becomes the foreground color. However, set Sample Size to 3 by 3 Average, and the Eyedropper looks at not only the pixel it's clicked upon, but also one pixel in every direction — making for a 3-pixel square, or 9 pixels in all. The Eyedropper averages the colors of those 9 pixels, and that average color becomes the foreground color. Likewise, setting Sample Size to 5 by 5 Average makes the Eyedropper look in a 5-pixel square, and it averages the colors of those 25 pixels.

And here comes The Weirdest Thing About Photoshop Elements: That Sample Size option in the Eyedropper's Options bar *affects the behavior of the Magic Wand.* If you set Sample Size to 3 by 3 Average and then use the Magic Wand, the Wand's selection will be based not just on the pixel it's clicked upon, but on the 3-pixel square of surrounding pixels. And likewise for 5 by 5 Average. Why? We don't know. It's spooky. It's weird. But it's true. And we thought you should know.

Selecting everything

When no part of an image is selected, the entire image is up for grabs. You can edit any part of it by using the paint or edit tools or any of about a billion commands. But you can also make the entire image available for edits by choosing Select➪All or Ctrl+A (⌘+A on a Mac) to select everything.

Beginning to see the mystery here? If you can edit any part of the image by deselecting it, why choose Select➪All, which also lets you edit everything? Because some operations require a selection, that's why. For instance, if you want to copy an entire image and paste it into another image (more on copying and pasting in Chapter 9), you need to select the entire image first. Sure, you could carefully drag around its perimeter with the Rectangular Marquee tool, but why bother when you can just Select All?

Deselecting everything

Before we plow into all that whiz-bang, awesome stuff that Elements lets you do to a selection outline, let's first touch on selection's exact opposite, deselection. Though this may seem at face value to be a ridiculously boneheaded topic — one that hardly merits space in a scholarly tome like *Photoshop Elements For Dummies* — deselecting is actually an integral step in the selection process.

Suppose, for example, that you select one part of your image. Then you change your mind and decide to select a different portion instead. Before you can select that new area, you have to deselect the old one. You can deselect an existing selection outline in several ways:

- ✔ Click anywhere in the image with the lasso or the marquee tools.

- ✔ To get rid of an existing selection and create a new one at the same time, just drag or click to create the new selection as you normally would. Elements automatically deselects the old selection when you create a new one.

- ✔ Click inside the selection with the Magic Wand. (If you click outside the selection, you not only deselect the selection, you create a new selection.)

- ✔ Choose Select➪Deselect or press Ctrl+D (⌘+D on a Mac).

- ✔ Choose Select➪Reselect or Ctrl+Shift+D (⌘+Shift+D on a Mac) to regain your most recent selection. You can do this even after you have performed numerous actions.

- ✔ Click the state preceding the final state in the History palette.

Editing Selections

The first selection outline you create is almost never perfect. Whether you use a lasso, a marquee tool, or the Magic Wand, there's almost always some problem with the selection. You didn't get the hair selected right, or a finger is clipped off. Whatever the problem, you can remedy it by adding to the selection outline or by subtracting from it.

Adding and subtracting from a selection

Elements gives you a very handy way to add to and subtract from your selections. The four selection modifier buttons in the Options bar, as pictured in Figure 8-7, enable you to make a new selection, add to a selection, subtract from a selection, or intersect a selection. Simply click on your desired selection modifier button and then drag. For instance, if you've made a rectangular selection with the Rectangular Marquee tool and you also need to make a circular selection, first switch to the Elliptical Marquee. Click on the second selection modifier button, "Add to selection." Now when you drag out your circular selection, the rectangular selection won't disappear; instead, the circular selection will be added to it.

Figure 8-7:
The four
selection
modifier
buttons
in the
selection
tools'
Options bar
let you
modify your
existing
selection.

Add to selection

Intersect with selection

Subtract from selection

New selection

It's also possible — and once you get up to speed with Elements, you'll prob-ably find it more convenient — to modify selections using the keyboard. Even if you do use the keyboard, the selection modifier buttons automatically become active when you press the appropriate keys anyway.

To add an area to the current selection, Shift+drag with a lasso or marquee tool, or Shift+click with the Magic Wand. It doesn't matter which tool you used to select the image previously, nor does it matter whether you Shift+click inside or outside the selection.

For example, if you're working with an obligatory person-holding-up-the-Tower-of-Pisa photo like the one in Figure 8-8, first select the tower by drag-ging around it with the Lasso tool, as shown in the left example. To add the woman to the selection, press the Shift key and drag the Lasso around her perimeter, creating the selection outline shown in the right example.

To remove an area from a selection, Alt+drag (Option+drag on a Mac) with a lasso or marquee tool or Alt+click (Option+click on a Mac) with the Magic Wand. To deselect the gap between the woman's legs in Figure 8-8, for exam-ple, you could Alt+drag (Option+drag on a Mac) with the Lasso tool. To dese-lect the area under her left arm, you could Alt+click (Option+click on a Mac) with the Magic Wand.

When you're adding to a selection, a little plus sign appears next to your cursor. When you're subtracting from the selection, a little minus sign appears. And when you're selecting the intersection of two existing selec-tions (as explained next), a little multiply sign appears. See, your math teacher was right — knowing arithmetic comes in handy in all kinds of situations.

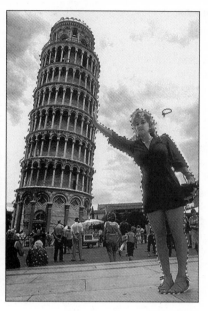

Figure 8-8:
To select both the tower and the woman, you can first select just the tower (left), and then press the Shift key and drag around the woman to select her, too (right).

Intersecting a selection with a selection

If you press the Shift and Alt (Option on a Mac) keys together while clicking with the Magic Wand or dragging with a lasso or marquee tool, you select the intersection of the previous selection and the newest one. (Like that made any sense, right?) Take a look at Figure 8-9. If you first drag around the black rectangle, then Shift+Alt+drag (Shift+Option+drag on a Mac) around the gray rectangle, you get the intersection of the two rectangles. Elements selects all portions of the second marquee that fall inside the first marquee and deselects everything else, leaving the selection shown in the right half of the figure. That's an *intersection*.

You can also use the Intersect selection modifier button (the last in the grouping of four buttons in Figure 8-7) in the Options bar to obtain an intersection.

Try selecting an area with the Lasso or one of the marquee tools and then Shift+Alt+clicking (Shift+Option+clicking on a Mac) inside the selection with the Magic Wand. Or click with the Magic Wand and then Shift+ Alt+ drag (Shift+Option+drag on a Mac) with one of the other selection tools. Either technique lets you limit the area of colors selected with the Magic Wand tool.

Figure 8-9:
To get the intersection of these two rectangles, first marquee the black rectangle and then Shift+Alt+ marquee (Shift+ Option+ marquee) around the gray rectangle (left). The right figure shows the intersection.

Avoiding keyboard collisions

There are a variety of ways to use the lasso and marquee tools while pressing keys. Pressing Alt (Option on a Mac) while using one of the lasso tools, you may recall, temporarily accesses one of the other lasso tools. Pressing Shift while using a marquee tool results in perfect squares and circles.

But what happens when you start combining those shortcut keys with all the add, subtract, and intersect shortcut keys we've just talked about? The following list answers your most burning questions:

✔ To add a square or circular area to an existing selection, start by Shift+dragging with the appropriate marquee tool. You get an unconstrained rectangle or oval, just as though the Shift key weren't down. Then midway into the drag — here's the catch — release the Shift key and then press it again, all the while keeping the mouse button down. The shape snaps to a square or circle with the second press of Shift. Keep the Shift key down until after you release the mouse button. Bet you didn't see that one coming.

✔ Pressing Alt (Option on a Mac) to temporarily access the Polygonal Lasso when the regular Lasso is active causes trouble when you have an existing selection. This is because pressing Alt (Option on a Mac) in that scenario sets you up to subtract from the selection. So, if you want to add or subtract a straight-sided selection, use the Polygonal Lasso — don't try to Alt+click (Option+click on a Mac) with the regular Lasso.

✔ The same advice goes if you want to find the intersection of a selection and a straight-sided shape.

Automatic selection discombobulators

Shift+dragging, Alt+dragging (Option+dragging on a Mac), and all those other wondrous techniques are wildly helpful when it comes to selecting complex details. But they aren't the only selection modifications you can make. Elements offers a handful of automatic functions that reshape selection outlines, blur them, and otherwise mess them up. All the commands discussed in the next few sections reside under the Select menu.

Extending the Magic Wand

Two commands, Grow and Similar, are extensions of the Magic Wand tool (for details on the Magic Wand, see "Wielding the wand" in this chapter). The Grow command expands the size of the selection to include still more continuous colors. For example, if clicking with the Magic Wand doesn't select all the colors you want it to, you can either increase the Tolerance value inside the Options bar and reclick with the tool, or just choose Select⇨Grow to incorporate even more colors. It's kind of a clunky method, especially because the Grow command doesn't have a keyboard shortcut. You'll usually get better results if you Shift+click with the Wand tool, but every once in a while, the Grow command works like you'd expect. (You can use the Grow command with selections made with tools other than the Magic Wand, by the way.)

The Similar command selects all colors that are similar to the selected colors regardless of whether they're interrupted by other colors. In other words, Similar selects all the continuous colors that Grow selects, as well as all similarly colored pixels throughout the image.

Both Grow and Similar judge color similarity exactly like the Magic Wand tool does — that is, according to the Tolerance value in the Options bar. So, if you increase the Tolerance value, the commands select more colors; if you decrease the value, the commands select fewer colors. For example, if you want to select all colors throughout the image that are exactly identical to the ones you've selected so far, enter **0** into the Tolerance option box, and choose Select⇨Similar.

Swapping what's selected for what's not

Sometimes it's easier to select the stuff you don't want to select and then tell Elements to select the deselected stuff and deselect what's selected. (It's certainly easier to *do* this than to *write* it.) This technique is called *inversing a selection,* and you do it by choosing Select⇨Inverse or pressing Ctrl+Shift+I (⌘+Shift+I on a Mac).

For example, suppose that you want to select the clock tower shown on the left side of Figure 8-10. A typical work of baroque madness, this building has more spikes and little twisty bits than a porcupine. Therefore, selecting it would prove a nightmare.

Selecting the sky, on the other hand, is quite easy. By clicking and Shift+clicking a couple of times with the Magic Wand tool (set to the default Tolerance of 32), you can select the entire sky in a matter of two or three seconds. Then choose Select⇨Inverse to "inverse" the selection so that the building is selected and the sky is deselected. To better show off the selection, it's filled with white in the example on the right.

Figure 8-10:
This building (left) is too darned ornate to select easily, but it's a snap to select the sky and then inverse the selection. Filling the selection with white shows how accurate the selection is (right).

Making the selection fuzzy around the edges

You can blur the edges of a selection created with the lasso or marquee tools by increasing the Feather value in the corresponding Options bar. But more often than not, you want to leave the Feather value set to 0 and apply your feathering after you finish drawing the outline.

To feather an existing selection, choose Select⇨Feather or press Ctrl+Alt+D (⌘+Option+D on a Mac). A dinky dialog box with a single option appears onscreen. Enter the amount of fuzziness, in pixels, that you want to apply to the selection and press Enter (Return on a Mac). The selection outline probably won't change very much, but you see a distinct blurring effect when you edit the selection.

You can use feathering to make an image appear to fade into view. For example, take a look at the kid-in-a-basket image shown on the right side of Figure 8-11. If you want to pull off the same effect on an image like the one shown on the left side of the figure, first encircle the little duffer with the Elliptical Marquee tool. Then use Select⇨Inverse to select the background instead and apply Select⇨Feather with a value of 8 pixels. Finally, use Ctrl+Backspace (⌘+Delete on a Mac) to fill the selection with white. The result should look something like the locket with fuzzy edges, as shown on the right side of Figure 8-11. This effect is also possible using the Vignette Frame from the Effects palette (see Chapter 17 for more information on Effects).

Figure 8-11: A tiny tot trapped in a basket (left) receives a classic feathering treatment (right).

Using Border, Smooth, and the rest

The remaining selection outline modifiers, found in the Select⇨Modify submenu, aren't quite as useful, but they do come in handy every now and then:

✔ The Border command selects an area around the edge of the selection. You tell Elements the width, in pixels, of the border you want to select. This command is probably the least useful command of the bunch. If you want to color the outline of a selection, it's easier to use stroking. (See the section "Grabbing a square or circle" earlier in this chapter for more on stroking.)

✔ Select⇨Modify⇨Smooth rounds off the corners of a selection outline. If the selection is very irregular and you want to straighten the twists and turns, use the Smooth command. Elements asks you to enter a value from 1 to 100 to tell it how far it can move any point in the outline. Enter 2 or 3 to be safe.

✔ If you want to increase the size of a selection a few pixels outward, choose Select➪Modify➪Expand and enter the number of pixels. The maximum value is 100 pixels; if you want to expand the outline farther, you have to choose Expand a second time.

✔ Select➪Modify➪Contract is the opposite of the Expand command. This command shrinks the selected area by 1 to 100 pixels all the way around.

Moving selections

To move a selection outline without moving the image inside it, select a tool other than the Move or Crop tool and nudge the selection with the arrow keys. You can also drag the selection if you choose one of the selection tools and position it within the selection. This is a great way to reposition a selection outline without disturbing so much as a single pixel in the image.

Hiding the Ants

One more thing about selection outlines — and it's a vital thing to know when working with Elements. Under the View menu, you'll find the item Selection Edges. When there's an active selection, Selection Edges has a checkmark next to it. If you select the command, the checkmark goes away. Select it again, and the checkmark comes back.

The Selection Edges command hides the "marching ants" of the active selection outline. This makes it much easier to see what you're doing as you work, particularly around the edges of the selection; those distracting ants turn invisible. Note, however, that this is not the same thing as deselecting the selection. When you toggle off Selection Edges, the selection is still active; the visible evidence of the active selection (the marching ants) has just become invisible.

While Selection Edges is a crucial command, it also leads to the number one most common mistake while working with Elements. You'll make a selection, choose Selection Edges to hide the selection, work inside your selection without distraction, and then move to working outside the selection — and nothing will happen. You won't be able to edit your image where you want. You'll get annoyed, start to fume, decide that the problem is that you're just not pressing on your mouse **HARD ENOUGH** — and then become convinced that Elements and your computer are plotting against you. Just take a deep breath, calmly ask yourself "Did I hide my selection edges?", answer yourself, "Yes, as a matter of fact, I did," and then hit Ctrl+D (⌘+D on the Mac). All is well. Phew.

Chapter 9

Layer Layer

*1*nsofar as "high art" is concerned, the heyday for surrealism was 70 to 80 years ago. But the problem with guys like Max Ernst, René Magritte, and even Salvador Dalí was that they never got around to learning how to use Photoshop Elements. Oh, sure, they were long dead by the time Elements debuted. But still, think of what they could have done with Elements' layers. A paintbrush is great, but it pales when compared to Elements as a means for merging photo-realistic images to create flat-out impossible visual scenarios.

Color Plate 9-1 provides ample evidence. No matter how hard you worked at it, you could never assemble these subjects in a photo shoot. It's just so darn difficult to squeeze a giant fish, the Reims Cathedral in France, and the planet Neptune into the same room. If you had talent streaming like fire-hydrant jets out your ears, you might be able to paint the image, but most of us would have thrown in the towel at the prospect of re-creating a High Gothic cathedral facade that took a team of thirteenth-century masters 65 years to carve.

But we live in a sparkling modern age, filled with more dazzling masterworks of automation than we know what to do with. Thanks to one such masterwork — we speak here of Elements, naturally — it's possible to throw together Color Plate 9-1 in a couple of hours. Altogether, the composition comprises eight separate images; however, it required not so much as a single stroke of a painting or editing tool. The images were simply selected, combined, blended together, and finally a few stray pixels were erased that weren't doing the final study in surrealism a lick of good. The blending was accomplished using blending modes, which Chapter 13 discusses.

Because it can be difficult to distinguish every one of the eight images, Figure 9-1 shows each one individually. The arrows indicate the order in which the images are stacked on top of each other. For example, the underwater kelp jungle in the lower-right corner of Figure 9-1 lies at the bottom of the composition in Color Plate 9-1; the photo of Neptune in the upper-left corner of the Figure 9-1 rests at the top of Color Plate 9-1. The image appears as if you cut out and pasted a picture of the kelp onto a page, pasted the fish on the kelp, pasted the astronaut in front of the fish, and so on.

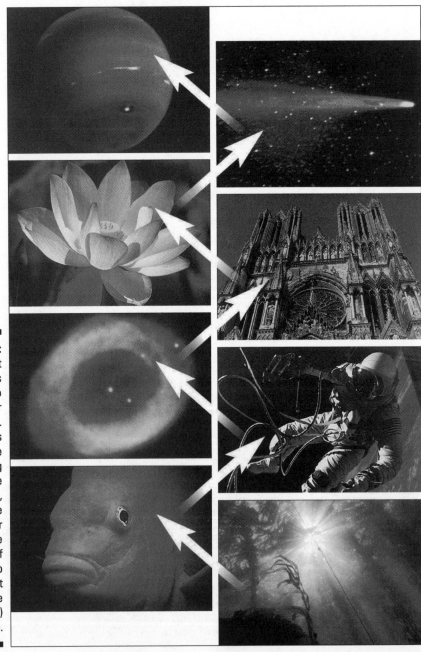

Figure 9-1:
The eight images used to create Color Plate 9-1. The arrows show the layering order of the images, from the kelp (lower right) at the bottom of the heap to the planet Neptune (upper left) at the top.

This is the point at which you ask, "Yeah, yeah, yeah, but how in the world do I begin to pull off something like this?" Well, wouldn't you know it — that's what this chapter is all about. And, remarkably, it's all a lot easier than you may think.

Pasting Images Together

Suppose that you want to paste the fish image from the bottom of Figure 9-1 into the neighboring kelp image. How do you go about it? Here's one approach:

1. **Open the fish image and select the fish. (To learn about selections, refer to Chapter 8.)**

2. **Click the Copy icon (the one with two pieces of paper and two arrows) in the Shortcuts bar or press Ctrl+C (⌘+C on a Mac).**

   Ctrl+C (⌘+C on a Mac) is the time-honored keyboard shortcut for the Edit⇨Copy command, which places a copy of your selection onto the clipboard. The *clipboard* is a temporary storage area for image data. The fish displaces any previous occupant of the clipboard (sent there via Edit⇨Copy or its close cousin, Edit⇨Cut).

3. **Open the kelp image.**

4. **Click the Paste icon (the one with a clipboard, a piece of paper, and an arrow) in the Shortcuts bar or press Ctrl+V (⌘+V on a Mac).**

   Ctrl+V (⌘+V on a Mac) is the shortcut for the Edit⇨Paste command, which dumps the current contents of the clipboard into your image. The original fish image remains intact because the fish you pasted into the kelp was merely a copy.

But these steps aren't the only way to combine images. You also have these options at your disposal:

- ✔ To cut a selection from one image and paste it into another, click the Cut icon (the pair of scissors) in the Shortcuts bar, or choose Edit⇨Cut. Then switch to the other image and click the Shortcuts bar's Paste icon, or choose Edit⇨Paste. The selection is removed entirely from the first image and planted in the second.

- ✔ You can clone a selection between images by dragging it with the Move tool or Ctrl+dragging (⌘+dragging on a Mac) it with any tool except the Hand or the Shape tools.

  This method of cloning between images is known in the computer world as *dragging and dropping,* by the way.

- ✔ The Copy command copies only the contents of the currently selected layer. To copy from all layers in the image, select Edit⇨Copy Merged.

✔ To transfer an entire image to another image window, choose Select⇨All or Ctrl+A (⌘+A on a Mac) before dragging or using the Cut or Copy commands.

✔ For a weird but occasionally useful trick, use Edit⇨Paste Into to paste an image inside an existing selection, as described in the upcoming section "Filling a selection with a selection."

When you use the Paste command, Elements places the pasted image on a new layer. When you drag and drop a selection from one image to another, Elements places the selection on a new layer as well. For more on working with layers, start reading at the section "Excuse Me, but What's a Layer?" and keep going to the end of the chapter.

Filling a selection with a selection

The Edit⇨Paste Into command lets you insert an image into an existing selection outline. For example, suppose you wanted to paste the fish behind some of the vegetation in the neighboring kelp image so that the fish would appear to be intertwined with its environment. As shown in the first example of Figure 9-2, select an area inside the kelp stalks and feather the selection by choosing Select⇨Feather. Then choose Paste Into or Ctrl+Shift+V (⌘+Shift+V on a Mac) to create the fish-inside-the-kelp shown in the second example. (Note that the selection has been deselected in the second example so that you can better see the transitions between fish and stalks.)

Elements pastes the selection to a new layer. You can then move and blend the pasted image just as though it were a floating selection. It's just that the pasted image is invisible outside the boundaries of the previous selection outline.

You can also paste into the unselected area of an image by pressing the Alt key (Option key on a Mac) as you choose Edit⇨Paste Into. If this had been done with the image in Figure 9-2, for example, the fish would show through the exact opposite area of the kelp bed that he does now.

Resizing an image to match its new home

When you bring two images together, you always have to deal with the issue of relative size. For example, the fish is too large for its surroundings. Here's how to ensure that the two images you want to combine are sized correctly:

1. **Magnify the two images to exactly the same zoom factor.**

   To see them side by side, a zoom ratio of 50% or smaller may be necessary.

Figure 9-2:
After
selecting an
area of kelp
(left), use
the Paste
Into
command to
introduce
the fish to
his new
kelpy home
(right).

2. **If either of the two images appears disproportionately large, scale it down (bad pun, we know) by using Image⇨Resize⇨Image Size.**

   In this case, you don't care at all about the dimensions or resolution of the image; all you care about is the file size — that is, the number of pixels comprising the image. If the image you want to copy or drag (fish) is too large, scale it down just enough to fit inside the destination image. If the destination image (kelp) is too large, reduce it as desired. Keep Ctrl+Z (⌘+Z on a Mac) ready in case you accidentally go too far. (See Chapter 4 for more information about the Image Size command.)

   Be careful not to over-reduce! Remember that you're throwing away pixels and, therefore, sacrificing detail. And you definitely don't want to enlarge the image after you've reduced it. Your image will turn to mush. (For more info on how to size your images safely, see Chapter 4.) If you go too far, you can always restore the original by choosing File⇨Revert, or undoing your steps using the History palette, as discussed in Chapter 7.

3. **Combine the two images.**

   Copy and paste or drag and drop — it's your call.

4. **Position the image more or less where you want it.**

5. **Choose Image⇨Resize⇨Scale.**

   This command lets you fine-tune the relative size of the imported image with respect to its new home. (More on this command at the end of the chapter in the section "Using the Transform tool.") A marquee with four corner handles surrounds the image.

6. **Drag a corner handle to scale the image.**

Shift+drag a handle to scale the image proportionally, as the first example in Figure 9-3 illustrates. After you release the handle, Elements previews how the resized image will look. Don't worry that the preview is a little choppy; the scaled image will be smooth.

Don't scale the image up; only scale it down. Otherwise, Elements has to make up pixels, which is most assuredly not one of the program's better capabilities.

7. **Move your cursor inside the transform box and double-click.**

After you resize the image as desired — you can drag the corner handles all you want — move your cursor inside the box. Double-click or press Enter (Return on a Mac) to accept the image's new size and tell Elements to work its magic. You can also click the Commit box (the checkmark icon) at the end of the Options bar. The resized image will appear perfectly smooth.

If you decide that you don't want to scale the image before you double-click or press Enter (Return on Mac), press Esc or Ctrl+period (⌘+period on a Mac) to get rid of the box. You can also click the Cancel button (the X icon) in the Options bar. If you've already double-clicked or pressed Enter (Return on Mac), you can restore the image to its original size by pressing Ctrl+Z (⌘+Z on a Mac).

Figure 9-3:
Use the Scale command to refine the image size.

Excuse Me, but What's a Layer?

Here's a little analogy to get things rolling. Imagine that you have three sheets of acetate — you know, like folks used to slide into overhead projectors to bore audiences before the days of multimedia presentations. Anyway, on one sheet you draw a picture of a fish. On a second sheet, you draw a fishbowl. And on a third sheet, you draw the table on which the fishbowl sits. When you stack all the sheets on top of each other, the images blend together to create a seamless view of a fish in his happy home. If you're familiar with animation, this is the same way a multiplane camera works.

Layers in Elements work just like that. You can keep different parts of your image on separate layers and then combine the layers to create a composite image. You can rearrange layers, add and delete layers, blend them together using different opacity values and blend modes, and do all sorts of other impressive things.

Another advantage of using layers is that you can edit or paint on one layer without affecting the other layers. That means you can safely apply commands or painting tools to one portion of your image without worrying about messing up the rest of the image — and without bothering to select the part you want to edit.

You aren't restricted to the layers that Elements creates automatically, however. You can create as many new layers as your computer's memory allows, up to a theoretical 8,000. In the case of the image shown in Color Plate 9-1, the kelp, fish, astronaut, nebula, cathedral, flower, comet, and Neptune were kept on separate layers. Though they may appear to blend together along the edges, they are, in fact, as distinct as peas in a pod.

Finding your way around the Layers palette

The Layers palette, shown in Figure 9-4, is Grand Central Station for managing layers. Here's what you need to know to navigate the Layers palette:

- ✔ The Background is the bottom layer in the image. Every image has a Background (unless the Background has been turned into a regular layer — read on to see how).

- ✔ The order of the layers in the Layers palette represents their order in the image. The top layer in the palette is the top layer in your image, and so on.

✔ You can edit only one layer at a time — the active layer. The *active layer* is the one that's highlighted in the Layers palette and that has a little Paintbrush icon to the left of its layer name. To make another layer active, just click on its name.

✔ Press Alt+] (right bracket) — Option+] on a Mac — to move up one layer; press Alt+[(left bracket) — Option+[on a Mac — to activate the next layer down. Press Shift+Alt+] (Shift+Option+] on a Mac) to move to the top layer; press Shift+Alt+[(Shift+Option+[on a Mac) to move to the Background or bottom layer.

✔ An eyeball icon next to a layer name means that the layer is visible. To hide the layer, click on the eyeball. To display the layer, click where the eyeball was to bring it back.

✔ To hide all layers but one, Alt+click (Option+click on a Mac) on the eyeball in front of the name of the layer you want to see. Alt+click (Option+click on a Mac) again to redisplay all the layers.

✔ If you hide the Background layer, you see a checkerboard pattern any- where the Background showed through. The checkerboard represents the transparent areas of the visible layers.

✔ This gray and white checkerboard can be customized in the Trans- parency section of the Preferences; you can specify the size and color of the squares Elements uses to represent transparency.

✔ To find out how to use the Blend Mode pop-up menu and the Opacity setting at the top of the palette, refer to Chapter 13.

✔ To create a new, blank layer, click on the Create New Layer icon at the bottom of the palette (refer to Figure 9-4). To create a duplicate of an existing layer, drag the layer to the Create New Layer icon.

When you create a layer in the manner mentioned in the preceding para- graph, Elements gives the layer a name like Layer 1 or Layer 2, and so on. If you want to name the layer, double-click on the layer name in the Layers palette and enter a name in the Layer Properties dialog box that appears. You can also select the layer and choose Rename Layer from the Layers palette or Layer menu.

✔ Alternatively, you can create the layer by choosing the New Layer or Duplicate Layer command from the Layers palette menu (click on the right-pointing arrow at the top of the palette), or choose Layer⇨New⇨ Layer or Layer⇨Duplicate Layer. If you use this method to create a layer, Elements prompts you to give the layer a name.

✔ To delete a layer, drag it to the Trash icon. Keep in mind that you're throwing away the layer along with the image on it. Layers can also be deleted via Layer⇨Delete Layer or by choosing Delete Layer from the Layers palette pop-up menu.

✔ If you ever want to create a selection outline around the objects on a layer, Elements gives you an easy way to do it. Just Ctrl+click (⌘+click on a Mac) on the layer name in the Layers palette.

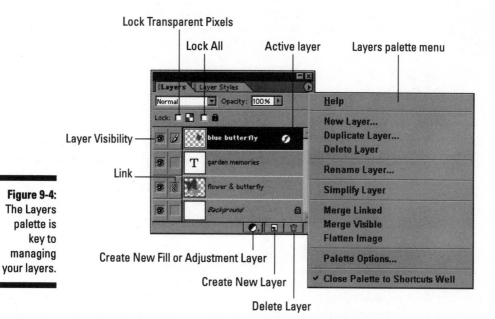

Lock Transparent Pixels

Lock All   Active layer   Layers palette menu

Layer Visibility

Link

Figure 9-4:
The Layers palette is key to managing your layers.

Create New Fill or Adjustment Layer

Create New Layer

Delete Layer

Moving and manipulating layers

Layers are flexible things — you can move them, shuffle their order, and rearrange them as though they were a deck of playing cards. Here's a look at some of the more common layer manipulation moves you may need to make:

✔ To move an image on a layer, drag it with the Move tool or Ctrl+drag (⌘+drag on a Mac) with any other tool except the Hand or Shape tools. To move the layer in 1-pixel increments, press an arrow key with the Move tool selected or press Ctrl (⌘ on a Mac) plus an arrow key with any tool but the Hand or Shape tools. To move the layer in 10-pixel increments, press Shift as you press the arrow key

✔ Check the Auto Select Layer in the Options bar to switch to a layer when you click with the Move tool on any part of that layer.

The Auto Select Layer option has a drawback, in that it makes it very easy to switch layers when you don't want to.

✔ The Show Bounding Box option, which also appears in the Options bar when the Move tool is active and is switched on by default, surrounds the contents of the layer (or the selection) with a box with handles. This box lets you transform a layer without choosing a command. (For more on transformations, see "Transforming Layers and Selections" in this chapter.)

✔ To link an active layer to another layer, click on the second column of the Layers palette — just to the left of the layer name — next to the layer that's not active. A Link icon appears in the column. Now you can move, scale, and rotate both layers at once. To remove the link, click on the Link icon.

✔ To delete linked layers in one fell swoop, select one of the layers in the group, and Ctrl+click (⌘+click on a Mac) the Trash icon in the Layers palette.

✔ Can't figure out which layer holds the object you want to edit? With the Move tool selected, press Alt+right-click (Control+Option on a Mac) on the object. Or Ctrl+Alt+right-click (⌘+Control+Option on a Mac) with any tool but the Hand or Shape tools. Elements automatically activates the appropriate layer. Or right-click (Control+click on a Mac) on the object. Elements tells you which layer the object resides on and enables you to *select* the layer, but doesn't automatically activate the layer upon clicking.

✔ After you get a few layers going, you can move one in front of or behind another by dragging it up or down in the list of layers in the Layers palette. A black line shows where the layer will be inserted. You can't reorder the Background or move any layer below the Background until you convert it to a layer. To convert, double-click on the Background in the Layers palette, enter a name for the layer, and press Enter (Return on a Mac). Or you can leave the default name of Layer 0 and press Enter (Return on a Mac).

✔ To convert the active layer into a Background layer, choose Layer⇨ New⇨Background From Layer.

✔ Another way to rearrange layers is to use the commands in the Layer⇨Arrange submenu. Click on the layer that you want to move in the Layers palette. Then:

   1. Choose Layer⇨Arrange⇨Bring to Front (Shift+Ctrl+]/Shift+⌘+]) to make the layer the topmost layer.

   2. Select Bring Forward (Ctrl+]/⌘+]) to move the layer up one level.

   3. Select Send Backward (Ctrl+[/⌘+[) to move the layer down one level.

   4. Select Send to Back (Shift+Ctrl+[/Shift+⌘+[) to move the layer to just above the Background layer.

✔ You can copy an entire layer to a new image by selecting the layer in the Layers palette and dragging and dropping the layer to the new image. The layer drops at the spot where you release the mouse button and resides one layer above the active layer in the new image.

Flattening and merging layers

Sadly, layers aren't all fun and games. To put it bluntly, they come at a steep price and require some concerted management skills. First, if an image contains layers, saving it in any format other than Elements' native Photoshop format, PDF, or TIFF merges all the layers into one (refer to Chapter 6 for more about saving). The Photoshop, TIFF, and PDF formats are the only formats that preserve layers. Second, every layer you add also makes your file size grow. And third, layers can really slow down Elements. To keep running at peak efficiency, it's best to juggle as few layers at a time as possible.

If you want to save your image for use in a different program that cannot utilize Photoshop, PDF, or TIFF formats, but you think you might need to revisit the layered version of the image at some point in the future, you can save the composition to a different file and flatten it — that is, smush all the layers together. To do this, choose File➪Save As. The Save As dialog box appears onscreen. Check the As a Copy option, and then select your desired file format from the Format pop-up menu. Notice that the Layers option is grayed out, meaning that Elements will automatically flatten the image for you upon saving.

Name the image and press Enter (Return on a Mac). Elements saves the flattened image to a different file.

But useful as that is, you're still going to want to merge layers every so often to keep your image manageable. Otherwise, operations can slow to a snail's pace, and that's an insult to the snail. Here are your merging options:

- ✔ To merge several layers into one, hide all layers except the ones you want to merge. In other words, eyeball icons should appear in front of the layers you want to merge. Hide the eyeball if you don't want to merge the layer. Then choose Merge Visible from the Layers palette menu (by dragging from that right-pointing arrowhead in the upper-right corner of the palette) or from the regular Layer menu at the top of the screen. Or, even simpler, press Shift+Ctrl+E (Shift+⌘+E on a Mac).

  You can merge one layer with other layers to which it has been linked. Choose Merge Linked from the Layers palette menu or from the top Layer menu. Easier yet, press Ctrl+E (⌘+E on a Mac). Note that the Merge Linked command changes to the Merge Down command if you have no linked layers selected. Merge Down will merge your selected layer with all layers residing below it.

- ✔ If you want to flatten the entire image and get rid of all the layers, choose the Flatten Image command from the palette menu or from the Layer menu.

Locking Layers

The last chapter talks about creating selections to limit the active working area — for instance, you can paint inside a selection outline to paint just the selection and leave the surrounding areas untouched. But when you send a selection to a layer, the selection outline disappears. So how do you paint only inside the image on a layer? For example, maybe you want to paint stripes on an object on a layer without going outside the lines.

The solution is to select the Lock Transparent Pixels check box near the top of the Layers palette, as shown in Figure 9-4. The transparent areas around the object stay transparent, letting you paint only inside the opaque and translucent pixels.

For a quick way to turn the Lock Transparent Pixels check box on and off, press the forward slash key (/). The Lock All option prevents you from painting, editing, moving, or transforming your layer. (But you can still make selections.)

Moving and Cloning Selections

The very end of Chapter 8 looks at moving a selection outline without moving the contents of the selection. Now that we have a working knowledge of layers, let's look at ways of moving selections along with the pixels they contain:

- ✔ To move a selection, grab the Move tool (press V to select the tool from the keyboard) and drag. A bounding box appears around the selection to show that you're about to move it from its current home. When you move the selection, the area where the selection used to be is filled with the Background color (assuming that you're working on the Background layer), as illustrated in Figure 9-5.

- ✔ You can temporarily access the Move tool by pressing Ctrl (⌘ on a Mac) when any tool but the Hand or one of the Shape tools is selected.

- ✔ To nudge a selection 1 pixel, press one of the arrow keys while the Move tool is selected. Or press Ctrl (⌘ on a Mac) and an arrow key when any tool other than the Hand or Shape tools is selected. The up arrow nudges the selection 1 pixel up; the right arrow nudges it to the right, and so on, just like you'd think. To nudge a selection 10 pixels, press Shift along with an arrow key while the Move tool is selected.

- ✔ To clone and move a selection, Alt+drag (Option+drag on a Mac) with the Move tool or Ctrl+Alt+drag (⌘+Option+drag on a Mac) with any tool other than the Hand or Shape tools. Your cursor changes into two arrowheads — a reminder that you're creating a clone of your selection.

Figure 9-5:
After
selecting
the
Washington
Monument
(top), it's
dragged to a
more
convenient
location
(bottom).

✔ To clone and nudge, select the Move tool and then press Alt (Option on
a Mac) and one of the arrow keys. Or, when any tool other than the Hand
or Shape tools is selected, press Ctrl+Alt (⌘+Option on a Mac) as you
press the arrow keys. Press Shift+Alt (Shift+Option on a Mac) with an
arrow key to clone the selection and move it 10 pixels.

> ✔ You can move and clone selections between images just as you would within a single image. Just drag the selection from its current window into the other image window.

Transforming Layers and Selections

The end of Chapter 4 looks at commands that can flip and rotate the entire canvas. Now let's take a look at the related subject of *transforming*. In Elements' parlance, transforming means spinning, stretching, and generally distorting. You can transform a layer or selection when there's a bounding box around it, such as the bounding box that appears by default when you select the Move tool. You can drag from the square handles of the bounding box to transform the layer or selection.

Using the Image menu's commands

The Image menu has three submenus that contain transforming commands: Rotate, Resize, and Transform. At the top of the Rotate submenu is the Free Rotate command (along with other commands that mirror the ones covered in Chapter 4). The bottom of the Resize submenu has the Scale command, and the Transform submenu has four different transforming commands.

These commands work with or without selections. If there is no selection, the commands work on the entire layer. If there is an active selection, the commands affect only the selected area. The only exception to this is the Background layer, which must have an active selection in order to be transformed.

Using the Transform tool

There's a secret tool hiding inside Elements that is nowhere to be found in the Toolbox: the Transform tool. Just choose one of the transforming commands or drag a handle of the Move tool's bounding box, and you'll see the Transform tool's mysterious icon appear on the far left of the Options bar (see Figure 9-6), exactly where you'd see, say, the Zoom tool's icon if you had the Zoom tool selected. This implementation in Elements is somewhat confusing; you can manipulate your transformation using the Options bar, or you can freely choose from among the six transforming commands under the Image menu. The latter option is by far the easiest, so let's take a closer look at the commands:

- ✔ **Free Rotate:** This is a scaled back version of the Free Transform tool, which only allows you to rotate and move the selection. Move the cursor toward the edges or outside of the selection to rotate; move the cursor toward the center to move the selection.

- ✔ **Scale:** Drag any handle to scale your selection. Press Shift+drag to maintain proportions. Press Alt+drag (Option+drag on a Mac) to scale from the center point outward. (This behavior is similar to that of the Crop tool, as covered in Chapter 4.)

- ✔ **Free Transform:** This option allows you to scale, move, and rotate the selection. Free Transform can be invoked from the keyboard by pressing Ctrl+T (⌘+T on the Mac).

- ✔ **Skew:** Skew permits distortion on a given axis.

- ✔ **Distort:** Distort enables handles to move independently with no axis restrictions.

- ✔ **Perspective:** When you drag a corner handle, the opposite corner handle on the same side moves as well.

Figure 9-6:
The Options
bar for the
stealthy
Transform
tool.

The most useful control found in the Options bar is the "Reference point location" option (the first icon on the left). This sets the point around which the transformation happens and is especially useful when rotating the selection.

Ending your transformation

After you finish transforming, press Enter (Return on a Mac) or double-click inside the transform box or click the Commit button (the check icon) in the Options bar. To cancel, press Esc or Ctrl+period (⌘+period on a Mac), or click the Cancel button (the X icon).

You have many more options available in the Layers palette — blend modes, text layers, adjustment layers, shape layers, fill layers — but we thought it was important to give you a basic introduction to the Layers palette relatively early on in the book. Don't worry: We'll peel away the many layers of the Layers palette as we proceed.

Part III
Realer Than Life

The 5th Wave   By Rich Tennant

"Well, well! Guess who just lost 9 pixels?"

In this part . . .

Photographs are supposed to be little records of a moment in time, right? Sure, it can be a drag to stop whatever fun you're having and smile for the camera. But in the back of your mind you know it's going to be worth it down the road because you can imagine yourself in the twilight of your years, reflecting on those halcyon days of yore (whatever that means). Was the sky really that blue? Was your face really that wrinkle-free? Was life ever really that brilliantly in focus?

If now, in the prime of your youth (did we lose anyone there?), you give your photos a working over with Photoshop Elements, the answers to those questions will be no, no, and no. You see, Elements has a phalanx of tools designed to make your images look better than they ever did in real life. And we're not just talking about cleaning the dust off a scanned photo or eliminating a case of flash-induced red eye — although Elements can certainly do those things. Elements can dig deep within the shadows and find hidden details, take a gray sky and make it blue, and soften up those wrinkles with no surgery required.

The three chapters in this part tell you how to use Elements to make your images look better — "realer" than life, if you will. Although doing this to your photos might give you a glorified sense of the past in your later years, there will be an easy remedy. Just take your 14 megapixel digital camera, snap a photo, import it into your 5 googolhertz computer, and get to work using Photoshop Elements Version 36.0. With all the advancements in technology, you'll be able to make the new reality look much better than the old reality ever could.

Chapter 10

Dusting Off Images
(Without the Lemony Scent)

· ·

In This Chapter

▶ Applying filters
▶ Using the Dust & Scratches filter
▶ Cleaning up an image with the Clone Stamp tool
▶ Using the Red Eye Brush tool

· ·

*I*f you've ever scanned an image, you know the story. You start with a lovely photograph that you've cherished all your life, place it carefully in your scanner, and the scan ends up looking like someone stuck it inside a dryer lint trap. Big, gnarly hairs wiggle across the image. Little dust flecks seem to have reproduced like rabbits. And if you really hit the jackpot, you may even spy a few fingerprints on your image. It's enough to make you clean the house, shave the cats, and have your fingerprints sanded off.

Ultimately, that won't get you anywhere. But the dust-busting tools discussed in this chapter can. With a keen eye and a little bit of elbow grease, you can scrub away those imperfections and make your image appear absolutely spotless.

Photoshop Elements offers two methods for dusting away the specks:

✔ The Dust & Scratches filter automates the removal of image imperfections, but it can do more harm than good by getting rid of important detail as well.

✔ The Clone Stamp tool lets you copy portions of an image to cover up blotches. This tool takes more time to use than the Dust & Scratches command and requires a considerable amount of clicking and dragging, but it also results in a better-looking picture.

And as soon as we've gotten the dust out of our eyes, we'll also take a clear gaze at the Red Eye Brush Tool, Elements' dedicated tool for exorcising that flash-induced demonic glowing look from the subjects in your images.

Introducing Filters

Before we look at the Dust & Scratches filter, we'd better back up and address the topic of filters in general. If you're a photographer or if you've taken a photography course or two, you know how photographic filters work. They refine or refract light to modify the image as it comes into the camera. A daylight filter strains some of the blue out of the image; a polarization lens eliminates reflected light; a fish-eye lens refracts peripheral imagery into the photo.

But real-life filters present some problems. They take up a ton of room in your camera bag, they generally bang around and get scratched, and you never know when you're going to contract a sudden case of butterfingers and drop a lens onto a marble floor. Also, you have to decide which filter you want to use while shooting the photo. Not only is it difficult to experiment through a viewfinder, but also whatever decision you ultimately make is permanent. If you go with a fish-eye lens, you can't go back and "undistort" the image later.

The Photoshop Elements filters are another story:

- ✔ All filters reside in a single palette (surprisingly called the Filters palette).
- ✔ You can undo a filter if you don't like the results.
- ✔ You can preview the outcome of almost every filter.
- ✔ You can apply several filters in a row and even go back and revisit a single filter multiple times.
- ✔ Most Elements filters have no real-world counterparts, which means that you can modify images in ways that aren't possible inside a camera.

If you're a professional photographer, you may want to forgo a few of your camera's filters and take up Elements' filters instead. Granted, you may still want to use corrective lenses to adjust color and keep out reflected light, but avoid a special-effects filter that makes the image look like more than what your eyes can see. Such filters merely limit the range of effects you can apply later inside Elements.

If you aren't a photographer, filters open up a whole new range of opportunities that no other Elements function quite matches. Filters can make changes automatically, so there's no need to be an artist (although an artistic vision certainly comes in handy). Filters can make poor images look better and good images look fantastic. And you can use them to introduce special effects, such as camera movement and relief textures. Frankly, filters turn Elements into a lean, mean (though good) photo-munching machine.

Applying filters

You have two basic ways to apply Elements filters: the Filter menu and the Filters palette. In the Filter menu, all filters are grouped into submenus, with the exception of the nonconformist Liquify filter, which hangs out at the top of the menu and won't consort with the other filters. Most filters, when applied using the Filter menu, present a dialog box that lets you tweak various aspects of the filter.

In the Filters palette, the Liquify filter has allowed itself to be categorized along with the Distort filters. You can switch between categories by using the drop-down menu at the top of the palette, or just set the menu to All if you like having your filters organized strictly by alphabetization. Each filter has a thumbnail showing the effects of the filter applied to a sample image. To apply a filter from the Filters palette, click on the filter and then click the Apply button at the top of the palette, double-click the filter in the palette, or just drag the filter from the Filters palette into the image window. If the Filter Options check box is checked at the top of the palette, you'll then be presented with the filter's dialog box (when applicable). If Filter Options is unchecked, Elements will (in almost every case) bypass the dialog box and just apply the default values for that filter. It's strongly recommended that you keep the Filter Options check box checked at all times in order to have the most control over your filters.

A few fast filter facts

Here are some important things to know about using filters:

- ✔ The Filters palette has two different viewing modes: List view and Thumbnail view. You'll probably find List view to be more helpful in the long run. One of the List view's best features is that it lets you view the thumbnail of your selected filter right beneath the Original view of the thumbnail image, making it easier to compare the before and after states of the thumbnail.

- ✔ If you select some portion of your image, the filter affects the selection and leaves the rest of the image unmodified. If you don't select a portion of the image, the filter affects the entire layer.

- ✔ To create smooth transitions between filtered and unfiltered areas in an image, blur the selection outline by choosing Select⇨Feather (see Chapter 8).

- ✔ After you apply a filter, you can reapply it with the same settings by choosing the first command in the Filter menu or by pressing Ctrl+F (⌘+F on a Mac).

✔ Most filters display a dialog box so that you can control how the filter is applied. If the last filter was one of these, press Ctrl+Alt+F (⌘+Option+F on a Mac) to redisplay the dialog box and apply the filter again using different settings.

✔ To undo the last filter, press Ctrl+Z (⌘+Z on a Mac) or click the Step Backward button in the Shortcuts bar. Unlike a canceled filter, an "undone" filter remains at the top of the Filter menu, so you can later apply it by pressing Ctrl+F (⌘+F on a Mac).

✔ Some filters take a few seconds or possibly even minutes to apply, depending on the size of your image. You can cancel such a filter in progress by pressing Esc. The name of the previous filter remains at the top of the Filter menu, so you can't press Ctrl+F (⌘+F on a Mac) to reapply a canceled filter.

Using the Dust & Scratches Filter

With that whirlwind tour of filters out of the way, let's see exactly how to use the Dust & Scratches filter. Automobile aficionados know that the only way to clean a car is to tenderly rub its surface with specially treated pieces of felt dipped in no-tears baby shampoo. They would never take their cars through one of those drive-through wash joints where big floppy pieces of blue plastic flog your car and take little bits of your paint job along with them. That's the main problem with the Dust & Scratches filter — it's akin to sending your image through a car wash. But just because we may not approve of the Dust & Scratches filter, that's no reason for you not to take a crack at it. Maybe you need to clean up an image in a hurry for that last-minute space in the company newsletter, and the car wash solution is the only one you have time to try.

The lab rat for today's outing is Figure 10-1. This figure demonstrates another variety of splatter that can plague images — old photo gunk. The lines, scratches, and dots in this image weren't introduced in the scanning process; they were a part of the original photo. Shot near the beginning of this century, this picture of Halley's comet has held up amazingly well over the years. We should all hope to look half as good when we're its age.

Incidentally, if you're a lover of things extraterrestrial, you can't go wrong with Corbis' "Space & Spaceflight" CD, which includes about as many views of the sun, moon, planets, and outlying nebula as a person could hope for.

To tidy up an image that presents similar symptoms, go to the Filters palette and scroll down to Dust & Scratches. You can also set the pop-up menu at the top of the palette to Noise, which will narrow your search down to just five filters, or even go up to the Filter menu and choose Noise⇨Dust & Scratches. Elements displays the strange and mysterious Dust & Scratches dialog box, shown in all its glory in Figure 10-2 and explained in the next two sections.

Figure 10-1:
Halley's comet as it appeared in 1910, replete with old photo gunk.

If you select a portion of your image before you choose the Dust & Scratches command, the command affects just the selected area.

Preview cursor   Preview box   Zoom buttons

Figure 10-2:
Like most filters, the Dust & Scratches dialog box provides a hefty supply of previewing options.

Previewing the filter effects

The makers of the Dust & Scratches dialog box know that at first glance it doesn't make a lick of sense, so they thoughtfully provide some preview options (shown in Figure 10-2) to enable you to see what happens when you make some otherwise-meaningless adjustment. Here's how these preview options work:

- ✔ The preview box shows how your modifications look when applied to a tiny portion of the image.

- ✔ If you move the cursor outside the dialog box, it changes to a hollow square. Click on an area in the image to capture it inside the preview box.

- ✔ You can also scroll the contents of the preview box by dragging inside the box. Your cursor changes to a little hand.

- ✔ To magnify or reduce the contents of the preview box, click on the plus or minus zoom button.

- ✔ You can also access the standard magnifying glass cursor inside the preview box by pressing the Ctrl (⌘ on a Mac) key to zoom in or the Alt (Option on a Mac) key to zoom out.

- ✔ As long as the Preview check box is selected, Elements previews your settings in the image window as well as in the preview box.

- ✔ You can even use the standard Hand and Zoom cursors inside the image window while the Dust & Scratches dialog box is open. Just press the spacebar to get the hand cursor or Ctrl or Alt (⌘ or Option on a Mac) to get the zoom cursors. This technique is a great way to preview a filter at two different zoom ratios, one inside the dialog box and one outside.

- ✔ If Elements seems to be slowing down too much as it tries to preview a filter in the image window, just click on the Preview check box to turn off the function.

Specifying the size of the speck

The Dust & Scratches dialog box offers just two options that affect the performance of the filter: the Radius and Threshold slider bars. The slider bars work as follows:

- ✔ Change the Radius value to indicate the size of the dust specks and the thickness of the hairs that you want to eliminate. In geometry, radius means half the width of a circle, so the Radius value is half the width of a dust speck. The minimum value is 1, meaning that the filter wipes out all specks and hairs up to 2 pixels thick.

"Ah, ha," you may think, "If I just crank up the Radius value as far as it goes (100 pixels), that should be enough to eliminate entire colonies of dust bunnies." Well, no. The Dust & Scratches filter doesn't really know a speck from a tiny bit of detail. So, if you have it rub out 100-pixel radius dust globs, it also rubs out 100-pixel details, such as Uncle Ralph's head. Figure 10-3 shows the effects of setting the Radius value to 1 on the left and 3 on the right. Notice how fuzzy the image becomes with a 3-pixel radius? A word of advice: Never set the radius value higher than 2.

✔ The Threshold value tells Elements how different the color of a dust speck has to be from the color of the surrounding image to be considered a bad seed.

The default Threshold value of 0 tells Elements that dust and image need only be 0 color levels different from each other. Because all colors are at least 0 levels different, Elements ignores the Threshold value and considers only the Radius value. Both images in Figure 10-3 were filtered with a Threshold value of 0.

Figure 10-3: The results of applying the Dust & Scratches filter with the Radius slider set to 1 pixel (left) and 3 pixels (right).

By raising the Threshold value, you tell Elements to be more selective. If you set the value to 10, speck and image colors must vary by at least 10 levels before Elements covers up the speck, as in the first example of Figure 10-4. If you raise the Threshold to 20 — as in the second example — Elements disregards still more potential impurities. Notice that the two horizontal streaks in the second image remain intact, having been ruled out by the Threshold setting. (By the way, the Radius value was set to 3 in Figure 10-4 — something you were warned against doing earlier — in order to make the effects of the Threshold setting more noticeable.)

If you set the Threshold value any higher than 100, the dust specks have to be white and the image black — or vice versa — to receive any attention. It's best not to use values over 15.

Figure 10-4:
With the Radius set to 3 pixels, here's the Threshold set to 10 (left) and then to 20 (right).

Even though the Dust & Scratches filter variously obliterated the detail in Figures 10-3 and 10-4, none of the images are completely free of spots and streaks. Admittedly, this old, moldy picture is a lot worse off than most of your images are likely to be, but the fact remains that the Dust & Scratches filter is an imperfect solution. Just like a cheap car wash, it gets rid of most of the dirt — but not all of it — and it takes away some of the paint and detailing along with it. Even if you go to the trouble of selecting each tiny dust speck individually and running Dust & Scratches on it, you might as well be expending that effort with a superior tool: the Clone Stamp tool.

Experimenting with the Highly Ethical Clone Stamp Tool

If you're willing to expend a little extra energy and you can stand up to your friends when they call you compulsive, the tool of choice for cleaning up images is the Clone Stamp tool. The second tool from the bottom on the left side of the Toolbox, the Clone Stamp tool lets you take a good portion of an image and paint it onto the bad portion. This miraculous process is called, quite naturally, *cloning*.

You can also clone part of your image by copying and pasting it, as described in Chapter 9. You should get familiar with both methods of cloning because both have their place in the retouching world. The Clone Stamp tool works well for fixing small flaws in images — a scratch in a snapshot; a bruise on a pear; a mole on someone's face; and for cloning images with soft drop shadows. Copying and pasting works well for single, standalone images or images on their own layers.

Stamping out splatters

Want to see how the Clone Stamp tool works? Try out these steps:

1. **Select the Clone Stamp tool from the Toolbox (see Figure 10-5).**

   To select the Clone Stamp tool from the keyboard, press the S key.

2. **Make sure that the Aligned box is checked in the Clone Stamp tool Options bar.**

   This option lets you clone from relative points in your image. You'll see how it works in a second.

3. **Start dragging randomly inside your image.**

   Whoops, you got an error message, didn't you? See, to use the Clone Stamp tool, you have to tell Elements which portion of your image you want to clone before you begin cloning it. Elements isn't a mind reader, you know.

   Now that you've grasped this valuable lesson, grab a pen and put a big X through Step 3 so that you never make the same mistake again.

Clone Stamp tool   Options bar

Figure 10-5:
The Clone
Stamp tool
and its
trusty
Options bar,
partners in
cloning.

4. **Alt+click (Option+click on a Mac) on the portion of the image that you want to clone.**

   For example, to fix that big goober near the beginning of the lower tail of Halley's comet, Alt+click (Option+click on a Mac) at a location that appeared to contain similar gray values to the comet stuff that surrounds the goober, as shown in Figure 10-6. The point is to pick a portion of your image that blends in with areas around the blemish you want to eliminate.

5. **Now click or drag on the offending blemish.**

   To apply the digital zit cream, just click directly on said goober. No muss, no fuss; the glitch is gone.

When you click or drag with the Clone Stamp tool, Elements displays a cross cursor along with the stamp cursor, as shown in Figure 10-7. (For clarity's sake, the cursors are set to Standard in the Display & Cursors section of the Preferences.) This cross represents the clone source, or the area that you're cloning from. As you move the mouse, the cross cursor also moves, providing a continual reference to the portion of your image that you're cloning. (Things work differently when you have the Aligned option unchecked in the Options bar, however, as explained in the next section.)

The dreaded cosmic goober

Alt+click with rubber stamp

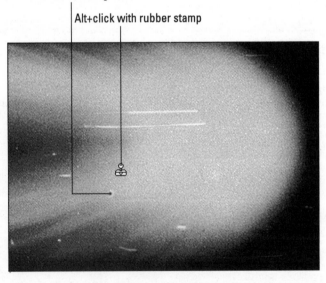

Figure 10-6: Alt+click (Option+click on a Mac) on a good portion of an image to establish the cloning source.

Clone source   Rubber stamp cursor

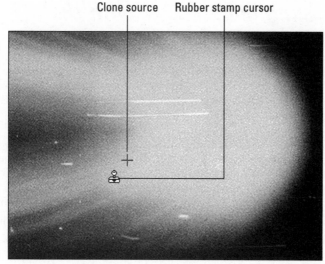

Figure 10-7:
When you use the Clone Stamp tool, a small cross follows to show you what part of the image you're cloning.

If the cloned area doesn't blend in well, just click the Step Backward button in the Shortcuts bar or press Ctrl+Z (⌘+Z on Mac) and then Alt+click (Option+click on a Mac) in the image with the Clone Stamp tool to specify a better source for your cloning. Click or drag with the tool to test out a different clone. You may have to do this several times to get it just right.

Just for the sheer heck of it, Figure 10-8 shows the comet after a 15-minute workout with the Clone Stamp tool. Now, isn't that way better than anything from Figures 10-3 and 10-4?

Figure 10-8:
Halley's comet, all dressed up and nowhere to go for 74 years.

Performing more magic with the Clone Stamp Tool

If you never find out another thing about the Clone Stamp tool, you'll be able to clean images quite easily after reading the preceding section. But the Clone Stamp tool is an amazing tool with more facets and capabilities than most Elements tools:

TIP

- ✔ To change the size or shape of the area that's cloned, change the brush size in the Brushes palette, located on the far left in the Options bar. Click on the downward-pointing arrow and choose from the first three rows of brushes. You can also change the size of the brush on the fly by tapping the [and] keys. For much more on brushes, see Chapter 14.

- ✔ To make the clone more translucent or less translucent, use the Opacity slider in the Options bar. Access the slider by pressing the black arrow to the right of the numeric setting. A setting of 100 makes your clone opaque.

- ✔ To clean up a straight hair or scratch, Alt+click (Option+click on a Mac) with the tool to specify the source for the cloning as you normally would. Then click at one end of the scratch and Shift+click at the other.

- ✔ If the first clone doesn't look exactly right but is pretty close, you may want to modify the clone slightly rather than redo it. Lower the Opacity setting in the Options bar by pressing a number key and then clone from a different position by again Alt+clicking (Option+click on a Mac) and dragging. This enables you to mix multiple portions of an image together to get a more seamless blend.

- ✔ Normally, the Clone Stamp tool clones from a relative location. If you move your cursor to a different location, the clone source moves with you. But what if you want to clone multiple times from a single location? In this case, leave the Aligned box unchecked in the Options bar. Now, you can Alt+click (Option+click on a Mac) once to set the source and click and drag multiple times to duplicate that source.

- ✔ The Pattern Stamp tool, which shares a flyout menu with the Clone Stamp tool in the Toolbox, clones an area with a repeating pattern. You can define your own pattern by selecting a rectangular area and choosing Edit⇨Define Pattern (if you don't define a selection, the entire canvas will be used for the pattern). Select your custom pattern from the Pattern drop-down palette in the Options bar. Drag with the Pattern Stamp tool, and you'll see the pattern appear. It's cool but generally not useful.

- ✔ Elements enables you to save multiple custom patterns. In addition, you have a variety of pattern presets available for use. You access both your custom patterns and the Elements presets via the Pattern drop-down palette and its accompanying menu.

✔ You can clone between images. If you have two images open, you can Alt+click (Option+click on a Mac) inside one image to specify the source and drag in the other image to clone. It's like painting one image onto another.

✔ Figure 10-9 shows an example Deke created of cloning between images. Starting with the two images on the left side of the figure (which he scaled to the same file size by using Image⇨Resize⇨Image Size, as discussed in Chapter 4), he Alt+clicked (Option+click on a Mac) inside the top image and then dragged with the Clone Stamp tool inside the bottom image. He cloned the woman's face and blouse using a large fuzzy brush and then switched to a smaller brush for the touch-ups. To match the skin tones in the forehead and the base of the nose, he cloned from the woman's cheeks at an Opacity setting of 50%. Pretty amazing, huh?

✔ If your image contains layers (as discussed in Chapter 9), remember that the Clone Stamp tool normally clones only from the active layer. If you select the Use All Layers check box in the Options bar, the Clone Stamp tool reads the pixels in all visible layers to create the clone. When you then click or drag with the Clone Stamp tool, Elements paints the clone onto the active layer.

Figure 10-9: By cloning from the top-left image onto the bottom-left image with the Clone Stamp tool, Deke was able to merge the two images to create the strange but nonetheless believable specimen on the right.

✔ The Clone Stamp tool also lets you clone using brush modes, which can create special effects by blending the colors of pixels. For a discussion of brush modes and blend modes, see Chapter 13. In the meanwhile, if you have half an hour to waste, play with the different modes and see what you can do. Or spend the time with a loved one instead. Nah, check out those brush modes.

The Clone Stamp tool is unquestionably one of Elements' two or three most useful tools. Take the time to get to know it well.

Getting the Red Out

If you've been on the business end of a modern camera recently, you've probably witnessed a startling display of light just before the picture snapped, something akin to a laser light show at your local planetarium. The multiple strobes that many camera flashes emit nowadays are all about shrinking your pupils to keep out red eye, the longtime scourge of photo takers everywhere. If the flash on a camera is too close to the lens, the light from the flash enters the eye, hits the retina, and bounces back into the lens, creating the glowing effect. The modern strobe flashes are indeed quite effective at stopping red eye before it happens.

And that's a very good thing, because red eye is very difficult to correct digitally. The reflected light actually blasts away detail, and there's usually no way to know even what color the person's irises are supposed to be. Elements' solution for this problem is the Red Eye Brush tool; if the red eye problem in an image isn't too severe, it can do the trick. The proof — as the popular saying goes — is in Color Plate 10-1.

The Red Eye Brush tool is located on the left side of the Toolbox, the third tool from the bottom. Here are the controls available to you inside the Red Eye Brush tool's Options bar:

✔ **Brush:** Select a brush size here. For more information, see the earlier section "Performing more magic with the Clone Stamp," or better yet turn to Chapter 14.

✔ **Current:** This is the color that will be replaced when you use the Red Eye Brush tool. When the Sampling pop-up menu is set to First Click, the Current color becomes the color of the pixel that the Red Eye Brush is currently over. With Sampling set to Current Color, you can click on the Default Colors button to automatically set the Current color to a serviceable reddish-brown, or click on the Current color box to select a different color from the Color Picker.

✔ **Replacement:** This is the color that will replace the Current color in the image when the Red Eye Brush tool is used. The actual color used to replace the Current color is usually a somewhat muted version of the chosen Replacement color.

✔ **Default Colors:** This sets the Replacement color to black. When the Sampling option is set to Current Color, the Default Colors button also sets the Current color to a reddish-brown.

✔ **Sampling:** When set to First Click, the Red Eye Brush will replace the color of the pixel it is clicked upon with the Replacement color. When set to Current Color, the Red Eye Brush will only function if it is clicked on a pixel within the Tolerance range of the Current color.

✔ **Tolerance:** This specifies how close a pixel has to be to the Current color before it is affected. A low setting means that the Red Eye Brush will only affect colors that are very close to the Current color; a higher setting means that the Red Eye Brush is more tolerant of different colored pixels, and will therefore affect them as well.

While the Red Eye Brush tool is certainly worth giving a spin, Elements actually has another tool that can eliminate red eye with more precision. We're speaking of the Replace Color command, which we'll get to in Chapter 12.

Chapter 11

What Kind of Tool Am I?

*B*ack in the old days, retouching a photograph was a formidable task. If you wanted to remove the reflection from someone's glasses, sharpen the focus of a detail, or tidy up a wrinkle or two, you had to paint or airbrush the photo and hope for the best. Anyone short of a trained professional would more often than not make a complete mess of the project and wish to heck it had never been started. Even the pros found it difficult to match flat colors on a palette to the ever-changing landscape of a photograph.

The beauty of Photoshop Elements is that you can paint not only with specific colors (as explained in Chapter 14) but also with colors and details already found in the image. Using the editing tools — Smudge, Blur, Sharpen, Dodge, Burn, and Sponge — you can subtly adjust the appearance of pixels by shifting them around, boosting contrast between them, or lightening and darkening them. And where the Blur and Sharpen tools leave off, the Blur and Sharpen filters pick up and go the extra mile. The results are edits that blend in with their surroundings.

Retouching images with Elements lets you work in ways that traditional photographers simply can't and also offers a built-in safety net. You can undo any change you make or simply revert to your original image if you don't like how your retouched image turns out. After you finish this chapter, you'll be so inspired to enhance and modify photographic details that you'll welcome problem images with open arms.

Touching Base with Retouching Tools

When push comes to shove, the editing tools are more like than unlike the painting tools. But the editing tools are sufficiently different from their painting cousins to confuse and perplex the unsuspecting neophyte. And unlike the Pencil, Paintbrush, and Airbrush, the editing tools don't have any common real-world counterparts. We can't say, "Elements' Smudge tool works just like the conventional Smudge tool that's hanging out in your garage right next to the leaf rake," because recent surveys have shown that almost no one has a Smudge tool hanging in the garage (or anywhere else).

Editing tools would be extremely useful in real life if only someone would get around to inventing them. Take the task of touching up the walls in your rec room. (Come on, everyone has a rec room! Where else would you do your recreating?) Using paintbrushes and rollers alone, this job can be a nightmare. The paint on the walls and the paint in the can may no longer exactly match. If you have to scrape away any dry paint, you'll have a heck of a time matching the texture. And, knowing you, you may very well trip over something and spill paint all over the carpet.

But scan the walls of the rec room into Elements and your problems are solved. Even if you have to retouch both paint and wallpaper, the editing tools, shown in Figure 11-1, can handle the job without incident:

- ✔ Use the Smudge tool to smear colors from a pristine area of the wall to the bare spots and the stains. You can smear the paint as far as you want, just as though it were still wet and in infinite supply. This is the editing tool you'll use most often. (The section "Smudging Away Imperfections," later in this chapter, discusses it further.)

- ✔ If the transitions between objects in the wallpaper are a little ragged — for example, if the pixels in the little polka-dot mushrooms don't seem to blend naturally with those in the cute little frogs sitting beneath them — you can smooth the pixels out with the Blur tool, which looks like a water drop. This tool blurs the edges between colors so that the colors blend together.

- ✔ To rebuild textures, drag with the Sharpen tool — which looks like someone took the Blur tool and, well, sharpened it. The Sharpen tool increases the amount of contrast between colors and builds up edges.

- ✔ Together, the Blur and Sharpen tools are known as *focus tools*. The former downplays focus; the latter enhances it. Both tools are eloquently explained later in this chapter in the section, "Focusing from the hip."

- ✔ To lighten a dark area in the wallpaper, drag with the Dodge tool, which looks like a circle on the end of a stick. This tool lightens up the area evenly.

✔ If an area on the wall has become faded over the years, you can darken it by using the Burn tool, which looks like a hand in the shape of an O.

✔ Are the colors just too darn garish? Or has the color been drained right out? Okay, so these aren't common rec room problems, but if they do occur, you can take up the Sponge tool to remedy them.

✔ The Dodge, Burn, and Sponge tools are called *toning tools,* meaning that they change the colors in an image.

Figure 11-1: Alas, the editing tools are not yet available at your local hardware store.

Blur tool — Sharpen tool
Sponge tool — Smudge tool

Dodge Tool   O
Burn Tool   O

See, don't you wish you had a crack at using these tools in real life? Seems to me that Bob Villa or Tim Allen should get to work on them. There are millions to be made.

Smudging Away Imperfections

The shark image shown in Figure 11-2 provides an ideal subject for demonstrating the powers of the proudest Elements editing tool, the Smudge tool. Like so many rough-and-tumble sharks that occupy the inner cities of our oceans, this guy is no stranger to the occasional toothy brawl. Frankly, his face is a mess. He looks like he had a bad time shaving this morning, except he doesn't have little bloodstained bits of tissue paper stuck all over his face. But when you're a shark, you're a shark all the way, and the marks on his face are probably the result of a violent rumble.

Figure 11-2:
This shark is
on the road
to ruin.

But whatever caused his scars, they can be fixed with the help of the Smudge tool. As you may recall from the earlier rec room analogy, the Smudge tool pushes color from one portion of your image into another. When you drag with this tool, Elements "grabs" the color that's underneath your cursor at the start of your drag and smears it in the direction of your drag.

The Smudge tool is a great contraption for smearing away scars, wrinkles, overly large noses, droopy ears, and all the other things that plastic surgeons keep their eyes out for. Figure 11-3 shows a magnified view of the shark receiving a thorough makeover with the Smudge tool. (The cursor has been set to Standard mode in the Display & Cursors panel of the Preferences.) The various sharkish defects are smoothed away to the point that the guy looks like he's made out of porcelain.

Light on the smudge, please

Notice that in Figure 11-3, the Smudge tool is being rubbed *with* the grain of the detail. It's tracing along the shark's gills, rubbing along the length of the shark's fins, and dragging up the shark's snout, all in short, discreet strokes. (It's very bad to rub a shark the wrong way.) You get more natural-looking results if you carefully trace along the details of your subject and don't simply drag haphazardly all over the place.

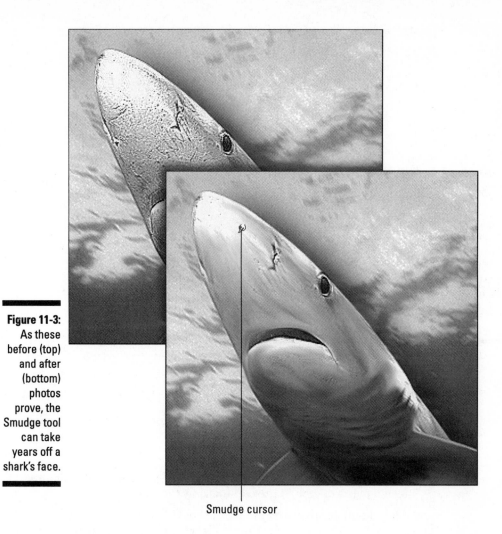

Figure 11-3:
As these
before (top)
and after
(bottom)
photos
prove, the
Smudge tool
can take
years off a
shark's face.

Smudge cursor

Retouching with the Smudge tool requires a certain amount of discretion. If you really go nuts and drag over every single surface, you get an oil-painting effect, like the one shown in Figure 11-4. You can create some cool stuff this way, but excessive smudging is not the same as retouching.

Figure 11-4:
You can
convert a
photo into
an oil
painting by
dragging the
Smudge tool
all over the
place.

Smudge-specific controls

You can modify the performance of the Smudge tool by using the Smudge
options (see Figure 11-5):

✔ Click and Shift+click to smudge in a straight line. You can also Shift+drag
to smudge horizontally or vertically. These Shift+click and Shift+drag
techniques work for all the edit tools, by the way.

✔ Select another brush size in the Brushes palette to enlarge or reduce the
size of the smudge brush. You can likewise change the brush size for all
the edit tools. To display the Brushes palette, click on the downward-
pointing arrow next to the Brush icon in the Options bar. (For much
more on changing brushes, see Chapter 14.)

✔ There are various smudge options in the Options bar. For example, you
can adjust the Pressure slider by clicking on the black arrow to the right
of the default setting of 50% to create more subtle retouching effects.
Increase the Pressure setting to make the effect more pronounced.

✔ Remember that you can change the brush size from the keyboard by
pressing the bracket keys and change the Pressure setting by pressing
the number keys.

Figure 11-5:
The options that affect the Smudge tool.

✔ The Modes drop-down menu gives you two options, Darken and Lighten, which let you smear only those colors that are darker or lighter than the original colors in the image. You also have the Color brush mode, which lets you smear the colors in an RGB image without harming the detail. Pretty nifty. The other brush modes — Hue, Saturation, and Luminosity — range from nearly useless to completely useless. Don't worry about them. And for general purposes, you won't really need to worry about the Modes menu at all when using the Smudge tool. For much more on brush and blending modes, see Chapter 13.

✔ Depending on your computer system, Elements may slow down dramatically when you increase the Pressure setting above 80% or 90%, select a large brush size, or change the brush mode. And if you do all three at the same time, the program may run so lethargically that you'll think you've crashed. Just go get a cup of coffee, and Elements should be finished when you get back.

✔ Select the Finger Painting check box to dip your brush into the Foreground color before smudging. Elements applies a little dab of Foreground color at the beginning of your drag and then begins to smear into the existing colors in the image as usual.

✔ The Use All Layers check box doesn't make any difference unless you're editing an image with layers. It enables you to pierce through and pick up the colors from all of your layers.

✔ The Liquify filter is sort of like the Smudge tool on steroids. Most of Smudge's capabilities are available there, as well as a host of other tools for smearing around your image in useful and amusing ways. To check out the Liquify filter, head on over to Chapter 13.

All Them Other Edit Tools

The remaining edit tools fall into a group that experts call "the other guys." Whereas you may pick up the Smudge tool every third day or so, it's questionable if you'll select one of the other guys once a week. Even so, they can prove fantastically helpful — well, moderately helpful anyway — if used properly. The upcoming sections contain choice bits of wisdom for using the other guys.

Dodge? Burn? Those are opposites?

Wondering why the Dodge and Burn tool icons look the way they do? It's because they have their roots in traditional stat camera techniques in which you shoot a photograph of another photograph to correct exposure problems. The Dodge tool is supposed to look like a little paddle that you wave around to block off light, and the Burn tool is a hand focusing the light. It may seem, therefore, that dodging would make the image darker and burning would make it lighter. But Elements is thinking in terms of negative film, where black is white, up is down, right is left, and Goofus is, of course, a Cornish game hen.

Here's a handy key for remembering which tool does what:

- ✔ The Dodge tool lightens images, just as a dodge ball lightens your body by about ten pounds when it knocks off your head.

- ✔ The Burn tool darkens images, just as a sunburn darkens your body and eventually turns it a kind of charbroiled color.

Or you could remember it this way: The D in Dodge stands for darken; the B in Burn stands for brighten. Except that that is totally incorrect.

Glad we could clear things up.

Generally, you adjust the performance of the Dodge and Burn tools just like the other edit tools and the paint tools. You can find all the tool options, including brush sizes, in the Options bar:

- ✔ The Exposure slider bar, accessed by pressing the black arrow to the right of the default setting of 50%, indicates how much an area will be lightened or darkened. As always, lower the value to lessen the impact of the tool and raise the value to increase the impact.

- ✔ The Range drop-down menu contains just three options: Highlights, Midtones, and Shadows. The default setting is Midtones, which lightens or darkens medium colors in an image and leaves the very light and dark colors alone. Figure 11-6 shows the result of dragging all over the shark with the Dodge tool while Midtones was the active range.

- ✔ The Shadows range ensures that the darkest colors are affected, while Highlights impacts the lightest colors. In Figure 11-7, the Dodge tool was scribbled with while the range was set to Shadows. The payoff is a shark that looks like it ate the world's supply of glowworms. Even the darkest shadows radiate, making the image uniformly light.

- ✔ To darken an image with similar uniformity, select the Burn tool and set the brush mode to Highlights.

You can use a variation of the Dodge and Burn tools in the form of the Color Dodge and Color Burn brush modes (explained in Chapter 13). When you use the regular Dodge and Burn tools, you simply lighten or darken your image. But if you use one of the painting tools with the Color Dodge or Color Burn brush modes, you can both lighten or darken and infuse the image with color. For example, if you want to lighten an image and give it a yellowish glow, paint with yellow and the Color Dodge brush mode.

Figure 11-6:
By setting the brush mode to Midtones and dragging indiscriminately with the Dodge tool, the shark was lightened without eliminating contrast.

Playing with the Color knob

The Sponge tool is designed for use on full-color images. Don't try using it on grayscale images because it doesn't do you any good. It's not that it doesn't work — it does — it just doesn't work correctly. On a grayscale image, the Sponge tool either lightens or darkens pixels like a shoddy version of the Dodge or Burn tool.

When you work on a color image, the Sponge tool increases or decreases saturation. Ever used the Color knob on an old television? Turn the knob up, and the color leaps off the screen; turn it down, and the colors look gray. What you're doing is adjusting the TV's saturation. Increasing saturation makes the colors more vibrant; decreasing saturation makes the colors more drab. The Sponge tool works in much the same way.

Figure 11-7:
Using the
Dodge
tool in
combination
with the
Shadows
brush mode
makes the
shark's
darkest
shadows
tingle with
light.

Here's how you use the Sponge tool:

1. **Select the Sponge tool.**

   Press the Q key (for "quench," maybe?). Elements then displays the appropriate Options bar.

2. **Select the desired Mode option from the drop-down menu in the Options bar.**

   Select Saturate to make the colors vibrant; select Desaturate to make the colors drab.

3. **Press a number key to change the Pressure value.**

   You can also drag the slider bar in the Options bar, which you access by clicking on the black arrow next to the numeric setting. Either way, the setting affects the impact of the Sponge tool.

4. **Drag with the tool inside a color image.**

   Watch those colors change.

One good use for the Sponge tool is to provide a focal point for your image. Suppose that you have a color photo of a group of people and want to have one person stand out among the others. Select your person (see Chapter 8 for selection methods) and then choose Select⇨Inverse. Now, carefully take the Sponge tool, set the Mode option to Desaturate in the Options bar, and drag over the other people. You see their colors wash out while your chosen person remains bright and stands out among the crowd. This technique works with any group of objects. You can also set the option to Saturate to make your chosen object brighter than the rest.

Focusing from the hip

From what we've learned about the Smudge tool, it's clear that it is a wonderful little device. But it's not always the right tool for the job. For example, suppose you have a harsh transition between two colors. Maybe one of the shark's teeth looks a little jagged, or you want to soften the edge of a fin. Which of the following methods would you use to fix this problem?

  ✔ Smear the colors a bit with the Smudge tool.

  ✔ Soften the transition between the colors by using the Blur tool.

Okay, you were tipped off by the preceding paragraph saying that the Smudge tool is "not always the right tool for the job," so naturally you chose the second answer. (You did choose the second answer, didn't you?) But a time will come when you run into this exact situation and your first reflex will be to reach for the Smudge tool.

So let's try to drive home the point a bit with the aid of Figure 11-8. The figure starts off with the harshest of all possible color transitions — that is between white and its archenemy, black. You want to smear the colors together so that they blend a little more harmoniously, so naturally you reach for the Smudge tool. The problem with this method (as shown in the second example in the figure) is that you can't get a nice, smooth transition between the two colors no matter how hard you try. Even if you Shift+drag with the Smudge tool, you get some inconsistent smudging. You also run the risk of smearing surrounding detail. All this happens because the Smudge tool is designed as a free-form smearing device, not as an edge softener.

Meanwhile, an edge softener is sitting nearby waiting for you to snatch it up. If you drag the Blur tool between the white and black shapes — whether you drag perfectly straight or wobble the cursor back and forth a bit — you get a softened edge like the one shown in the final example of Figure 11-8.

Here are a few other items about the focus tools:

  ✔ Just as the Blur tool softens transitions, the Sharpen tool firms the transitions back up.

  ✔ At least, that's what the Sharpen tool is supposed to do. In practice, it tends to make an image overly grainy. Use this tool sparingly.

Harsh transition

Smeared with Smudge tool

Figure 11-8:
The parable
of the harsh
transition,
the Smudge
tool and the
Blur tool.

Softened with Blur tool

✔ You can adjust the impact of the Blur and Sharpen tools by changing the Pressure settings in the Options bar. As a jumping-off point, try working with the pressure set to about 60% for the Blur tool and 30% for the Sharpen tool.

✔ When you work with the focus tools, you have access to the same brush modes as you do when using the Smudge tool. The important ones are Darken, Lighten, and Color. Any of the three can help downplay the effects of the Sharpen tool and make it more usable. For more on brush modes and blending modes, see Chapter 13.

If you want to adjust the focus of large areas of an image — or an entire image — your best bet is to go with the Blur and Sharpen filters. These commands work much more uniformly than the focus tools.

Sharpening Those Wishy-Washy Details

No matter how good an image looked before you scanned it, chances are that it appears a little out of focus onscreen. The image in Figure 11-9 is an exaggerated example. Snapped around the time Stonehenge was built, this photo has suffered the cruel scourges of time. It probably wasn't that sharply focused in the first place, but all these many years later, it looks so soft you'd swear that it was sculpted out of gelatin.

The solutions to softness are the four filters found under the Sharpen category of the Filters palette. The following sections explain how these filters work and when — if ever — to apply them.

Figure 11-9:
Antique
images
such as this
one are
notoriously
soft on
focus.

The single-shot sharpeners

The first three sharpening filters — Sharpen, Sharpen Edges, and Sharpen More — are *single-shot filters*. You choose them, and regardless of the Filter Options check box, they do their work without complex dialog boxes or other means of digital interrogation. These filters, with their straightforward names, are a breeze to use.

Unfortunately, when it comes to Elements, you get back what you put in — mentally, that is. In other words, if you don't have to work at it, it's liable to deliver rather mediocre results. As demonstrated in Figure 11-10, all three of these Sharpen filters sharpen, but none satisfactorily remedies the image's focus problems.

Figure 11-10 shows the results of applying each of the three single-shot sharpeners to a detail from the image. In each case, the filter was applied once (as shown in the middle row) and then a second time (as shown in the last row). For the record, here's what each of the filters does:

✔ Sharpen enhances the focus of the image very slightly. If the photo is already well focused but needs a little extra fortification to make it perfect, the Sharpen filter does the trick. Otherwise, forget it.

✔ The Sharpen More filter enhances focus more dramatically. Although it's easily the most useful of the three single-shooters, it's still fairly crude. For example, the center image in Figure 11-10 isn't sharp enough, whereas the bottom image is so sharp that little flecks — called *artifacts* — are starting to form in the woman's dress. Boo, hiss.

✔ The Sharpen Edges filter is a complete waste of time. It sharpens the so-called edges of an image without sharpening any of the neutral areas in between. In the figure, for example, the filter sharpens the outline of the guy's face but ignores the interior of his jacket. The result is an inconsistent effect that eventually frays the edges and leaves non-edges looking goopy by comparison.

Figure 11-10:
The effects of applying each of the single-shot sharpeners are shockingly shabby.

As you may have gathered by now, we don't whole-heartedly recommend these filters. Still, you may want to go ahead and apply Sharpen or Sharpen More to an image to see whether it does the trick. If a single-shot sharpener turns out to be all you need, great. If not, click that Step Backward button in the Shortcuts bar and try out the Unsharp Mask command, explained next. It's a little scarier, but it works like a dream.

Unsharp Mask: The filter with a weird name

If the Photoshop Elements programmers had been in charge of naming Superman, they would have called him "Average Guy from Krypton." Rather than describing what the guy does, the programmers describe his origins. That's exactly what they did with the Unsharp Mask filter. Rather than calling the filter "Supersharpen," which would have made a modicum of sense and may have even encouraged a few novices to give it a try, they named it after a 40-year-old stat camera technique that a few professionals in lab coats pretend to understand in order to impress each other.

So forget Unsharp Mask and just think "Supersharpen." To use the "Supersharpen" command, choose Unsharp Mask. The "Supersharpen" dialog box appears, as shown in Figure 11-11.

Figure 11-11:
Experts agree that the Unsharp Mask dialog box really should be called the *Super-sharpen* dialog box.

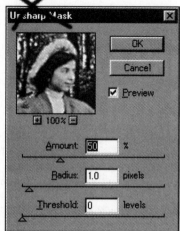

Like the Dust & Scratches dialog box (see Chapter 10), the Unsharp Mask dialog box, shown in Figure 11-11, enables you to preview what happens when you change the values in the three option boxes. You can preview the filter inside the dialog box and in the main image window. If you can't quite remember how these previewing functions work, check out Chapter 10. To sharpen an image, use the three slider bars like so:

✔ Change the Amount value from 1% to 500% to change the amount of sharpening. This may strike you as obvious, but just to be sure, higher Amount values produce more sharpening.

✔ Adjust the Radius value to specify the width of the edges you want to sharpen. If the image is generally in good shape, use a Radius of 0.5. If the edges are soft and syrupy, like the ones in Figure 11-9, use a Radius of 1.0. And if the edges are almost nonexistent, go with 2.0. Generally, you don't want to go any lower than 0.5 or any higher than 2.0 (though 250 is the maximum).

✔ You don't have to enter 1.0 or 2.0 into the Radius option box. A simple 1 or 2 will suffice. It's just that you can enter $\frac{1}{10}$ values — such as 1.1 and 1.9 — if you're in a particularly precise mood.

✔ As with the Threshold option in the Dust & Scratches dialog box, the Unsharp Mask Threshold option determines how different two neighboring pixels must be to be considered an edge. (See Chapter 10 for a review of this concept.) The default value of 0 tells Elements to sharpen everything. By raising the value, you tell Elements not to sharpen low-contrast pixels.

This idea is great, but the implementation in Elements leaves something to be desired. The filter creates an abrupt transition between sharpened and ignored pixels, resulting in an unrealistic effect. Therefore, it's usually a good idea to leave Threshold set to 0.

Some sharpening scenarios

Figure 11-12 demonstrates the effects of several different Amount and Radius values on the same detail to which the piddly little Sharpen More command was applied in Figure 11-10. Throughout Figure 11-12, the Threshold value is 0.

Figure 11-12 is organized into two rows. In the first image in the top row, the Amount value is 200% and the Radius is 0.5. Then the Amount value was halved and the Radius value was doubled in each of the next two images. Though the effect is similar from one image to the next, you can see that the right image has thicker edges than the left image. The differences are subtle; you may have to look closely. Put on your glasses (where applicable).

The bottom row of the figure features more pronounced sharpening effects. The first image in the bottom row has Amount and Radius values of 500% and 0.5. Then the Amount value was progressively halved, and the Radius value was progressively doubled. Notice that the edges in the right image are thicker, and the left image contains more artifacts (those little flecks in the jacket and hat).

After experimenting with a few different settings, the best setting seems to be an Amount of 250% and a Radius of 1.0. Figure 11-13 shows the final image sharpened with these settings.

Figure 11-12: The effect of a whole bunch of Amount and Radius values on detail from an ancient photo.

200%, 0.5   100%, 1.0   50%, 2.0

500%, 0.5   250%, 1.0   125%, 2.0

Figure 11-13: The image from Figure 11-9 sharpened with an Amount value of 250% and a Radius value of 1.0.

Blurring Adds Depth

If you want to make a portion of your image blurry instead of sharp, you can apply one of the commands from the Blur category of the Filters palette. Right off the bat, you quick thinkers are thinking, "Blurry? Why would I want my image to be blurry?" This is a classic problem. You're thinking of blurry as the opposite of sharp. But blurry and sharp can go hand in hand inside the same image. The sharp details are in the foreground, and the blurry stuff goes in the background.

Take Figure 11-14, for example. In this image, the background was selected and blurred. The scene becomes a little more intimate, as though the background were far, far away. It also has the effect of making the foreground characters seem more in focus than ever.

To make the effect complete, the lower-right corner of the image was selected, feathered, and blurred. The result is a gradual blurring effect, as though the ground were becoming progressively out of focus as it extends beyond our field of vision.

For the most part, then, blurring is a special effect. Unlike sharpening, which has the effect of correcting the focus, blurring heightens reality by exaggerating the depth of an image. In other words, you never have to blur an image — and you probably won't do it nearly as frequently as you sharpen — but it's a lot of fun.

The first two commands in the Blur category — Blur and Blur More — are the Dumb and Dumber of the blur filters. Like their Sharpen and Sharpen More counterparts, they produce predefined effects that never seem to be quite what you're looking for.

The "Superblur" command — the filter that offers the powers you need to get the job done right — is Gaussian Blur. The filter is named after Karl Friedrich Gauss, a dusty old German mathematician who's even older than the photograph from Figure 11-9. But just think "Superblur" — or, as Mr. Gauss would have put it, *Ueberblur*.

When you choose Gaussian Blur, Elements displays the dialog box shown in Figure 11-15. The Radius value determines the number of pixels that get mixed together at a time. You can go as high as 250.0, but any value over 10.0 enters the realm of the legally blind. In Figure 11-14, the background was blurred with a Radius value of 4.0 and the lower-right patch of ground with a Radius of 2.0.

Figure 11-14:
Blurring the
background
as well as a
small tip
of the
foreground
(bottom
right) brings
the family
up close
and
personal.

Ueberblur!!!

Figure 11-15:
Specify the
exact
amount of
blur you
want in the
Ueberblur
dialog box,
also known
as the
Gaussian
Blur
dialog box.

Of all the tools and filters we look at in this chapter, the most valuable to you will be the Unsharp Mask filter. It's not a miracle worker — you can't take an image that's blurred beyond recognition and expect Unsharp Mask to pull details from it. But on soft-to-slightly blurry photos, it's the deal. Odd name and not exactly user-friendly controls aside, Unsharp Mask is without question one of the top ten most important tools that Elements puts at your disposal. In fact, let's really go out on a limb: There's probably not a digital image out there that wouldn't benefit (or that hasn't already benefited) from being given a working over with Unsharp Mask.

So the next time you're in a movie theater and the screen goes all blurry because the projectionist is making out with his girlfriend and not paying attention to his job, lean your head back and scream at the top of your lungs: "Unsharp Mask! Unsharp Mask!" You'll feel better, and you'll suddenly find you have a lot of empty seats around you in the theater. Isn't digital imaging a great thing?

Chapter 12

The Rainbow Correction

*H*ere's a common scenario for you: You get some pictures or slides back from the photo developer — we're talking regular photos here, not the digital kind — and one of them catches your eye. The color is great, the composition is fantastic, everyone's smiling; it ranks among the best pictures you've ever shot. It's not 100 percent perfect, but you figure you can fix the few glitches with Photoshop Elements.

So you scan the image, open it up, and your heart sinks to the pit of your stomach. The image is dark, colorless, and generally a big, fat disappointment. The snapshot from the photo developer looks far better than this murky mess onscreen.

In a perfect world, this would never happen. But scanning is an imperfect process, and even if your scanner isn't one of those $50 "bargains," seeing a scanned photo onscreen for the first time can be discouraging.

Take Color Plate 12-1, for example. The original slide looked something like the example on the right, but when it was opened in Elements, the image appeared as shown on the left. Sure, it's an old slide — that's Deke in the striped shirt, so you know that a couple of years have passed — and the composition leaves something to be desired. (Deke has a fake tree growing out of his shoulder and his sister seems to be balancing a flower-adorned globe on her head.) But, come on, it didn't look this bad. Is this an audition for the remake of *20,000 Leagues Under the Sea* or what?

If you run into a similar problem, never fear — you have cause to be optimistic. The colors may not look like much now, but chances are good that you have enough colors to get by. Though it may be hard to believe, your image very likely contains a few million colors; it's just that they're all squished toward the dark end of the spectrum. Your job is to bring these colors back to life.

Want proof? The image on the right side of Color Plate 12-1 isn't a different scan; it's just a color-corrected version of its neighbor on the left. In fact, Deke revived the color by using only two commands — Levels and Variations. No painting or editing tools, no selection outlines, no adding colors to the image. The existing colors are merely stretched across the spectrum.

Elements offers many color-correction commands, but you need only a few of these to get the job done. In this chapter, you'll see how these miracle commands work. You'll also learn how to use adjustment layers, which let you do some of your color correcting on an independent layer, thereby providing you with extra flexibility and safety.

Color-Correcting Correctly

You'll find the basic Elements color-correction commands in the Enhance menu. Of these commands, you'll probably find Levels and Variations absolutely indispensable.

Levels and Variations

Before we dig into these two commands, let's talk about Levels' sidekick, the Auto Levels command, for a minute. If Levels and Variations are your good and loyal friends, Auto Levels is sort of like that weird uncle you basically like, but you're not quite sure you can trust.

Choose Enhance⇨Auto Levels or press Ctrl+Shift+L (⌘+Shift+L on a Mac) to automatically correct the contrast of an image. For example, Figure 12-1 shows a typical low-contrast image composed entirely of cheerless grays. The inset squares show the lightest and darkest colors in the image as well as some sample shades in between. With the Auto Levels command, Elements automatically makes the lightest gray white and the darkest gray black and stretches out the colors in between. Figure 12-2 shows the result.

Figure 12-1:
What a dismal scene: Come to this gas station and get your tank filled with depression. The Grim Reaper will change your oil.

Figure 12-2:
The Auto Levels command brings out some strong blacks and whites, but the grays remain dark and dreary.

Unfortunately, Auto Levels doesn't always do the trick. Figure 12-2, for example, contains strong blacks and whites, but the grays appear overly dark (as witnessed by the shades in the inset squares). Furthermore, although it's not an issue in a black and white image like this one, Auto Levels has been known to introduce color casts to images. Auto Levels works its magic on each color channel individually, and this can definitely throw the color balance out of whack.

The solution is Enhance⇨Brightness/Contrast⇨Levels, which you can access from the keyboard by pressing Ctrl+L (⌘+L on a Mac). The Levels command takes some getting used to, but it lets you adjust the medium grays as well as the darkest and lightest pixels. (We cover the command in detail later in this chapter, in the section "Leveling the Contrast Field.") And as far as color images go, Levels can improve the contrast of your image without the possibility of introducing a color cast. Figure 12-3 shows the Gulf station running in tip-top condition, thanks to the Levels command. See how much clearer the details in the cars now appear?

Figure 12-3:
A nice, even transition of grays makes a day at the gas station seem like a walk through the park.

Unlike Levels, which serves grayscale and color images equally well, Enhance⇨Variations is specifically designed to correct full-color images. (You can use the command on grayscale images, but it merely duplicates some of the options inside the Levels dialog box.) You can increase or decrease the intensity of colors or tint the image to remove a color cast. For example, if an image is too yellow, you can add blue to it, as in the first example in Color Plate 12-2. If the image is too blue, add yellow, as in the second example. In both cases, Variations preserves non-blue and non-yellow colors. Throughout, for example, the Christmas tree remains true to its natural color of pink.

Upcoming sections explain how to use Levels, Auto Levels, and Variations in detail. But just for the record, here's the general approach to take when color correcting an image in Elements:

1. **Try the Auto Levels command.**

   You may well see an improvement in the contrast of your image, but it's also possible you'll see an unpleasant shift in the colors. If you like what you see, you can skip all the other steps. If you think Auto Levels actually made your image look worse, click the Step Backward button in the Shortcuts bar. If you think Auto Levels made an improvement but some more tweaking is still in order, proceed to Step 2.

2. **Apply the Levels command.**

   Use this command to change the contrast of the image and to lighten or darken the medium colors.

   If you're editing a grayscale image, this command is the end of the line. If your full-color image looks a little drab, however, keep correcting.

3. **Choose the Variations command and select the Saturation radio button.**

   The options inside the Variations dialog box let you boost the intensity of colors in an image, as discussed in the section "Variations on a Color Scheme," later in this chapter.

   If the colors now look the way you want, press Enter (Return on a Mac) and get on with your life. Continue only if you need to remove a color cast.

4. **Choose the Color Cast command (E̲nhance⇨C̲olor⇨Color Cas̲t).**

   This command is hardly foolproof, but it couldn't be simpler and is worth a try. For information on this command, see the section "Removing that color cast sure feels good" later in this chapter. If you can't get rid of your image's color cast using the Color Cast command, click Cancel and proceed to Step 5.

5. **Apply Variations again, select the Midtones radio button, and adjust the colors in the image.**

   Note: Again, the section, "Removing that color cast sure feels good," tells all.

Those "other" color correctors

There are several other color-correction commands in Elements that range from useful-but-complex to simple-but-completely inept. Here's the rundown:

✔ **Equalize:** The Equalize command (I̲mage⇨A̲djustments⇨E̲qualize) takes the brightest and darkest pixels from among the three color channels in the image and maps them to white and black. It then tries to evenly distribute the rest of the pixels between them in terms of brightness. This produces a higher-contrast image but isn't generally as effective as even Auto Levels.

- **Gradient Map:** The Gradient Map command (Image⇨Adjustments⇨ Gradient Map) enables you to map any gradient to the grayscale values in your image. You can produce some interesting special effects with this command.

- **Invert:** The Invert command (Image⇨Adjustments⇨Invert) changes the color of every pixel to its opposite. White becomes black, blue becomes yellow, and so on. The end result resembles a photographic negative, making Invert useful for special effects but not much else.

- **Posterize:** The Posterize command (Image⇨Adjustments⇨Posterize) limits each color channel to a specified number of brightness levels, redrawing your image with fields of solid color. Again, a nice effect, but not useful on a day-to-day basis.

- **Threshold:** The Threshold command (Image⇨Adjustments⇨Threshold) turns every pixel in your image either white or black, based on its brightness value according to a threshold you set. If you need it, there it is.

- **Auto Contrast:** Avoid using Auto Contrast (Enhance⇨Auto Contrast). Stick with correcting contrast in an image by using the Levels command, which gives you more control.

- **Hue/Saturation:** This command (Enhance⇨Color⇨Hue/Saturation) is powerful for changing color and color intensity. The section, "Using the Replace Color command," at the end of this chapter covers most of its functionality.

- **Remove Color:** This command (Enhance⇨Color⇨Remove Color) is just the thing for draining the color from a selected area and leaving it black and white. But if you want to convert an entire image to grayscale, see Chapter 5.

- **Brightness/Contrast:** The Brightness/Contrast command (Enhance⇨ Brightness/Contrast⇨Brightness/Contrast) is utterly and completely worthless. Seriously. If you've never used it, don't start. If you have used it, stop — you're hurting your images.

Leveling the Contrast Field

Not one image in this book — except the gloomy-looking Figure 12-1 — has escaped a thorough going-over with the Levels command. This command is one of the most essential functions inside Elements. In fact, if an image displays any of the following symptoms, you can correct it with Levels:

- The image is murky, without strong lights and darks, like the one in Figure 12-1.

- The image is too light.

✔ The image is too dark.

✔ The image is gaining weight, losing hair, and developing bags under its eyes.

Whoops, that last item sneaked in by mistake. If an image gains weight, loses hair, and develops baggy eyes, you have to send it on a three-week cruise in the Caribbean. And tell it to stop writing books.

Fiddling with adjustment layers

Elements offers a feature to use in conjunction with the Levels command, as well as with several other color correction tools: adjustment layers. Adjustment layers are just like the layers discussed in Chapter 9, except that you use them expressly to apply color correction commands.

Sharing space with adjustment layers are fill layers. You can use fill layers to add a layer of solid color, a gradient, or a pattern. Other than the masking abilities that fill layers share with adjustment layers (see the Technical Stuff icon below), there's really nothing you can do with fill layers that you can't do just by selecting an ordinary layer and filling it with color. Fill layers really have nothing to do with color correction, but it'll be convenient to take a look at them here, too.

Adjustment and fill layers offer several advantages over ordinary layers:

✔ The color correction of adjustment layers affects all the underlying layers in the image. If you don't use an adjustment layer, the color correction affects only the active layer.

✔ You can create as many different adjustment layers as you want. So, if you want a few layers to use one set of color correction settings and the rest of the image to use another set, you just create two different adjustment layers. You can also create as many fill layers as you desire.

✔ Because the color correction "exists" on its own layer, you can experiment freely without fear of damaging the image. If, at some point, you decide that you don't like the effects of the color correction, you can edit the adjustment layer or just delete it entirely and start fresh. You can also edit or delete fill layers.

✔ You can blend adjustment and fill layers with the other layers using the Opacity and Blend Mode settings in the Layers palette, just as you can with any layer. (More on blend modes in Chapter 13.) These features give you even more control over how your image appears.

To create an adjustment layer, do the following:

1. **In the Layers palette, click on the layer that you want to color correct.**

   When you create an adjustment layer, Elements places it directly on top of the active layer in the Layers palette. This adjustment affects the layer or layers underneath, depending on whether you turn on the Group with Previous Layer check box as mentioned in Step 2 below.

   If you select a portion of your image before creating the adjustment layer, the color correction affects only the selected area across all underlying layers.

2. **Choose Layer⇨New Adjustment Layer and then select your desired adjustment from the submenu. For this example, let's choose Levels.**

   The New Layer dialog box appears. Here's a field guide to your options: If you want to give your adjustment layer a specific name, enter the name into the top option box.

   Skip the Opacity and Mode drop-down menus; if you want, you can change these settings later in the Layers palette. For now, skip the Group with Previous Layer check box. We'll look at this a little later in the chapter.

   You can also click the "Create new fill or adjustment layer" icon at the bottom of the Layers palette and select an option from the drop-down menu. This bypasses the New Layer dialog box.

3. **Press Enter (Return on a Mac).**

   Elements adds the adjustment layer to the Layers palette and displays the Levels dialog box, which is explained in the next section.

Creating a fill layer is just as easy. Simply choose Layer⇨New Fill Layer and select solid color, gradient, or pattern from the submenu.

If you are wondering what that extra thumbnail is, shown in Figure 12-4, here's a brief explanation. Elements adds a layer mask to every adjustment or fill layer. In short, layer masks are like pieces of clear acetate that hover over the layer. You paint on them to selectively hide or display either the adjustment or fill effect, or in the case of regular layers, pixels. Applying black pixels on the layer mask hides, white pixels show, and any gray color in between displays or hides in varying degrees of transparency. In other words, to display the full strength adjustment or fill over the image, leave the layer mask white (the default). To remove the adjustment or fill over the image, paint the mask with black. To partially display the adjustment, paint the mask with gray. To isolate only one portion of an image, leave it white and paint the rest of the layer mask black. Any painting tool can be used on the mask, but best results are usually achieved by using the Airbrush, Paintbrush, or Gradient.

The easiest way to paint on the layer mask is by Alt+Shift-clicking (Option+ Shift-clicking on the Mac) on the layer mask thumbnail. As you then start to paint with black or gray in the image window, you'll see a pink overlay appear on the image. Where things are darkest pink, the layer mask is totally blocking the effect of the adjustment layer. Where things look normal, there's little or no blocking going on. You can also Alt-click (Option-click on the Mac) to view just the mask in grayscale without the underlying image. Shift-click on the layer mask thumbnail to turn off the effects of the mask temporarily. Performing either of those commands again will set things back to normal.

Clipping Group icon   Fill layer

Figure 12-4: The Layers palette sporting adjustment and fill layers.

Layer Mask | Adjustment layer

New fill or adjustment layer

Remember that an adjustment or fill layer works just like any other layer in the Layers palette. You can vary the effects of the adjustment by playing with the Opacity slider and blend modes; you can move the layer up or down in the Layers palette to affect different layers; and you can merge the layer with an underlying layer to permanently fuse the color correction or fill to the image. (You can't, however, merge an adjustment or fill layer with another adjustment or fill layer.)

If you ever want to change the settings for an adjustment or fill layer, just double-click on the adjustment or fill layer icon in the Layers palette. You can also select the adjustment or fill layer and choose Layer➪Layer Content Options. Elements redisplays the appropriate dialog box, where you can modify the settings. To delete the adjustment or fill layer, drag it to the Trash icon in the Layers palette.

To change the type of your adjustment or fill layer, choose Layer➪Change Layer Content and select the new type of adjustment or fill you want.

You can flip back and forth between a view of your corrected image and your uncorrected image by clicking on the eyeball icon next to the adjustment layer name in the Layers palette. When the eyeball is present, the layer is visible, showing you the color corrected image. When the eyeball is hidden, so is the layer, giving you a "before" view of your image. You can do the same with fill layers.

Before moving on to dissect the Levels command, let's have a brief explanation of the Group with Previous Layer option we told you to skip earlier. If you check this box in the New Layer dialog box, the adjustment or fill layer will affect only the pixels of the immediately underlying layer. Any layers below that will be unaffected. This technique is referred to in Elements' higher circles as a *clipping group*. A clipping group is where you combine multiple layers into a group in which the lowest layer in the group masks the others. You can also create clipping groups with regular layers. In addition to selecting this option in the New Layer dialog box, you can also create a clipping group by selecting the adjustment or fill layer in the Layers palette and choosing Layer⇨Group with Previous or Ctrl+G (⌘+G on a Mac). Or simply press the Alt key (Option key on a Mac) and click on the horizontal line between the two layers. Notice that your cursor icon changes to an arrow with two circles and a small down-pointing arrow, and appears on the top layer after you click (see Figure 12-4). To remove the clipping group, simply Alt-click (Option-click on Mac) again or choose Layer⇨Ungroup or Ctrl+Shift+G (⌘+Shift+G on a Mac).

Making friends with the Levels dialog box

To apply the Levels command, you can create a new adjustment layer, as described in the preceding section, or choose Enhance⇨Brightness/Contrast⇨ Levels, or press Ctrl+L (⌘+L on a Mac). If you choose the command from the Enhance menu or press the keyboard shortcut, the color correction is applied directly to the image and affects only the active layer.

Either way, the dialog box shown in Figure 12-5 appears. Luckily, you don't need to address all the options that inhabit this dialog box. So, before you break into a cold sweat or shriek at the top of your lungs (or do whatever it is you do when you see terrifying sights like Figure 12-5), let's try to distinguish the important options in this dialog box from the stuff you won't use in a month of Sundays:

✔ The options in the Channel drop-down menu let you adjust one color channel in a full-color image independently of the other channels. (This is proof-positive that those red, green, and blue color channels we told you about in Chapter 5 are really there.) These options are helpful if you know what you're doing, but they're not terribly important.

✔ The three Input Levels option boxes control the settings of the darkest, medium, and lightest pixels in your image, in that order. These options are important, which is why we cover them thoroughly in the next section.

✔ That black birthmark in the middle of the dialog box is called a *histogram*. It shows you how the colors in your image are currently distributed. It also rates the Seal of Importance.

✔ The slider bar directly beneath the histogram provides three triangles, one each for the darkest, medium, and lightest pixels in your image. These triangles are the most important options of all.

✔ The Output Levels option boxes and the accompanying slider bar let you make the darkest colors lighter and the lightest colors darker, which is usually the exact opposite of what you want to do. Mark these options Not Particularly Important on your screen with a grease pencil. (Just kidding.)

✔ The OK and Cancel buttons are as important as always. One applies your changes, the other doesn't. No news here.

✔ Press the Alt key (Option key on a Mac) to change the Cancel button to a Reset button. Click on the button while pressing Alt (Option on a Mac) to reset the settings to the way they were when you entered the dialog box. Very helpful.

✔ Clicking on the Auto button is exactly like applying Auto Levels. The only time you might want to use this button is if you should want to apply the Auto Levels command on an adjustment layer.

✔ When you press the Alt key (Option key on a Mac), the Auto button changes to an Options button. We tell you about this feature only because you may notice it for yourself when you press the Alt key (Option key on a Mac) to access the Reset button. But whether you notice it or not, the Options button is totally unimportant. And if you do notice it, don't muck with the settings that become available to you when you click on the button.

✔ The three eyedropper icons let you click on colors in your image to make them black, medium gray, or white. Steer clear of these icons except to stamp them Not Important, Ditto, and Doubly So.

✔ The Preview check box lets you view the effect of your edits inside the image window. It's very important that you turn this option on.

Figure 12-6 shows the Levels dialog box as it appears after you strip it down to its most important components. (Don't try this at home.) As you can see, the Input Levels options — which include the three option boxes, the histogram, and the slider bar — represent the core of the Levels command. The other options are just icing on the cake.

Figure 12-5:
The complicated-looking Levels dialog box contains many options that you don't need to worry about.

Histogram

You say you want to be able to admire the quiet beauty of a histogram, but not have any distracting controls in sight that could actually make your image look better? You're in luck! The Histogram command (choose Image⇨Histogram) gives you a view of the histogram for your image, along with a whole bunch of theoretically helpful statistics. But you can't actually *do* anything with this information — not until you close the Histogram, at least. Ah well, at least the Histogram command tells you how many pixels you have in your image, in case you were wondering. Although this count may be inaccurate, so perhaps you should count them for yourself. (Oh my, we hope you know that we're kidding.)

Figure 12-6:
When you strip the Levels dialog box of its excessive regalia, it becomes far less daunting.

Darkest pixels   Lightest pixels

Brightness and contrast as they should be

The histogram from the Levels command seen in Figure 12-6 is a graph of the color in the uncorrected image in Figure 12-7. The graph is organized from darkest colors on the left to lightest colors on the right. The peaks and valleys in the histogram show the color distribution. If the darkest colors were black, the histogram would start on the far-left edge of the slider bar. If the lightest colors were white, it would continue to the far-right edge. But as it is, the left and right edges taper off into flatlands. This means that the darkest and lightest pixels in the image are not as dark or light as they could be.

Figure 12-7:
Though they lived in a time when Elements was not available, these uncorrected characters still managed to find something to smile about.

If some of that information went a little over your head, not to worry. Some folks like graphs, while graphs make other folks think that they're in a board meeting and start to nod off. Either way, remember that the histogram is provided for your reference only. All that matters is how you adjust the slider triangles underneath the histogram:

- ✔ To make the darkest pixels black, drag the left slider triangle to the right so that it rests directly under the beginning of the first hill in the histogram. Figure 12-8 shows the dragged triangle and its effect on the image.

- ✔ To make the lightest pixels white, drag the right-hand triangle to the left so that it lines up directly under the end of the last hill in the histogram, as in Figure 12-9.

Figure 12-8: Dragging the first triangle affects the darkest pixels in the image.

Figure 12-9: The image lightens up when the white triangle is dragged to the left.

✔ The most important triangle is the middle one. Called the *gamma point,* this triangle lets you change the brightness of the medium colors in your image. Drag to the right to make the medium colors darker. But more likely, you want to drag to the left to make the medium colors lighter, as demonstrated in Figure 12-10.

Figure 12-10:
Dragging
the middle
triangle
brings out
the detail in
an image.

The values in the three option boxes above the histogram update as you drag the slider triangles. The left and right values are measured in color levels. Just like the RGB values in the Color Picker — where you define colors (see Chapter 5) — 0 is black and 255 is white. So if the left value is 45, as it is in Figures 12-8 through 12-10, any pixel that is colored with a level of 45 or darker becomes black. The gamma value — the middle one — is measured as a ratio . . . er, forget it, it doesn't make any sense, and it matters even less. The point is, a value of more than 1 lightens the medium colors; a value less than 1 darkens them.

If you want to see the effect of the Levels command on a full-color image, you need look no further than Color Plate 12-4. Nestled in this quiet corner of the book is a homemade Italian gate. Starting with the uncorrected image in the upper-left corner, each of the slider triangles was adjusted, eventually arriving at the much superior color balance shown in the lower-right image. It just goes to show you, Levels is bound to be good for any image.

If you notice a loss of color in your image after you apply the Levels command, don't worry. You can get that color back by using the Variations command, discussed later in this chapter.

Using the Adjust Backlighting and Fill Flash commands

The Adjust Backlighting and Fill Flash commands (both found under the Enhance menu) are designed to easily compensate for common photographic lighting problems. You probably have more than a few photos where the subjects in the foreground are in the shadows, yet the background behind them is extremely bright. (You guessed it: The flash didn't go off.) Fill Flash can help bring out details in the foreground, while Adjust Backlighting can increase the contrast of the background. (Bear in mind that Elements has no idea what the "foreground" and "background" of the image are; it just looks at the brightness values of the pixels.)

What's so special about these commands is that they perform a correction that you can't pull off just by applying the Levels command to your image. Adjust Backlighting brings out details in bright areas without wiping out details in dark areas as much as Levels would. And likewise, Fill Flash brings out details in dark areas without wiping out details in light areas as much as Levels would.

These commands are only slightly more difficult to use than Auto Levels. There's just one slider: Drag it around until things look better. Figure 12-11 shows the results.

Before   Adjust Backlighting   Fill Flash

Figure 12-11: The image on the left can benefit from applications of both Adjust Backlighting (center) and Fill Flash (right).

Variations on a Color Scheme

One negative effect of manipulating the brightness levels in an image is that it can weaken some of the colors, particularly if you lighten the medium colors by dragging the gamma point in the Levels dialog box to the left. To bring the colors back to their original intensity, choose Enhance⇨Variations.

While Elements has a dedicated Color Cast command, the Variations command can also cure color casts, in which one color is particularly prominent in the image. A photograph shot outdoors, for example, may be overly blue; one shot in an X-rated motel room may be a shade heavy in the reds. Whatever color predominates your image, the Variations command can tone it down with elegance and ease. But first we'll examine how Variations can boost the colors in a Levels-corrected image.

Turning plain old color into Technicolor

To bolster the intensity of colors in your image — for what it's worth, color intensity is called *saturation* in image-editing vernacular — follow these pleasant steps:

1. **Choose Enhance⇨Variations.**

   The enormous Variations dialog box erupts onto your screen, filled with about a million small previews of your image.

2. **Select the Saturation radio button in the upper-right corner of the dialog box.**

   Most of the small preview images disappear. Only five remain, as shown in Figure 12-12. The three previews in the middle of the dialog box represent different color intensities. The top two previews show the image as it appeared before you chose the Variations command and how it looks now, subject to the changes in the Variations dialog box.

3. **Drag the slider triangle in the upper-right corner to the left, toward Fine.**

   This slider controls the extent of the changes made inside the Variations dialog box. If you drag the triangle toward Coarse, the changes become more drastic; drag it toward Fine, and they become more gradual. The setting is reflected inside the left and right previews in the middle of the dialog box. The changes become more subtle.

   Because color intensity is a very sensitive function inside Elements, it's best to set the slider to one of the first two notches so that you can make gentle, incremental changes.

4. **To increase color intensity, click on the preview labeled More Saturation.**

   Clicking once increases the intensity by a gradual amount, owing to the slider bar setting. To add more intensity, click again. Each time you click, the Current Pick previews update — one in the middle and one at the top — to reflect your latest change.

Figure 12-12:
Click on
the More
Saturation
preview to
boost the
intensity of
the colors in
an image.

If inconsistently colored pixels begin to emerge, Elements is telling you that these colors are outside the CMYK color range and will cause problems for professional printers. Don't worry about it until the weird pixels take over a third or more of your image. You can always turn off the Show Clipping check box to view the pixels normally.

If at any time you want to reset the Current Pick preview to the original image, just click on the preview labeled Original in the upper-left corner of the dialog box.

5. **When you're satisfied with the increased color intensity, press Enter (Return on a Mac).**

Elements applies your settings to the original image, just as they were shown in the Current Pick preview. No surprises with this dialog box.

Changes you make via the Variations dialog box affect only the active layer. Unfortunately, you can't apply the Variations command using an adjustment layer as you can the Levels and Auto Levels commands.

Color Plate 12-3 shows the difference between a butterfly whose splendor was completely destroyed using the Levels command and that same butterfly restored to its original luster and brilliance via the Variations command. To achieve this radical transformation, the slider bar inside the Variations dialog box was set to the second notch over from the left and the More Saturation preview was clicked on a total of six times.

Removing that color cast sure feels good

Images are like people in that they hate to wear casts. When your image is encumbered by a color cast, it becomes uncomfortable and downright crotchety. Take the first image in Color Plate 12-5, for example. To the inexperienced eye, this image may appear happy and at peace with itself. But in truth, its life is a living heck, made miserable by a decidedly yellow color cast.

The Color Cast command

Elements has a command that is solely dedicated to removing color casts. It should come as no surprise that we're talking of the Color Cast command (Enhance⇨Color⇨Color Cast). Using it is a breeze. Just select the command and use the Eyedropper tool to click in your image on an area that should be devoid of color — either white, black, or gray. Color Cast will perform the necessary correction to drain the clicked area of color, adjusting the entire image accordingly.

This command either works, or it doesn't, and whether or not it works depends entirely on your image. It's certainly possible that your image may not contain any areas that ought to be white or black; in that case, move on to Variations as a color cast correction tool.

While experimenting with Color Cast, make sure you click the Reset button after every unsatisfactory click in the image. The effects of Color Cast are cumulative, and things can get ugly quickly.

The Variations command

To remove a color cast once and for all, revisit the Variations command:

1. **Choose Enhance⇨Variations.**

   The Variations dialog box takes over your screen.

2. **Select the Midtones radio button in the upper-right corner of the dialog box.**

   This option lets you edit the medium colors in your image. (You can also edit the dark or light colors by selecting Shadows or Highlights, but these options produce extremely subtle effects and have little impact on your image.)

   After you select Midtones, the central portion of the dialog box fills with seven previews, as shown in Figure 12-13. These previews let you shift the colors in the image toward a primary color — green, yellow, red, magenta, blue, or cyan. As usual, the Current Pick preview in the center of the cluster updates to show the most recent corrections applied to the image.

The three previews along the right edge of the Variations dialog box let you lighten and darken the image. But because they're less capable than the gamma point control in the Levels dialog box, you can feel free to ignore them.

3. Click on one of the More previews to shift the colors in the image toward that particular color.

First, identify the color cast. Then click on the preview opposite to that color. In the case of the horse image from Color Plate 12-5, the cast is clearly yellow and, to a lesser extent, green. To eliminate the yellow cast, More Blue was used. To eliminate the green cast, More Magenta did the trick.

Check out Color Plate 5-2, which shows that yellow ink filters out blue light and magenta ink filters out green light. This filtering means that yellow and blue are direct opposites, as are magenta and green. Such opposite colors are termed *complementary.*

Figure 12-13:
Click on the More Blue preview to add blue and remove yellow in an image. Click on More Magenta to add magenta and remove green.

4. If you go too far toward one color, just click on the opposite color to step backward.

In Color Plate 12-5, for example, the More Blue preview was clicked on twice, More Magenta was clicked on twice, and then More Blue was clicked again. But it became apparent that the color cast correction had gone too far. The resulting image — shown in the bottom-right corner of the color plate — was too blue and too magenta. So the More Yellow button was clicked on to remove the last application of blue and More Green was clicked on to remove the last application of magenta. The lower-left example in the color plate shows the result.

As when you adjust color saturation, you can vary the impact of the previews on the image by dragging the slider triangle toward Fine or Coarse. The images in Color Plate 12-5 were all created with the triangle set in the center, as it is by default.

If your image has more than one layer, Variations' color cast manipulations affect only the active layer.

Using the Replace Color command

Up to now, this chapter has dealt with color correction commands that are designed to make your images look more like real life. But the Replace Color command approaches the concept of color "correction" from a slightly different angle — more like "That red ribbon I won really *should* have been blue!" Replace Color excels at isolating a single color in an image and turning it into a different color.

To apply Replace Color, choose Enhance➪Color➪Replace Color. The Replace Color dialog box appears, as nobly depicted in Figure 12-14. The dialog box is divided into two parts: Selection and Transform.

To use the Replace Color command, do the following:

1. **Apply Replace Color either to your entire image, or to a selection.**

   If there are areas of color in your image similar to the one you want to replace, it might be a good idea to draw a rough selection around your target area. For more on selections, see Chapter 8.

2. **Click the Image radio button.**

   The image or the selected portion appears in the preview.

3. **With the Eyedropper tool, click in your target area either within the preview or within the image window.**

4. **Switch to the Selection radio button.**

   You should see the results of your selection in the preview window in white. Black areas in the Selection preview are totally unselected, white areas are completely selected, and gray areas are partially selected.

5. **Adjust your selection with the Add Eyedropper, the Subtract Eyedropper, and the Fuzziness slider.**

   Hopefully the Add and Subtract Eyedroppers are self-explanatory. The Fuzziness slider expands or contracts your selection. Higher Fuzziness values select more colors, and lower values select fewer colors. If you make an arbitrary change to the color using the Transform sliders, you'll be able to see the selection within the image window as well. This can help you judge the quality of your selection.

6. **Once you're happy with your selection, change the color using the Transform sliders.**

You can adjust the Hue (the "color" of the color), Saturation (the richness of the color), and Lightness (how light or dark the color is). The Sample swatch shows you the resultant color of the Transform sliders.

7. **When you're happy, click OK.**

The color of the selected area has been replaced with your new color.

The Replace Color uses a very sophisticated selection method, which yields results that equal or surpass those of any of the standard selection tools. Replace Color is a very versatile command; as noted in Chapter 10, it's actually a more powerful alternative to the Red Eye Brush Tool. Just draw a selection around your subject's eyes, apply Replace Color, select the red glow, and change its Saturation and Lightness.

Figure 12-14: The Replace Color command can isolate and replace an area of color within your image.

Part IV
The Inspiration/ Perspiration Equation

The 5th Wave   By Rich Tennant

"Why don't you try blurring the brimstone and then putting a nice glow effect around the hellfire?"

In this part . . .

Thomas Alva Edison supposedly once said "Genius is 1 percent inspiration and 99 percent perspiration." (Unfortunately there's no record of him actually saying this, as he hadn't invented the phonograph at the time.) While this quote brings to mind visions of sweat dripping down Mr. Edison's neck and into open lightbulb sockets, he does have a point. A brilliant idea is nothing without the hours of back-breaking hard labor necessary to bring it to fruition.

Then again, Edison never used Photoshop Elements. (Recently unearthed evidence shows he never got beyond MacPaint 1.0.) With Elements, it's so easy to get the flashes of genius out of your head and on to the screen that it completely throws Edison's inspiration/perspiration equation out of whack. We're talking 90/10 . . . maybe 85/15 at the *most*. The five chapters in this part of the book deal with the ways Elements lets you express yourself, packing your most inspired, creative, and imaginative thoughts into your images. From painting and drawing to applying drop shadows and bevels, from adding text to stretching faces like Silly Putty — it's all here. We'll also look at some automated features that Elements offers; these amazing commands push the inspiration/perspiration equation to about 99/1, in actuality.

But first, you are going to have to perspire just a teeny bit while we help you learn to master these powerful tools. Feel free to rip the pages from this book one by one as you finish reading them and mop your fevered brow with them. We'll be proud to know that we've provided you with such absorbing literature.

Chapter 13

The Stylish Retouch

ome on, admit it. You're so ready for this chapter, you can taste it. Already, as you were working through the last Part of this book, learning ways to make your images look more like reality, mischievous little ideas began to pop into your head. Maybe you were using the Clone Stamp tool on a scanned image to get rid of some dust specks in the sky, and the thought snuck into your brain: "Gee, you know, this Clone Stamp tool is doing such a good job of cloning bits of sky and obscuring these dust flecks, that I guess — in theory — I could keep using this tool . . . to completely clone away my brother's head!"

Or maybe you were using the Replace Color command to gently tweak the color of your Uncle Waldo's cardigan sweater, and the thought occurred to you: "Well, gee whiz, this Replace Color command is doing such a nice job of changing the color of this sweater, that I guess — in theory — I could instead select Uncle Waldo's skin . . . and turn his head a virulent shade of screaming purple!"

Now if anything like these thoughts occurred to you, don't feel bad. It's perfectly normal to come to the realization that Photoshop Elements' carefully crafted, painstakingly perfected image-correction tools could not only be used, but also abused. Don't feel bad for having that thought. (It was just a *thought,* right?)

In truth, Elements has a host of other tools designed to let you inject your images with your own personal sense of style — no matter how funky, bizarre, or downright perverse that sense of style may be. Some of these tools, like the Layer Styles, you'll probably want to use every day. Some of them, like Blending Modes, are very useful for special effects. And then there are some — like the Liquify command — that are more-or-less digital torture devices, letting you vent your aggressions against your foes by pushing around a few pixels.

Add these tools to your Elements arsenal, and you'll not only be able to make your images look more real than life; you'll be able to infuse that life with your personal sense of style.

Using Layer Styles to Shine and Shadow

If you want to create a dimensional-looking Web button or imbue your text with a true sense of depth, this is the place to be. Elements makes the application of effects like drop shadows, glows, and bevels mere child's play with the Layer Styles palette. Layer Styles can be applied to regular layers and type layers (see Chapter 16), but not to the Background layer. Layer Styles are linked to the contents of a layer. If you edit the contents, the styles are updated dynamically, which makes using Layer Styles incredibly flexible.

Here is a step-by-step guide to applying a layer style:

1. **Start with an object on an active layer.**

   You'll see the best results if there's transparency around the edges of the object. Text on a text layer is a great place to start.

2. **Activate the Layer Styles palette.**

   By default, it's hiding behind the Layers palette, sharing the same window.

3. **Choose a Layer Styles category from the drop-down menu at the top of the palette.**

   You can choose between Bevels, Drop Shadows, Inner Glows, Inner Shadows, Outer Glows, Visibility, Complex, and Glass Buttons.

4. **Click on a layer style within your chosen category.**

   You should see the style immediately applied to your object.

We describe the various effects and their settings in the following list, yet a picture is worth a thousand words. See Figure 13-1 for some examples.

- ✓ **Drop Shadow:** Applies a soft shadow behind the object, giving the illusion that your layer is floating above the layers behind it. The Outline, Fill/Outline, and Neon Drop Shadows create strange, unrealistic effects.

- ✓ **Inner Shadow:** Applies a shadow on the object itself. This creates the effect that the object has been "cut out" from the layer behind it, with a light source beneath the object. Try it, and you'll see what we mean.

- ✓ **Outer Glow:** Creates a glow or halo effect around the object.

- ✔ **Inner Glow:** Makes the object itself glow.

- ✔ **Bevel:** Creates a chiseled 3D effect around the edge of the object.

- ✔ **Visibility:** Lets you make the object itself translucent or invisible, while keeping the layer style visible.

- ✔ **Complex:** Just as complex as it sounds, these are pre-made styles with intricate combinations of layer styles, textures, and colors.

- ✔ **Glass Buttons:** As simple as it sounds, these are pre-made styles that can turn your objects into a multitude of different-colored glass buttons.

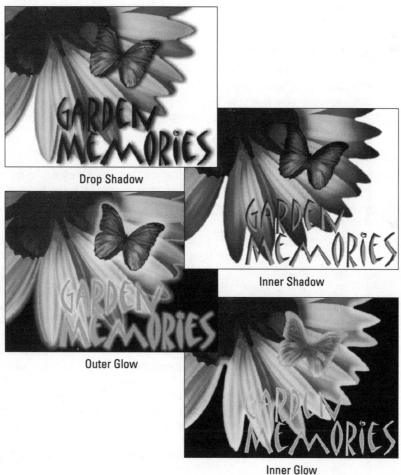

Drop Shadow

Inner Shadow

Outer Glow

Inner Glow

Figure 13-1:
The Layer
Styles
palette
makes it
easy to
apply
shadows,
glows, and
other
effects to
images and
type.

In addition to just clicking on the style in the Layer Styles palette to apply it to the active layer, there are other ways of applying styles:

✔ Drag and drop the style from the Layer Styles palette onto the desired layer in the Layers palette. To do this, you may have to separate the Layer Styles palette and the Layers palette from the common window they share by default. Just click on the tab of either palette and drag it out of the window onto the desktop.

✔ Drag and drop the style from the Layer Styles palette onto the desired object within the image window.

Here are some other handy things to know about layer styles:

✔ Click the Default Style (None) at the top of each Style category to clear all layer styles from a layer.

✔ You can switch between Thumbnail view and List view by clicking the buttons at the bottom of the Layer Styles palette, or by choosing the desired view from the Layer Styles palette menu (click the right-pointing triangle button in the upper-right corner of the palette.)

✔ You can copy and paste layer styles from one layer to another by choosing commands from the Layer➪Layer Style submenu.

✔ You can clear or hide the layer styles for a layer by choosing commands from the Layer➪Layer Style submenu. If you hide the layer styles for a layer, choose Layer➪Layer Style➪Show All Effects to reveal the layer styles again.

✔ You can globally scale up or down the layer styles applied to a layer by choosing Layer➪Layer Style➪Scale Effects. This can be very helpful if you change the size of the object the layer styles are applied to.

For instance, let's say you have a circular object on a layer with several layer styles applied to it. You decide the circle is too large, so you choose Image➪Resize➪Scale, and drag a corner handle of the bounding box to scale down the circle. (You can tell precisely how much you're scaling down the circle by first opening the Info palette and watching the scaling information in the upper-right corner of the palette.) You decide that your circle looks good at 50% of its former size, so you hit the Enter key (Return key on a Mac). While your layer style is, of course, still applied to the circle, the style itself hasn't been scaled down. A bevel that looks great on a large circle might be too big for a small one. No problem — just choose Layer➪Layer Style➪Scale Effect, enter 50% in the option box, and click OK. The layer style will be scaled down in proportion to the resized object.

It's also possible to edit layer styles with much greater control after they've been applied, as explained in the next section.

So the High Drop Shadow is too high, and the Low Drop Shadow isn't high enough? Don't despair: Tweak instead! Choose Layer⇨Layer Style⇨Style Settings — or easier still, just double-click on the little "*f*" in a circle on the layer in the Layers palette — to open the Style Settings dialog box, pictured in the rosy blush of its eternal youth in Figure 13-2.

Figure 13-2:
The Style
Settings
dialog box
gives you
exacting
control
over the
appearance
of layer
styles.

Here's the lowdown on the various controls contained therein:

- **Lighting Angle:** Determines the direction of the light source for Bevels and Shadows. Type in a value in degrees — or just drag the little circular dial to set the desired angle.

- **Use Global Light:** Checking this option keeps the Lighting Angle consistent for all layers in the same image. And this is usually a very good thing, as it makes the various objects in an image seem to exist together in the same "room," so to speak. If this option is checked for all the layers in an image, then making a Lighting Angle or Shadow Distance adjustment for one layer affects all the layers in the image.

- **Shadow Distance:** This sets the distance of the Drop Shadow from the object, and therefore creates the illusion of the object being closer or farther away from the layers beneath it. You can adjust this by dragging the slider, or by dragging the shadow itself within the image window. Notice that dragging the shadow can also affect the Lighting Angle.

- **Outer Glow Size:** Affects the size of the Outer Glow.

- **Inner Glow Size:** Affects the size of the Inner Glow.

- **Bevel Size:** Affects the size of the Bevel. (Boy, writing these books is easy!)

- **Bevel Direction:** Affects the direction of the . . . oh, okay, perhaps a bit more explanation is in order here. Bevel Direction can be used to make concave surfaces look convex, and vice versa. If the bevel is making your object look like it's protruding from the image, switching the Bevel Direction to Down will make it look as if it's recessed into the image.

A layer style is *live,* meaning that it updates itself as the contents of the layer change. For instance, the left image in Figure 13-3 shows a circle with a Simple Sharp Inner Bevel layer style applied. If you then apply the Ripple filter to the circle, as shown in the middle image of Figure 13-3, the Ripple filter is theoretically applied *before* the layer style, meaning that the Bevel applies itself to the rippled edges of the circle. If this isn't what you want — if, instead of a rippled circle with a bevel, you want a beveled circle that's been rippled — you have to Simplify the layer first before you apply the filter. Choose Layer⇨Simplify Layer. This will cause Elements to *rasterize,* or render the layer style into just plain pixels. The layer style will look exactly the same, but it will lose its "live," editable status. Then you can apply the filter at will. The end result of this process is shown in the right image of Figure 13-3.

Figure 13-3:
A circle with a layer style applied (left); the same circle with the Ripple filter applied (middle); the first circle after first being Simplified, then with the Ripple filter applied (right).

Layer styles also work splendidly well in conjunction with the Shape tools — so well, in fact, that they can be applied directly from the Shape tools' Options bar. This enables you to quickly create dimensional-looking geometric objects (such as buttons for Web pages), which can be resized at will without any loss in quality. If you resize an object drawn with a Shape tool, it should come as no surprise to you that the layer style changes to accommodate the shape. For more on the Shape tools, see Chapter 14.

Tending Your Many Splendid Blends

A layer with a layer style applied is a layer proud of its individuality. "Look at me!" it fairly shouts. "I'm not like you other guys milling around in the Layers palette. I've got style, baby! Get a load of that drop shadow. And check out this bevel — am I cut, or what?"

But some layers pride themselves on working as a team, blending together to create an interesting cumulative effect. That's where blending modes can help. At its core, a blending mode is a mathematical formula for combining the pixels in two different layers. It's possible to achieve some bizarre and beautiful effects with modes, and they can be hard to predict. Before we dive into blend modes, let's look at a method of blending layers together that's the oldest trick in the book: changing opacity.

Fooling with layer opacity

One neat trick to try with a layer is to make it partially translucent by using the Opacity slider in the Layers palette. In Figure 13-4, for example, the fish was made partially translucent by setting the Opacity to 70%. In the second example, he was made even more ghostly by lowering the Opacity to 30%. Whether the image is on its own layer or temporarily floating, you can use the Opacity slider bar in the Layers palette to achieve this effect. To access the slider bar, click on the right-pointing arrow to the right of the Opacity numeric setting.

To change the Opacity setting for a layer from the keyboard, make sure that any tool that doesn't have its own Opacity option in the Options bar is selected and press a number key. Press 9 for 90%, 8 for 80%, and so on, down to 1 for 10%. To return to 100%, press 0. You can also enter more specific Opacity values — such as 72 — by typing the digits quickly.

Keep in mind that the Opacity setting can't be changed for the Background layer because nothing lies behind it. You'd be looking through the Background into the empty void of digital space, a truly scary prospect. The same is true for the blend modes discussed in the next section.

Opacity: 70%   Opacity: 30%

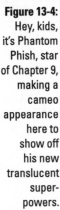

Figure 13-4:
Hey, kids,
it's Phantom
Phish, star
of Chapter 9,
making a
cameo
appearance
here to
show off
his new
translucent
super-
powers.

Playing around with blend modes

Many of the options that appear in the Blend Mode drop-down menu in the upper-left corner of the Layers palette are the same ones we've seen in the Mode menu of Options bar for some of the editing tools (see Chapter 11). You have Darken, Lighten, Hue, and the rest of the gang. These tools use brushes, so their modes are often referred to as brush modes. But these options aren't called brush modes when they're applied to layers because no brush is involved. You can call them overlay modes or blend modes; some high-falutin' folks call them *calculations.* But just plain modes is fine for us regular faluters.

Here's a brief description of how the most important ones work:

- ✔ **Multiply and Screen:** Multiply burns the floating image into the images behind it, darkening all colors where they mix. Screen does just the opposite, lightening the colors where they mix.

- ✔ **Difference:** The Difference mode has no real-world analogy. It creates a photo negative — or inversion — of the blended images according to their colors. Where one of the images is black, no inversion takes place. Where the images are light, you find lots of inversion.

- ✔ **Overlay, Soft Light, and Hard Light:** These are similar options. Overlay multiplies the dark colors and screens the light ones. Soft Light produces a more subtle effect. Hard Light is more dramatic than Soft Light or Overlay.

- ✔ **Color and Luminosity:** Like Multiply and Screen, the Color and Luminosity modes produce exactly opposite effects. The Color mode blends the color of the layer with the detail from the underlying images. Luminosity keeps the detail from the layer and mixes it with the colors of the underlying images.

- ✔ **Color Dodge, Color Burn, and Exclusion:** For some other interesting effects, experiment with the Color Dodge, Color Burn, and Exclusion modes. Suppose that you have two layers, a Background layer and Layer 1. Color Dodge lightens the pixels in the Background layer and infuses them with colors from Layer 1. Color Burn darkens the pixels and infuses them with color. Exclusion works similarly to Difference; it turns all black pixels white, all white pixels black, and all medium colors gray.

- ✔ **Darken:** This is another mode that can be useful. Say that you want to composite something like a scanned handwritten letter or sheet of music over an image. Obviously, you want only the handwriting or music notes to appear and not the white paper, which would obscure the underlying pixels. By choosing Darken, only the dark pixels appear, the light area appears transparent. Lighten does just the opposite — displays the light pixels and makes the dark pixels transparent.

- ✔ **Dissolve, Hue, and Saturation:** You can skip these other blend modes. They range from boring to duller than dull, and they rarely come in handy.

Just so you know, you can mix a translucent Opacity setting with a blend mode, but you can't select more than one blend mode at a time. It would be fun to combine Luminosity with Multiply, for example — you know, to apply detail that only darkens — but you just can't do it. Oh well.

For a look at some of what you can do with blend modes, refer back to Color Plate 9-1. Here's a rundown of some of the blend modes used:

- ✔ The Multiply mode was used to blend the nebula with the fish to create the black eye effect.

- ✔ The spray coming out of the fish's mouth is actually the spray from the comet, blended with the Screen mode.

- ✔ The Reims Cathedral and Neptune were blended with Luminosity and Hard Light, respectively.

We'll look more at blend modes in the guise of brush modes in the next chapter.

Those Phunky Philters

So far in this book we've looked at filters that can make your images look better, from removing dust and scratches to sharpening and even blurring. But this doesn't even begin to scratch the surface where Elements' filters are concerned. In fact, you'll probably find that there are more filters designed to make your images look weirder than there are to make them look "better." But hey, it's all subjective, isn't it? One man's "freaky" is another man's "normal." Here are a few ideas for imbuing images with your own personal whacked-out style.

Creating motion and puzzle pieces

In addition to Blur, Blur More, and that ueberblurrer Gaussian Blur, the Blur category in the Filters palette contains three additional filters — Motion Blur, Radial Blur, and Smart Blur — all of which are exclusively special-effects filters. The Motion Blur filter makes an image appear to move in a straight line; the Radial Blur filter can be used to move the selection in a circle or to zoom it outward toward the viewer. The Smart Blur option finds the edges in your image and then blurs only between the edges — it's as though Elements is carving your image up into puzzle pieces and then blurring each piece. If you apply the effect in heavy doses, the result is an image that resembles a watercolor painting and isn't too far removed from the effect created by the Artistic category's Watercolor filter.

Of the three filters, Motion Blur is the filter you're most likely to use. First, the filter lets you see the preview within the image window, making this filter accessible and predictable. Second, it's much easier to use. Finally, when compared with Radial Blur, it takes a lot less time to use; Radial Blur is one of the slowest Elements filters.

When you choose Motion Blur, Elements displays the Motion Blur dialog box. The filter smears pixels at a specified angle and over a specified distance. Enter the angle and distance into the appropriately named option boxes. You can also drag the spoke inside the circle on the right side of the dialog box to change the Angle value.

For example, Figure 13-5 shows a couple of discrete applications of the Motion Blur filter. (To see this image without the Motion Blur, take a gander at Figure 11-13 in Chapter 11.) To blur the boy, select him, feather the selection, and apply Motion Blur with an Angle value of 90° — straight up and down — and a Distance of 30 pixels. To blur his sister's arm — the one nearest her beaming brother — use an Angle of 45° and a Distance of 6 pixels. As you can see, Distance values over 20 smear the image into oblivion; smaller Distance values create subtle movement effects.

Figure 13-5:
Two unlikely
applications
of the
Motion Blur
filter.

Giving your images that gritty, streetwise look

Located quite logically in the Noise category is the Add Noise filter. Not to be confused with the as-yet-uncompleted Adenoids filter, Add Noise randomizes the colors of selected pixels. The result is a layer of grit that gives smooth images a textured appearance.

Apply Add Noise to display the Add Noise dialog box, shown in Figure 13-6. Here's how to use the options found therein:

✔ Drag the Amount slider triangle or enter a value between 0.10% and 400% to control how noisy the image gets. Low values permit a small amount of noise; high values permit more. Anything over 50% pretty much wipes out the original image.

✔ Select a Distribution radio button to control the color of noise. The Uniform option colors pixels with random variations on the shades it finds in the original image; the Gaussian option — which should be labeled High Contrast — colors pixels with more exaggerated light and dark shades. Therefore, Gaussian produces a noisier effect, about twice as noisy as Uniform. For example, an Amount value of 12.5% combined with Gaussian produces a similar visual effect to an Amount value of 25% combined with Uniform.

Figure 13-6:
This filter
adds
"noise" to
your image
to give it a
gritty
texture.

✔ The Monochromatic check box adds grayscale noise to full-color images.
When you turn off the option, Elements adds all colors of noise. (The
option has no effect on grayscale images except to shift the pixels
around a little.)

Stamping your image in metal

Another intriguing and sometimes useful filter is Emboss, located in the
Stylize category. This filter makes your image appear as though it were
stamped in metal. The edges in the image appear in relief, and the other
areas turn gray.

When you choose Emboss, Elements displays the dialog box shown in
Figure 13-7. You enter the angle of the light shining on the metal into the
Angle option box. The Height value determines the height of the edges,
and the Amount value determines the amount of contrast between blacks
and whites.

We're breezing over these options because they aren't the most useful gang
in the world. In fact, they can be big time wasters. Here's the important stuff
to know:

✔ How you set the Angle value doesn't matter. Feel free to drag the spoke
on the circle until you get what you want, but don't expect big differences between one angle and another.

Figure 13-7:
Use the
Emboss
filter to
stamp
images into
sheets of
metal
(figuratively,
of course).

✔ Set the Height value to 1 or 2. Any value over 2 can impair detail.

✔ Okay, the Amount value is useful. Enter 50% for a very subtle effect, 100% for a medium Emboss effect, and 200% for added drama. You can go as high as 500%, but higher values make the contrast between blacks and whites too abrupt for most tastes.

Like Add Noise, Emboss isn't the kind of filter you go around applying to an entire image. After you've done it once or twice, it gets a little old. Rather, you'll want to apply it to selected areas.

To achieve the thrilling mottled metal effect on the far right of Figure 13-8, first select the dark areas in the mother and son image and apply the Emboss filter with an Angle of 45°, a Height of 2, and an Amount of 200%. Then blur the selection using the Gaussian Blur filter set to a Radius of 2 pixels, as shown in the middle example. Finally, apply Unsharp Mask with an Amount of 500% and a Radius of 2 pixels.

Your reaction may be one of, "Whoa, hold up a minute here. First you blur and then you sharpen? What kind of crazy logic is that?" Well, pretty sound logic, actually. After applying Gaussian Blur, the image turned overly gray, as you can see in the second example in the figure. Luckily, one of the properties of Unsharp Mask is that it increases the amount of contrast between dark and light pixels. So, to bring the blacks and whites back from the dead, the Radius value inside the Unsharp Mask dialog box was set to the exact value used in the Gaussian Blur dialog box — that is, 2.0. Using this value ensured that Unsharp Mask was able to correctly locate the blurred edges and boost their contrast. It's a great technique.

Figure 13-8:
After selecting the dark portions of the image, the selection was embossed (left), blurred (middle), and sharpened (right), creating a soft relief.

Emboss   Gaussian Blur   Unsharp Mask

Merging colors in flaky images

The next two filters — Facet and Median — average the colors of neighboring pixels to create areas of flat color. Both throw away detail, but they're great for smoothing out the imperfections in old, cruddy images such as the one that keeps popping up in this book.

Located in the Pixelate category, Facet is a single-shot filter that roams the image looking for areas of similarly colored pixels and then assigns the entire area a single color. Figure 13-9 shows the elder daughter from way back in Figure 11-9, before she was sharpened. The middle example shows Facet applied. See how the image is now divided into a bunch of globby areas of color? To make the image clearer, Unsharp Mask was applied to the far-right example, using an Amount value of 250% and a Radius value of 0.5.

Located in the Noise category, Median averages the colors of so many neighboring pixels. To tell Elements the "so many" part, choose Median and enter a value anywhere between 1 and 100 into the Radius option box.

Figure 13-10 shows the result of applying various Radius values to the elder daughter. The top row shows the effects of the Median command; the bottom row shows what happened when Unsharp Mask was applied to each image. Notice how higher values melt away more of the image's detail. A Radius value of 3 makes the image gooey indeed; any higher value is pure silliness.

Figure 13-9:
Starting with the original image (left), the Facet filter was applied (middle) and then the edges were reinforced with Unsharp Mask (right).

Original Facet Unsharp Mask

You can use Facet and Median to blur background images, just as we did earlier with Gaussian Blur. Or you can combine them with the Add Noise and Emboss filters to create special effects.

Keep in mind that the real beauty of these more specialized filters is in combining them and applying them to small, selected portions of your image.

Figure 13-10:
The Median filter applied with three different Radius settings (top row) and then sharpened (bottom row).

Radius: 1 Radius: 2 Radius: 3

Median

Unsharp Mask

Making Taffy with the Liquify Filter

You thought Elements couldn't possibly give you any more ways to take your image out of the realm of reality, right? Well, hold on to your mouse, because the Liquify filter is in the house.

The Liquify filter, among other things, lets you warp, twirl, pucker, and bloat your image. It's enough to make a grown Elements user downright queasy! So take a deep breath and prepare to become "liquified."

Select the area of the image that you want to distort and follow these steps:

1. **Open an image and decide whether you want to distort the whole image or just a portion.**

   You can use an area selected with one of the tools described in Chapter 8. Or you can select a single layer (see Chapter 9). When you select an area, the unselected areas become *frozen* or protected from distortion. In Figure 13-11, the woman's head and a bit of the surrounding background were selected. She looks like she could use a good warping or two.

2. **Choose Filter⇨Liquify.**

   You can also find Liquify in the Filters palette. Just activate the palette, switch the drop-down menu to "Distort," and you'll see it there. Drag it out of the palette and into the image window, or click on the Liquify filter and click the Filters palette's Apply button. Or you can press Ctrl+Shift+X (⌘+Shift+X on the Mac). A huge dialog box appears, as shown in Figure 13-11.

3. **Select your desired brush size and pressure in the top-right portion of the dialog box.**

   Enter a numeric value or access the slider via the right-pointing arrow. Notice how a pinkish tint covers the non-selected area.

4. **And now, time for the fun stuff.**

   Use any one of the following tools to wreak havoc on your image. Check out the effects of each in Figure 13-12.

   - **Warp tool:** Pushes the pixels forward under your brush as you drag, creating a stretched effect. This tool gives the most "taffy-like" effect.

   - **Twirl Clockwise tool:** Rotates the pixels clockwise under your brush as you either drag or hold down the mouse.

   - **Twirl Counterclockwise tool:** Ditto the above, only in a counter-clockwise direction.

- **Pucker tool:** Moves the pixels toward the center of your brush as you drag or hold down the mouse, giving a kind of pinched look.

- **Bloat tool:** The opposite of Pucker — moves pixels away from the center, creating a kind of spherical effect.

- **Shift Pixels tool:** Shifts pixels perpendicular to the direction you move the brush. (In Figure 13-12 the brush was dragged up; ditto for the Reflection tool.)

- **Reflection tool:** Copies pixels from the area perpendicular to the direction you drag.

Twirl Clockwise tool

Warp tool

Twirl Counterclockwise tool

Pucker tool

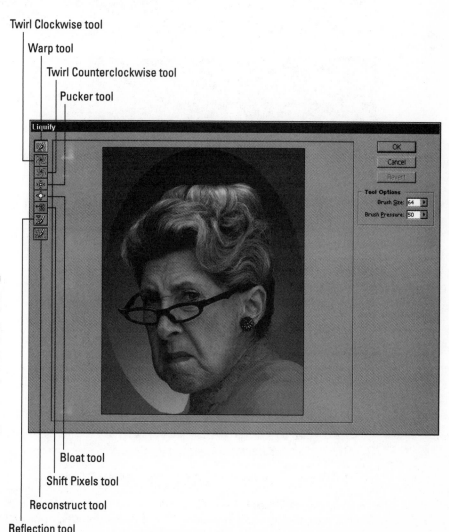

Figure 13-11:
The Liquify dialog box is where you can distort your image into another dimension of reality.

Bloat tool

Shift Pixels tool

Reconstruct tool

Reflection tool

Warp

Twirl Clockwise

Twirl Counterclockwise

Pucker

Bloat

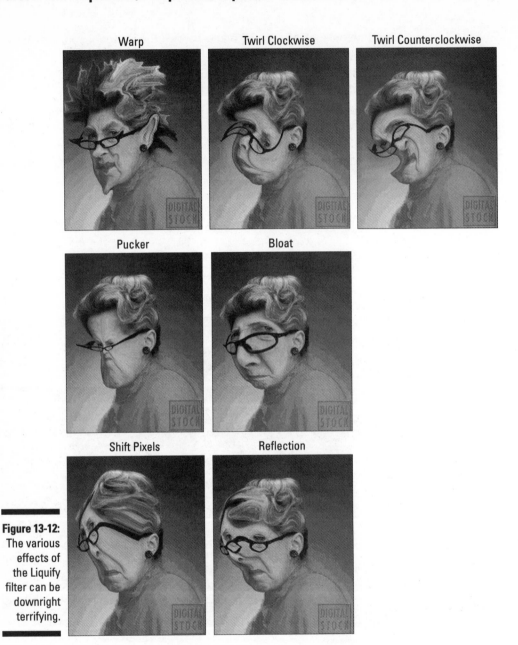

Shift Pixels

Reflection

Figure 13-12:
The various
effects of
the Liquify
filter can be
downright
terrifying.

5. Click on OK and show off your crazed masterpiece.

The best advice there is for understanding the inner-workings of the Liquify
filter is play, play, play. If you have a few spare moments, open an image and
do some freestyle reality altering of your own.

Chapter 14

If a Picture Paints a Thousand Words . . . Then Shut Up and Paint

• •

In This Chapter

▶ Using the Pencil, Paintbrush, and Airbrush tools

▶ Drawing straight lines with the painting tools

▶ Selecting brushes

▶ Wiping away pixels with the eraser tools

▶ Drawing on the Shape tools

• •

No, no, the title of this chapter isn't telling *you* to shut up. Heck, we're the ones using up all the words around here. But speaking of painting, as a novice or casual Photoshop Elements user, you fall into one of two camps: artist or nonartist. Some people are so comfortable with a paintbrush that they feel as though they were born with the device. But a much larger group of Elements users falls into a camp that modern sociologists call "artistically challenged."

Take this quick test to determine where you fall:

✔ After doodling in the phone book, are you so horrified by the results that you rip out the page, pour ketchup on it, and feed it to your dog?

✔ When you're asked by someone to draw a map to your house, do you give them a blank piece of paper and try to assert that you live with a pack of polar bears in a snowstorm in the Arctic?

✔ Do you have recurring dreams in which you suddenly remember that today is the day your final project is due in the art class you've forgotten to attend all year? And as you attempt to quickly paint a lounging model, you notice that the model is fully clothed and you're the one who's naked?

If you answered "Yes" to one of the preceding questions, you can safely assume that you belong to the non-artists camp. If you answered "Yes" to two of the questions, you are so firmly entrenched in the non-artistic tradition that completing a dot-to-dot picture seems like an immense and terrifying project. And if you answered "Yes" to two of the questions and "Oh, wow, I had that exact dream just last night!" to the third, here's one more question: How much does your analyst charge?

Whatever your level of artistic skill, though, a time will probably come when you'll want to rub a couple of the Elements painting tools against an image. But don't worry; the Impressionist Brush can make you look like you're an artist even if you aren't, and of course Elements also gives you several tools for erasing your work. For that matter, the Shape tools eliminate much of the need for an artistic hand anyway. So take a deep breath, and follow us.

Doodling with the Pencil, Paintbrush, and Airbrush

Elements offers just three painting tools — the bare minimum for artists and nonartists alike. Shown in Figure 14-1, they work like so:

- **Pencil:** The Pencil tool draws hard-edged lines of any thickness.

- **Paintbrush:** The Paintbrush tool draws soft lines with slightly blurry edges to create more natural transitions.

- **Airbrush:** The Airbrush tool paints soft lines like the Paintbrush. The only difference is that this tool pumps out color continuously — even when you hold it in place — as long as the mouse button is down. By contrast, the Pencil and Paintbrush tools paint only as you drag.

Airbrush — Paintbrush

Pencil

Figure 14-1:
There's no reason to be afraid of the three Elements painting tools.

You can select each of the painting tools from the keyboard. Press J to select the Airbrush, press B to select the Paintbrush, and N to select the Pencil.

"But wait," we can practically hear you say. "What about that brushy-looking tool below the Pencil? Isn't that a painting tool?" Actually, the Impressionist Brush isn't a painting tool for one simple reason: It doesn't apply new color to the canvas. Rather, it swirls the existing colors around in a truly weird fashion. Check it out and see what we mean — or better yet, wait until later in this chapter when we deal with it properly.

When you select the painting tools, Elements, by default, displays a cursor that matches the brush size exactly. If you press the Caps Lock key, however, the cursor changes to a crosshair cursor that can occasionally make it easier to see precisely what you're doing. The crosshair shows you the very center of the brush, regardless of how thick you've made it. (The upcoming section, "Switching the brush size," explains how to change brush sizes.) Press Caps Lock again to return to the brush-sized cursor.

If you prefer, you can make your painting tool cursors look like their icons: a little paintbrush, little airbrush, or little pencil. To make the cursor reflect the icon, press Ctrl+K (⌘+K on a Mac) to display the Preferences dialog box. Then choose Display & Cursors from the top drop-down menu or press Ctrl+3 (⌘+3 on Mac) to get to the cursor options. Select Standard from the Painting Cursors radio buttons and press Enter (Return on a Mac). Although they're kind of cute, these so-called "standard" cursors are really the least helpful of all.

The painting tools are small, nonpoisonous, and good with children. So why not take them for a walk and see how you like them? To use the Paintbrush, Pencil, and Airbrush tools to create the friendly Mr. Sun image shown in Figure 14-4 (go ahead, flip forward to take a look), just follow these steps:

1. **Click the New icon in the Shortcuts bar, choose File⇨New, or press Ctrl+N (⌘+N on a Mac) to create a new canvas.**

   Elements displays a dialog box that asks what size to make the new canvas. The dialog box offers Width, Height, and Resolution options, as does the Image Size dialog box discussed in Chapter 4.

2. **Make the canvas about 400 pixels wide by 400 pixels tall.**

   That's about 5½ x 5½ inches with a Resolution value of 72 ppi or 4 x 4 inches with a Resolution of 100 ppi. Alternatively, you can select Pixels from the Width and Height drop-down menus, enter **400** into each, and forget about the Resolution value. Also, make sure the Mode drop-down menu is set to RGB Color, and that White is selected in the Contents section.

3. **Press Enter (Return on a Mac).**

   The new empty canvas appears in a new window.

4. **Click the Default icon at the bottom left of the Toolbox or press the D key to set the Foreground color to black.**

5. **Select the Paintbrush tool.**

   Click on the Paintbrush icon in the Toolbox or press the B key. That's B for "brush;" get it?

6. **Draw a circle in the middle of your new canvas.**

   A rude approximation of a circle is fine. Experts agree that a lumpy circle has more personality.

7. **Paint some rays coming off the circle.**

   Figure 14-2 shows more or less how your image should look so far.

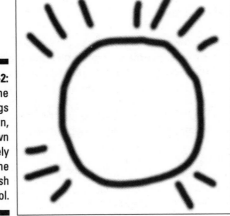

Figure 14-2:
The beginnings of a sun, drawn exclusively with the Paintbrush tool.

8. **Select the Pencil tool.**

   To access the Pencil from the keyboard, press N. That's N for . . . the third letter of "pencil."

9. **Draw a little face inside the sun.**

   Using the Pencil, you get hard-edged lines, as shown in Figure 14-3.

10. **Select the Airbrush tool.**

    Press J to access the Airbrush from the keyboard. That's J for . . . um . . . okay, you're on your own here.

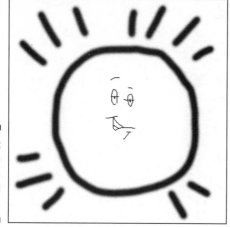

Figure 14-3:
A face
drawn with
the Pencil
tool.

11. **Change the Foreground color to orange.**

    Click the Foreground Color icon to get the Color Picker. Use the color slider and the color field to get a nice orange, or enter 255 for R, 150 for G, and leave B at 0.

12. **Click on and hold — without moving your mouse — inside the sun.**

    Notice that the Airbrush continuously pumps out paint. Neither the Paintbrush nor the Pencil does this.

13. **Paint some shading in the lower-right region of the sun.**

    Figure 14-4 shows a general idea. The Airbrush is useful for shading images. Of course, the real sun can't possibly have a shadow, but it doesn't have a face either, so we can allow room for some personal expression.

That's good enough for now. You may want to save this image, because we come back to it later in this chapter. Then again, if something goes wrong and you don't save the sun, no biggie. You can always re-create it or experiment with a different image.

Remember that at any stage in the previous exercise — or during any other painting mission upon which you may embark — you can always travel backward in time by clicking the Step Backward button in the Shortcuts bar or pressing Ctrl+Z (⌘+Z on a Mac). Everyone makes mistakes, and as we saw in Chapter 7, Elements gives you plenty of ways to correct yours.

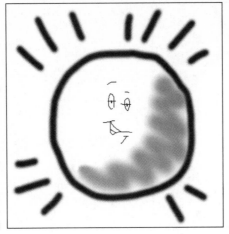

Figure 14-4:
Use the
Airbrush to
paint a
highly
unrealistic
shadow on
the sun.

Performing Special Painting-Tool Tricks

Dragging with a tool inside the image window is obviously the most common way to paint in Elements. But it's not the only way, as the following list makes clear:

- ✔ To create a straight line, click at one point in the image with any of the three painting tools, and Shift+click at another. Elements automatically creates a straight line between the two points.

- ✔ To create a straight-sided polygon, continue to Shift+click at various points in the image with any of the three painting tools. This method is great for creating triangles, five-pointed stars, and all sorts of other geometric shapes.

- ✔ To create a straight line that's exactly vertical or horizontal, click and hold with one of the painting tools, press and hold the Shift key, and then drag with the tool while the Shift key remains down. In other words, press Shift immediately after you begin to drag, and hold Shift throughout the length of the drag. If you release the Shift key while dragging, the line resumes its naturally free-form and wiggly ways.

- ✔ You may have noticed that there's a Line tool hidden away amongst the Shape tools — the heart-shaped Custom Shape tool is visible in the Toolbox by default. While you can draw straight lines with it too, it's really not a painting tool, but rather a whole different kind of animal. We'll explore the Shape tools later in this chapter.

- ✔ Alt+click (Option+click on a Mac) to lift a color from the image. Then drag to start painting with that color.

Choosing Your Brush

If the preceding two sections covered everything about the painting tools, Elements would be a royal dud. But as we all know, Elements is not a dud — far from it — so there must be more to the painting tools than we've seen so far. (This is classic Sherlock Holmes-style deductive reasoning at work here. Element-ary, my dear Watson.)

You can modify all three tools to a degree that no mechanical pencil or conventional paintbrush can match. For starters, you can change the size and shape of the tip of the tool, as explained in the next few sections. You can draw thick strokes one moment and then turn around and draw thin strokes the next, all with the same tool. This holds true of any tool that works like a brush, including the editing tools in Chapter 11.

Switching the brush size

To change one tool tip — called a brush size, or just plain brush — for a different one, click on the Brushes drop-down menu, which you can reach by clicking the arrow to the right of the word Brush in the Options bar. Elements displays the Brushes palette, shown in Figure 14-5. Here you can find a total of 36 brushes (assuming default settings), all free for the taking.

Figure 14-5: The Brushes palette lets you switch one size brush for another.

The numbers below the brush icons represent the diameters of the brushes. (In case that year of high school geometry has altogether removed itself from your brain, diameter is merely the width of a circle measured from side to opposite side.) To change the brush size for a tool, select the desired tool and then click on the Brushes drop-down palette in the Options bar. The left column of Figure 14-6 shows how each of the predefined brushes affects the performance of the Paintbrush tool. (In each case, an icon from the Brushes palette is shown directly to the left of a stroke created with that brush.)

Notice that some of the brushes have soft edges, whereas the others have downright blurry edges. When you begin using the brush, the palette puts itself back in its hiding place. You can also press Enter (Return on a Mac) or Esc to close the palette.

You can also check out the textured brushes in the Brushes palette below the round brushes. These can be fun to experiment with, but usually aren't practical for day-to-day use.

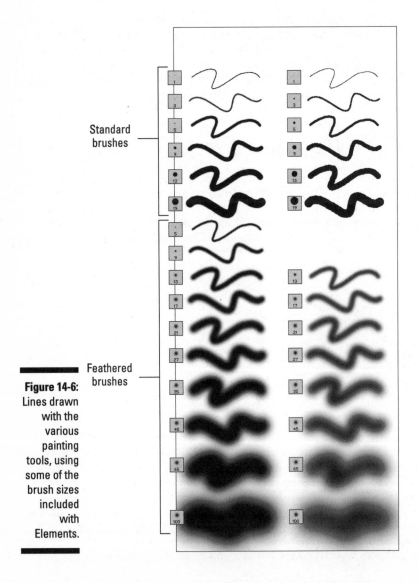

Standard brushes

Feathered brushes

Figure 14-6: Lines drawn with the various painting tools, using some of the brush sizes included with Elements.

You can view the Brushes palette in five ways — large and small thumbnails (the default), text only, or a large or small list (a combo of text and thumbnails). Access the Brushes palette drop-down menu to select any of these viewing options.

Right-click (Control+click on a Mac) on the canvas to display the Brushes palette underneath your cursor. Select a different brush and continue painting. The palette then disappears.

As we learned in Chapter 8, soft edges are said to be *anti-aliased,* whereas blurry edges are *feathered.* Both terms are proof positive that computer professionals actually don't want to be understood by the greater public. They prefer to speak in their own private code.

Figure 14-6 also shows the effect of some of the brushes on the Pencil and Airbrush tools. As the top six examples in the right column show, the Pencil tool draws a harsh, jagged line no matter which brush you select. Even the feathered brushes produce jagged lines when used with the Pencil. The Airbrush generally produces softer lines than the Paintbrush, as shown in the eight examples at the bottom of the right column.

Making your own brush

You may think that 36 brushes are enough to keep you happy well into your declining years. But rest assured, one day you'll want a brush size that's a little thicker than Option A and a little thinner than Option B. So you'll have to modify one or the other to come up with a custom brush of your own.

To edit a brush, just click on the brush icon in the Options bar. In response to your click, Elements displays the drop-down dialog box, shown in Figure 14-7. Here's how you modify the brush:

- ✔ Drag the Diameter slider to make the brush bigger or smaller. If you know the exact width value you need, enter it into the option box on the right side of the slider. This value is measured in pixels.

- ✔ The Hardness value represents the blurriness of the brush size. A value of 100% is hard, like the first six options in the Brushes palette. Anything else is progressively fuzzier. The 12 feathered options in the Brushes palette have Hardness values of 0%.

- ✔ Don't change the Spacing value. And don't even think about turning off the Spacing check box. The Spacing option determines how many dollops of paint are applied to your canvas and should only be changed for very specialized purposes.

✔ Before we talk about the Angle option, which comes next, you need to understand how Roundness works. (You see, the Angle value doesn't have any effect unless you first change the Roundness value.) The Roundness option lets you make the brush oval instead of round. A value of 100% is absolutely circular, as are most of the predefined brushes; anything less results in a shape that is shorter than it is wide.

✔ If you want an oval brush to be taller than it is wide or some other variation on its present state, you can rotate it by changing the Angle value. Keep in mind that 360 degrees represents one complete counterclockwise turn, so 90 degrees is a quarter-turn, 180 degrees is a half-turn, -90 degrees is a clockwise quarter-turn, and so on.

✔ You'll find it much easier to use the diagram in the lower-left corner of the dialog box to change the Angle and Roundness settings. Drag one of the two circular handles on either side of the circle to make the brush oval. To rotate the brush, either drag the gray arrowhead or just click at the position where you want the arrow to point. The labels in Figure 14-7 tell the story.

Create new preset

Figure 14-7:
The inner workings of a brush size.

Drag to rotate

Drag to change roundness

As you change the settings, the brush icon in the Options bar shows the effect of the modified settings on the brush. After you finish editing the brush, press Enter (Return on a Mac) to accept your changes. Note that this action creates a brush for temporary usage. You can also edit or create a brush and save it for later use. Once you've created your brush, give it a name and click the Page Icon button. You'll find your new brush at the bottom of the palette.

Going nuts with the Brushes palette

What we've seen so far would be plenty of brush options for an ordinary program. But Elements is no ordinary program. Elements is never satisfied to supply you with anything short of everything. You have to admire that in a program.

Here's what else Elements offers you:

- ✔ You don't need to manually click on a brush icon in the Brushes palette to select it. You can change the brush size from the keyboard, even when the Brushes palette is hidden. Press the right bracket key ( ]) to select a larger brush in varying increments. Increments are as follows: 1 pixel in brushes from 1–10 pixels in size; 10 pixels in brushes from 10–100 pixels in size; 25 pixels in brushes from 100–200 in size; 50 pixels in brushes from 200–300 in size; 100 pixels in brushes from 300–900 in size; and finally it jumps to 999 (the max). Press the left bracket key ([ ) to select a smaller brush by the same increments.

- ✔ To raise the hardness of a brush in 25 percent increments, press Shift+]. To lower the hardness, press Shift+[.

- ✔ To delete a brush size option from the palette, Alt+click (Option+click on a Mac) on it. If you press the Alt key (Option key on a Mac), you get a miniature pair of scissors. That's how Elements tells you that you're ready to clip a brush into oblivion.

- ✔ You can load additional custom brushes by choosing the Load Brushes command from the palette menu. (Click on the right-pointing arrow in the palette to display the menu. This is very similar to loading Swatch libraries into the Swatches palette.) When you choose the command, you see a dialog box similar to the standard Open dialog box. Go to the Adobe Photoshop Elements folder, then to the Presets folder, and finally to the Brushes folder, where you find numerous brush libraries. Try Assorted Brushes.abr. That's a fun one. Click on Load to add the custom brushes to the Brushes palette. As with the Swatches palette, the preset collections of brushes are also available at the bottom of the drop-down menu inside the Brushes palette.

- ✔ To return to the default collection of brushes, choose Reset Brushes from the palette menu. You will lose any brushes you may have created, so make sure you first choose Save Brushes from the Brushes palette's drop-down menu.

Exploring More Painting Options

Figure 14-8 shows the Options bar that appears when the Paintbrush is active. With a few exceptions, these options are the same ones that appear when you select the Pencil and Airbrush tools. Here's how the options work:

✔ The first icon on the far left is the tool identifier, which lets you know which tool is active. If you click the icon, you get a drop-down menu where you can either reset the default options for the specific tool, or do the same for all the tools. We discussed the Brushes palette options earlier in the section, "Choosing Your Brush."

✔ The Mode drop-down menu provides access to a bunch of different brush modes that control how the Foreground color applied by the tool mixes with the existing colors in the image. These modes function identically to the blend modes talked about in Chapter 13. You'll see some fun tricks to perform with some of the modes in the next section.

✔ Available when you use the Pencil or Paintbrush, the Opacity slider bar controls the translucency of the foreground color you're applying. A setting of 100% ensures that the paint is opaque so that you can't see the colors underneath. (When you use a feathered brush, the edges are translucent even at 100%, but the center is opaque.) Any Opacity setting lower than 100% makes the brush translucent.

✔ If you can't quite see your way through to how the Opacity slider works, a visual depiction will make everything clear. Figure 14-9 shows four lines drawn with the Paintbrush, two using a standard soft brush and two using a feathered brush. In each case, one line is set to 100% Opacity, and the other line is set to 40%.

✔ When you select the Airbrush, the Opacity slider bar changes to the Pressure slider bar. Rather than producing translucent lines at lower settings, the Airbrush applies less paint, as though you tightened the nozzle on a real airbrush.

Standard brush, 100%

40%

Feathered brush, 100%

40%

Figure 14-9:
Here's what it looks like when you paint over a sea anemone at different Opacity settings.

✔ Just as with a layer's opacity, you can change the Opacity or Pressure value for tools in 10% increments by pressing a number key. As long as you have one of the painting tools selected, pressing 9 changes the setting to 90%, 8 changes it to 80%, and so on. Press the 0 key to change the setting back to 100%. If you want a more precise setting — say, 75% — just type the value in quickly.

✔ The Wet Edges check box appears only when the Paintbrush tool is selected. You can select this option to make your lines translucent with dark edges, as though the lines were drawn with a magic marker. Give it a try with an Opacity lower than 100%. For a variation on the effect, choose the Multiply mode from the Mode drop-down menu.

✔ The Auto Erase check box appears when you select the Pencil tool. You can select this option to draw in the Background color whenever you click or drag on a pixel painted in the Foreground color (the accepted practice in other painting programs). It's very useful for making touch-ups with the single-pixel brush — click to add the Foreground color and click again to change it to the Background color.

✔ Click on the Brush icon at the far right of the Options bar to display the Brush Dynamics options.

You can choose to fade out the stroke or line over the course of several steps (1–999). One step is equal to one mark of the brush tip. You can also specify which options of the brush stroke — size, opacity/pressure, and color — you want to fade or change. Size is obvious. Opacity affects the translucency of the stroke. Color makes the color fade in intensity. The Stylus option affects how pressure-sensitive drawing tablets work in Elements. While they can be a nifty way to draw onscreen, we're assuming that you don't have one for now.

Experimenting with brush modes

If you read about blend modes in Chapter 13, you saw how they can be used to combine the colors of pixels in layers. Brush modes work in the same way, except that they combine the painted Foreground color with whatever is underneath it. Here are a few specific effects you can achieve using brush modes.

For example, consider the sun image shown back in Figure 14-4. Suppose that you want to color in the sun with yellow and the sky with blue.

The problem is, if you try to color in the sun and sky with one of the painting tools — even the Airbrush — you end up covering the face inside the sun with yellow and the rays outside the sun with blue. You can't fix the problem by lowering the Opacity value, because doing that just results in washed out colors, and you still obscure some of the sun's detail.

The two images in Color Plate 14-1 illustrate the problem. In the left image, we painted the sun and sky with the Paintbrush tool at 100% Opacity — obviously a bad move. In the right image, we repainted the image with the Opacity lowered to 40%. The image looks like it's been smeared all over with chalk. Yuck.

The solution is to select a brush mode. Change the Opacity back to 100% by pressing the 0 key. Then select Multiply from the Brush Modes drop-down menu in the Options bar. Miraculously, you can now paint both sky and sun without covering up the rays and the face. This is because the Multiply option darkens colors as though you had painted with watercolors. The Multiply option mixes the colors together to create darker colors. The upper-left example in Color Plate 14-2 shows the result.

Here are some additional brush modes and other information on this subject that you may find interesting:

✔ The Screen Mode is the exact opposite of Multiply. Multiply mixes colors as though they were pigments, which is why the colors get darker. By contrast, Screen mixes colors as though they were lights, which is why they get lighter. In the upper-right example of Color Plate 14-2, the Screen mode made it possible to apply color exclusively inside the black outlines and orange shadow. Nothing happened when the white areas were painted over, because any color mixed with white just makes more white.

✔ The Overlay Mode darkens dark colors and lightens light colors, resulting in a heightening of contrast. In the case of the sun, Overlay creates halos around the black lines because it darkens the inside of the lines and lightens the feathered edges. The lower-left example in Color Plate 14-2 makes it clear.

✔ The Difference brush mode is the loopiest mode of them all and the most likely to surprise you. It creates a photo-negative effect by mixing colors and finding their opposites. Check out the final example in Color Plate 14-2 to see the resulting plum sun against a tomato sky. Way cool.

✔ You can also have some fun experimenting with Difference's cousin, Exclusion. It sends all blacks to white, all whites to black, and all medium colors to gray.

✔ Use the Color brush mode to colorize grayscale images or change the color of portions of RGB images. Suppose that you want to change the color of the sky in the upper-left example of Color Plate 14-2 from blue to green. You can't use the Normal Mode because that wipes out the rays and the other lines. And you can't use Multiply again because that further darkens the sky. The answer is the Color Mode, which replaces a color with the foreground color without harming underlying detail.

✔ The Color Dodge and Color Burn brush modes offer an interesting new twist on the Dodge and Burn tools discussed in Chapter 11. In case you haven't discovered the Dodge and Burn tools yet, you drag with the Dodge tool to lighten a portion of your image and drag with the Burn tool to darken a portion of your image. If you use one of the painting tools and the Color Dodge mode, you can lighten your image and infuse it with color. Using Color Burn, you can darken and infuse with color. For example, to darken your image and give it a greenish tint, you paint with green using the Color Burn brush mode.

✔ To paint normally again, just select the Normal brush mode.

Shift+right-click (Shift+Control-click on a Mac) on your canvas with a painting tool to bring up a shortcut menu that provides access to the Edit Brush command and all the brush modes.

Six of the preceding brush modes — Multiply, Screen, Overlay, Difference, Color, and Normal — are super-useful, the kinds of modes you want to get to know on a first-name basis. Exclusion, Color Dodge, and Color Burn are also worth some attention. The others aren't nearly so useful. In fact, they're mostly boring and obscure. But who knows? Maybe you'll feel differently.

"Painting" with the Impressionist Brush

The Impressionist Brush allows you to paint in impressionistic swirls. (Although it's not, strictly speaking, a paintbrush, we'll still refer to what the Impressionist Brush does as "painting," for lack of a better word.) The Impressionist Brush is not — we repeat, not — a tool used to clean the lint off Rich Little. (Not that we're saying Mr. Little has a lint problem. Those are just vicious rumors and nothing more.)

Go ahead and open up an image. Press A to select the Impressionist Brush, and just start moving it around on your image. You'll instantly get an idea of what the Impressionist Brush is all about. Figure 14-10 shows an image before and after a grueling workout with the Impressionist Brush. Pretty groovy, huh?

The performance of the Impressionist Brush depends on the settings in the Options bar, pictured in Figure 14-11. Here are the options:

- **Mode:** This drop-down menu assigns a brush mode to the tool. See "Experimenting with brush modes" in this chapter for details.

- **Opacity:** Lower this value to create translucent strokes. To lower the Opacity from the keyboard, just press a number key any time the Impressionist Brush is active.

Figure 14-10:
An original image (left) and the same image brought to life with the Impressionist Brush (right).

Figure 14-11:
The Options
bar offers
numerous
settings for
the Impres-
sionist
Brush.

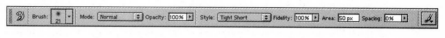

✔ **Style:** The Impressionist Brush paints with randomly generated cork-screws of color. You can decide the basic shapes of the corkscrews by selecting an option from the Style drop-down menu. Combine these options with different brush sizes to vary the detail conveyed by the impressionistic image.

✔ **Fidelity:** As it lays down corkscrews, the brush colors each corkscrew according to the color lifted by the cursor. Lowering the Fidelity value enables the corkscrew color to drift away from the source color. This produces random coloring (true to the impressionist tradition), but it also slows down the brush's response.

✔ **Area:** This value defines the area covered by a single dollop of paint. Larger pixel values generally mean that the brush lays down more strokes at a time; reduce the value for a more sparse look.

✔ **Spacing:** Change this value to give more or less tolerance to where the Impressionist Brush can paint within the image.

If impressionism interests you, experiment with this brush. If not, give this brush a slip. While it's pretty nifty, it definitely falls under the heading of Whimsical Creative Tools to Play with When You're Not under Deadline.

The Powers of the Eraser

What artist's toolbox would be complete without an eraser? Elements' Toolbox wouldn't be complete without three erasers — the Eraser tool, the Background Eraser tool, and the Magic Eraser tool.

To switch between the three eraser tools from the keyboard, press Shift+E.

Working with the regular ol' Eraser tool

The Eraser tool, directly under the Paint Bucket tool in the Toolbox, lets you erase in a couple of ways:

- ✔ If you drag with the Eraser in an image that contains only one layer, the tool paints in the Background color, which is white by default. Technically this may be erasing, but it's really just painting in a different color. Who needs it?

- ✔ If your image contains more than one layer (we discuss layers in Chapter 9), the Eraser works a little differently and becomes a lot more useful. If you drag the Eraser on the Background layer, the Eraser paints in the Background color, as usual. But on any other layer, the pixels you scrub with the Eraser become transparent, revealing pixels on underlying layers. (This assumes that the Lock Transparent Pixels box is unchecked in the Layers palette. If you check the Lock Transparent Pixels box, the Eraser paints in the Background color.)

The Eraser tool comes in four delicious eraser flavors. To switch flavors, select an option from the Mode drop-down menu in the Options bar.

Three erasers are named after painting tools — Paintbrush, Airbrush, and Pencil — and work exactly like these tools, down to the inclusion of the Wet Edges check box for the Paintbrush option. This means that you can change the brush size in the Brushes palette and adjust the Opacity setting to partially reveal the image or, in a layered image, make pixels only partially transparent.

The fourth option, Block, changes the eraser to the square, hard-edged, fixed-size eraser. The options in the Brushes palette don't affect the Block eraser, nor do the Opacity slider bar or any of the other settings in the Options bar. The Block Eraser can be useful when you want to completely erase general areas, but you probably won't take it up very often.

Trying out the somewhat Magic Eraser

Of the Background and Magic erasers, the Magic Eraser is the easier to use and the less capable. If you're familiar with the Magic Wand (see the section on using the Magic Wand in Chapter 8), the Magic Eraser is a cinch to use. The two tools operate virtually identically, except that the Wand selects and the Eraser erases.

When you click on a pixel with the Magic Eraser, Elements identifies a range of similarly colored pixels, just as it does with the Magic Wand. But instead of selecting the pixels, the Magic Eraser makes them transparent, as demonstrated in Figure 14-12. Bear in mind that in Elements, transparency requires a separate layer. So if the image is flat (without layers), Elements automatically floats the image to a separate layer with nothing underneath: hence the checkerboard pattern shown in the second example in the figure — transparency with nothing underneath.

Figure 14-12: To delete a homogeneously colored background, like the sky at top, click inside it with the Magic Eraser (bottom).

Notice in Figure 14-12 that the Magic Eraser deleted some of the blue sky, but not all of it. This is a function of the Tolerance value in the Options bar. Just like the Magic Wand's Tolerance value, the Magic Eraser's Tolerance value determines how similar a neighboring color has to be to the clicked color to be made transparent. A higher value affects more colors; a lower value affects fewer colors. Therefore, if you want to erase a larger section of the sky in Figure 14-12, you can raise the Tolerance value and click again. (Remember, any change to the Tolerance value affects the next click you make; it does not affect the existing transparent area.)

The other options in the Options bar work as follows:

- **Anti-aliased:** To create a soft fringe around the outline of your transparent area, leave this option turned on. If you prefer a hard edge — as when using a very low Tolerance value, for example — turn this check box off.

- **Contiguous:** This check box is inside both the Magic Eraser Options bar and the Magic Wand Options bar. When turned on, the Magic Eraser deletes contiguous colors only — that is, similar colors that touch each other. If you prefer to delete all pixels of a certain color regardless of their location, turn the Contiguous check box off.

- **Use All Layers:** When turned on, this check box tells Elements to factor in all visible layers when erasing pixels. The tool continues to erase pixels on the active layer only, but it erases them according to colors found across all layers.

- **Opacity:** Lower this value to make the erased pixels translucent instead of transparent. Low values result in more subtle effects than high ones.

For a more detailed description of these options as they affect the Magic Wand tool, read the section on using the Magic Wand in Chapter 8.

Using the more magical Background Eraser

The Magic Eraser is as simple to use as a hammer and every bit as indelicate. It pounds away pixels, but it leaves lots of color fringes and shredded edges in its wake. You may as well select an area with the Magic Wand and press the Backspace key (Delete key on a Mac). The effect is the same.

The more capable, more scrupulous tool is the Background Eraser. As demonstrated in Figure 14-13, the Background Eraser deletes background pixels as you drag over them. (Again, if the image is flat, Elements floats the image to a new layer to accommodate the transparency.) The tool is intelligent enough to erase background pixels and retain foreground pixels provided — and here's the clincher — that you keep the cross in the center of the eraser cursor squarely centered on a background pixel. Move the cross over a foreground pixel, and the Background Eraser deletes foreground pixels as well. As Figure 14-14 demonstrates, it's the position of the cross that counts.

Figure 14-13: Drag around the edge of an image with the Background Eraser to erase the background but leave the foreground intact.

Like the standard Eraser tool, the Background Eraser responds to the brush size specified in the Brushes palette. You can use the bracket keys [and] to make the brush size larger or smaller.

You can also modify the performance of the Background Eraser using the options in the Options bar. Here are your options:

- ✔ **Limits:** By default, the Background Eraser deletes colors inside the cursor as long as they are contiguous with the color immediately under the cross. To erase all similarly colored pixels, whether contiguous or not, set the drop-down menu to Discontiguous.

- ✔ **Tolerance:** Raise the Tolerance value to erase more colors at a time; lower the value to erase fewer colors. Low Tolerance values are useful for erasing around tight and delicate details, such as hair.

- ✔ **Brush Dynamics:** Indicated by a Paintbrush icon at the right end of the Options bar, this drop-down menu lets you specify the rate at which a brush stroke fades based on tolerance and/or size. If you own a pressure-sensitive tablet, such as the Intuos from Wacom, you can use the Stylus setting to specify whether pen pressure affects the size and tolerance of the eraser.

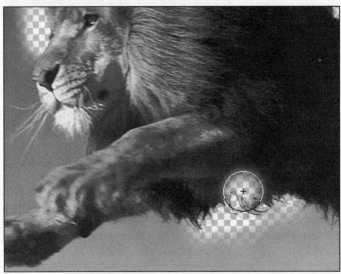

Figure 14-14:
Keep the cross of the Background Eraser cursor over the background you want to erase (top). If you inadvertently move the cross over the foreground, the foreground gets erased (bottom).

Isn't Elements Just a Paint Program?

Perish the thought. Elements also includes Shape tools, which are very handy at drawing geometric objects to be used for things like Web buttons. Shapes are exceptions to the way things generally work inside Elements, since they're not actually pixel-based. The Shape tools draw *vector objects,* which can be scaled to any size with no loss in quality. If you painted a circle in Elements on a very small canvas — say, roughly 20 pixels by 20 pixels — and then scaled your canvas up to around 2000 pixels by 2000 pixels using the Image Size command, the edges of your circle would look very fuzzy. But use the Ellipse Shape tool to draw a circle on that 20 by 20 canvas, scale it up to 2000 by 2000 with Image Size, and the Ellipse-drawn circle will look perfect, with razor-sharp edges. See the difference?

The Shape drawing tools

There are six different Shape tools — the Rectangle, Rounded Rectangle, Ellipse, Polygon, Line, and Custom Shape tools. In addition, there's the Shape Selection tool, which we'll get to in a minute. To experiment with the Shape tools for the first time, do the following:

1. **Select a Shape tool from the Toolbox.**

   The Custom Shape tool is visible by default. To access one of the other shapes, click and hold your cursor on the visible Shape tool, and a fly-out menu will appear. Or, just click on the visible Shape tool in the Toolbox and then choose the specific Shape tool you want from the Options bar, as pictured in Figure 14-15. (If you've experimented with the Shape tools at all before, go over to the Shape tool icon on the very far left, click it, and choose Reset Tool.)

Figure 14-15:
The Shape Options bar provides a plethora of options for the Shape tools.

Geometry options   Shape area buttons

2. **Drag with the tool to draw a shape on the canvas.**

   It really helps to have the Layers palette open while you work with the Shape tools. (For more on the Layers palette, see Chapter 9.) If you have the Layers palette open, you'll see that you just created a new layer. Most layers only have one thumbnail, but just like a fill layer or adjustment layer, Shape layers have two thumbnails: one for the color of the layer and one for the shape itself.

   By default, the color of the shape will be the Foreground color, but after drawing the shape, you can change the color by clicking the Color box in the Options bar to bring up the Color Picker.

3. **Draw another shape.**

   You'll see that you've created another layer. This happened because the Create New Shape Layer button is selected by default. This button is the left button in the shape area option buttons in the Options bar. Selecting one of the other four buttons will keep the next shape you draw on the same layer, and each of the four buttons has its own options for combining shapes on the same layer. See Figure 14-16 for a visual reference to the effects of the shape area buttons.

4. **Press the Step Backward button in the Shortcuts bar to undo the last shape you drew, click the Add to Shape Area button (the next button over from the Create New Shape Layer button), and draw a shape again.**

   This time make sure your new shape overlaps the old one. Use Step Backward again and experiment with the other three buttons, drawing overlapping shapes. Lather, rinse, repeat.

The drop-down menu in the Options bar at the right end of the row of Shape tools gives you access to Geometry options for the tools. The options here vary from tool to tool, but here's a rundown of what they all do:

Add
Subtract

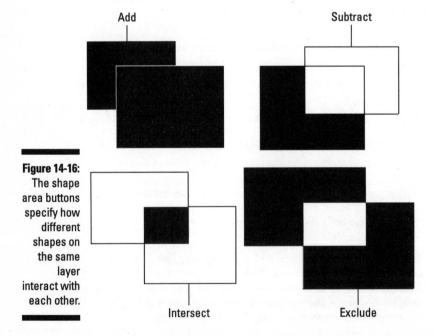

Figure 14-16:
The shape area buttons specify how different shapes on the same layer interact with each other.

Intersect
Exclude

- **Unconstrained:** Enables you to draw your shape freely, stretching or squashing it if you wish as you draw.

- **Square:** Enables you to draw a square with the Rectangle and Rounded Rectangle tools.

- **Fixed Size:** Enables you to draw a shape with a set width and height.

- **Proportional:** Lets you draw a shape with a proportional ratio of width and height.

- **From Center:** This option enables you to draw from the center out, rather than from a corner.

- **Snap to Pixels:** Aligns the shape perfectly with the "pixel grid" of the image. This ensures that straight lines will always appear crisp.

- **Radius:** Sets the width of the polygon.

- **Smooth Corners:** Makes smooth polygon corners.

- **Indent Sides By:** Creates the spikes of a star when the Polygon tool is selected. A larger value makes sharper and spikier points.

- **Smooth Indents:** Curves the sides of a star.

- **Circle:** Similar to the Square option, this constrains the Ellipse tool to draw a perfect circle.

- **Arrowheads:** Enables you to specify the placement of the arrowhead, the shape of the arrowhead, the width of your line, and the concavity (or curvature) of the arrowhead for the Line tool.

- **Defined Proportions:** The opposite of Unconstrained, this keeps you from distorting a Custom Shape as you draw it.

- **Defined Size:** Constrains drawing Custom Shapes to the size at which they were created.

Some tools have other options available in the Options bar:

- **Radius:** Specifies the amount of curve on the corners of the Rounded Rectangle tool.

- **Sides:** Specifies the number of sides for the Polygon tool.

- **Weight:** Specifies the thickness of the Line tool.

- **Shape:** Gives you access to the Shapes palette with the Custom Shape tool. From here you can select a different shape to draw. Click the drop-down menu in the Shapes palette to access 14 different libraries of shapes. The drop-down menu also lets you choose from several different viewing options for the Shapes palette.

The Options bar also makes it easy to add layer styles, which we cover in Chapter 13. And the final button in the Options bar is the Simplify button. No, the Simplify button doesn't simply make all the confusing Shape tools disappear. Clicking the Simplify button *rasterizes* your shape layer. Rasterizing is the process of converting your vector shape to pixels, meaning the shape loses its special resizable status. However, simplifying is necessary if you want to add filters and effects to your shape.

The Shape Selection Tool

If you're not happy with where you drew a shape, that's when that last Shape tool can come in handy. The Shape Selection Tool lets you click on a shape and drag it to a new location, but it also has a few other tricks up its sleeve:

✔ After you've clicked on a shape, go to Image⇨Transform Shape. This gives you access to four different commands — Free Transform Shape, Skew, Distort, and Perspective — wherein you can distort your shape in any number of interesting ways.

✔ Selecting the Shape Selection Tool gives you access to the Combine button in the Options bar, which combines various shapes on a single layer into one complex shape.

If all this painting and drawing seems a little daunting at first, don't give up. Just keep on plugging away. Remember, everything's daunting at some time. Heck, feeding yourself once seemed impossible, and yet look how well you do that today. Sure, not as well as some folks, but you're still getting there. Keep your chin up (and wipe it, for good measure.)

Chapter 15

The Digital Stencil

. . . .

In This Chapter

▶ Painting and editing inside a selection outline

▶ Using the Paint Bucket tool

▶ Using the Fill command

▶ Applying different types of gradients

▶ Stroking a selection

. . . .

A s we saw in the last chapter, Photoshop Elements has a whole mess of tools that replicate the process of drawing or painting on a canvas. But have you ever spray painted using a stencil? In case you've never engaged in this riveting pastime, here's how it works:

1. **Hold the stencil up to the surface you want to paint.**

2. **Spray recklessly.**

When you take the stencil away, you discover a painted image that matches the shape of the stencil. It's the epitome of a no-brainer.

In Elements, you can use a selection outline (see Chapter 8 for more on selections) in the same way. Just as a stencil isolates the area affected by the spray paint, a *selection outline* isolates the area affected by a paint or edit tool. You can also fill a selection outline with color or trace around the selection outline.

In this chapter you're going to learn every nuance of painting, filling, and tracing selections. While Chapter 8 explains how to create and manipulate selection outlines, this chapter shows you what to do with them.

Painting within the Lines

If some portion of an image is selected, Elements treats all deselected areas as protected. You can use any paint or edit tool inside the selection without worrying about harming areas outside the selection.

This chapter utilizes a jar-in-a-nook, which has a certain austere beauty about it — it's just the sort of prop that would look right at home in a hoity-toity kitchen of the idle rich. It's such a lovely object that during the course of this chapter we will, or course, completely muck it up. Specifically, we'll paint the inside of the jar without harming the background. To this end, do the following:

1. **Select the jar.**

   This is the only step that takes any work. You can start out by selecting the body of the jar with the Elliptical Marquee tool. If you have problems getting the marquee exactly on the jar — it's hard to know where to start dragging so that it comes out right — just make sure that the marquee is approximately the right size, select one of the marquee or lasso tools, and then use the arrow keys to nudge the outline into position. You can also temporarily hold down the spacebar as you're dragging to reposition the selection outline on the image. After you select the body to your satisfaction, you can Shift+drag with the Lasso tool to incorporate the neck of the jar into the selection as well.

2. **Make any modifications you deem necessary.**

   In this case, you may want to blur the selection outline a tad using Select➪Feather, as explained in Chapter 8. If your selection outline isn't dead on, the Feather command helps to fudge the difference a little.

   You'll probably also want to choose View➪Selection Edges to hide the selection after you've made it. Remember that the selection is still active; choosing Selection Edges just makes those distracting marching ants invisible, making it easier to see what you're doing.

3. **Paint and edit away.**

   Feel free to use any tool you want. You can paint with the Paintbrush, Airbrush, or Pencil; edit with the Smudge, focus, or toning tools; clone with the Clone Stamp — all with the assurance that the area outside the selection will remain as safeguarded from your changes as the driven snow (or whatever the saying is).

In Figure 15-1, the inside of the jar was painted using a single tool — the Airbrush — with a single brush size and only two colors, black and white. As a result, the jar is transformed into a kind of marble. Looks mighty keen, and there's not so much as a drop of paint outside the lines.

This stenciling feature is so all-fired handy that you'll almost always want to select an area before applying a paint or edit tool. The fact is, the selection tools are easier to control than the painting or editing tools, so you may as well take advantage of them.

Figure 15-1:
Using the
Airbrush,
we painted
the inside
of the
selected jar.

Dribbling Paint from a Bucket

Elements enables you to fill a selection with the Foreground color, the
Background color, a pattern, or a gradual blend of colors called a *gradient*.
But before we look at any of these eye-popping options, let's spend a moment
kicking around the Paint Bucket tool, which is part selection tool and part fill
tool. The Paint Bucket tool (it looks like a tilted bucket of paint) lets you fill
an area of continuous color by clicking on the area.

In Figure 15-2, for example, the Paint Bucket tool was clicked on the row of
broccoli in the jar with the Foreground color set to white. Elements filled the
broccoli with white, turning it into a rough facsimile of cauliflower.

To adjust the performance of the Paint Bucket, access the Options bar, also
shown in Figure 15-2. As with the Magic Wand tool, the Tolerance value determines how many pixels in your image the Paint Bucket affects. The only difference is that the Paint Bucket applies color instead of selecting pixels. You
can also select the Anti-aliased check box to soften the edges of the filled
area. (In Figure 15-2, the Tolerance value is 32, and Anti-aliased is turned on,
as it is by default.)

Paint Bucket tool

Figure 15-2:
The Paint
Bucket
fills a
continuous
area of
color with a
different
color.

The problem with the Paint Bucket tool is that it's hard to get the Tolerance value just right. You usually end up Stepping Backward several times and resetting the Tolerance value until you find the value that colors only the pixels that you want to color. Overall, the Paint Bucket is not the best tool for filling areas in Elements. If you select an area in your image by using the Magic Wand tool, which chooses pixels of similar color surrounding the cursor (discussed in Chapter 8) and then fill the area with a color (described in the next sections), you produce the same effect as with the Paint Bucket, *and* you have more alternatives at your disposal.

If you decide to ignore this advice and take up the Paint Bucket at your earliest opportunity, you can select the tool quickly by pressing K.

Applying Color to Selection Innards

The Paint Bucket isn't the best way to fill a selection outline. So what is the best way? Read on:

- To fill a selection with the foreground color, press Alt+Backspace (Option+Delete on a Mac).

- To fill a selection with the background color, press Ctrl+Backspace (⌘+Delete on a Mac).

- When you're working on a layer and want to fill the opaque part of a selection with the foreground color and leave the rest of the selection transparent, press Shift+Alt+Backspace (Shift+Option+Delete on a Mac). Press Ctrl+Shift+Backspace (⌘+Shift+Delete on a Mac) to fill the opaque area with the background color. (And if all this makes no sense at all, you may want to turn to Chapter 9, which explains layers and transparency.)

- Choose Edit⇨Fill to display the Fill dialog box, which also lets you fill the selection with translucent color or a pattern.

- Drag with the Gradient tool to create a gradient (a gradual blend) between two or more colors.

Two of these options — Edit⇨Fill and the Gradient tool — require more discussion, which is why the rest of this chapter is so filled to the gills with text.

Fill, I Command You!

Choose Edit⇨Fill to display the Fill dialog box, shown in Figure 15-3. The Use drop-down menu lets you specify the color or stored image with which you want to fill the selection; the Blending options let you mix the filled colors with the colors already inside the selection. We discuss all these options in more detail in this section.

You can also display the Fill dialog box by pressing Shift+Backspace (Shift+Delete on a Mac).

Figure 15-3:
Specify how you want to fill a selection by using the options in the Fill dialog box.

Fill

Contents
Use: Foreground Color

Custom Pattern:

OK
Cancel
Help

Blending
Mode: Normal
Opacity: 100 %
☐ Preserve Transparency

Selecting your stuffing

The most important part of the Fill dialog box is the Use drop-down menu. Here you select the stuff you want to use to fill the selection. The options are as follows:

- The Foreground Color option fills the selection with the foreground color, and the Background Color option fills the selection with the background color. Hopefully you're not surprised by this news.

- The next option, Pattern, fills a selection with a repeating pattern. You can define a pattern by selecting a rectangular area and choosing Edit⇔Define Pattern. If you don't define a selection, Elements creates the pattern from the entire canvas. You can access the patterns you've created, along with a variety of preset patterns, via the Custom Pattern drop-down menu.

- The last three options — Black, 50% Gray, and White — fill the selection with black, medium gray, and white, respectively. What's the point? Not much. If the foreground and background colors are set to blue and orange and you don't want to change them, you may find these options useful. And pigs may fly. You just never know.

Mixing colors the wrong way

You can enter a value into the Opacity option box of the Fill dialog box to mix the fill color or pattern with the present colors in the selection. You can also mix the fill and the selected color using the options in the Mode drop-down menu, which include Multiply, Screen, Difference, and other wacky blend modes (see Chapter 13).

Notice that we said you *can* do these things, not that you should. The truth is, you don't want to use the Fill dialog box's Blending options to mix fills with selections. Why? Because the Fill dialog box doesn't let you preview the effects of the Blending options. Even seasoned professionals have trouble predicting the exact repercussions of Opacity settings and blend modes, and it's likely that you will, too. And, if you don't like what you get, you have to undo the operation and choose Edit⇔Fill all over again.

The better way to mix fills with selections is to copy the selection to a new layer, fill it, and experiment with the Opacity slider and mode options in the Layers palette. Naturally, you have no idea what this means if you haven't read the supremely insightful Chapters 9 and 13. Until you do, take this valuable advice and be content to ignore the Opacity and Mode options in the Blending area at the bottom of the Fill dialog box.

The Preserve Transparency check box comes into play when you're working on a layer other than the Background layer, as discussed in Chapter 9. If the check box is turned on, only the opaque pixels in a selection are filled when you apply the Fill command — the transparent areas remain transparent. If the check box is turned off, the entire selection is filled. The option is dimmed if the Preserve Transparency option in the Layers palette is turned on.

Gradients: The Ever-Changing Color Sea

The Gradient tool lets you fill a selection with a fountain of colors that starts with one color and ends with another. By default, the two colors are the Foreground color and Background color.

But Elements can do more than create simple two-color blends. You can create custom gradients that blend a multitude of colors and vary from opaque to transparent throughout the blend. Elements has five gradient types: Linear, Radial, Angle, Reflected, and Diamond. And the Options bar offers settings that enable you to play with blend modes, opacity, and color reversals.

Checking out the Gradient tool

The following steps provide one of those in-depth introductions to the Gradient tool that folks find so helpful nowadays:

1. **Select some portion of your image.**

   In Figure 15-4, we selected the jar again. Just love that jar. It's so pristine; it just begs to be messed up.

   If you don't select a portion of your image before using the Gradient tool, Elements fills the entire image with the gradient. (Or, if you're working on a layer, as discussed in Chapter 9, the gradient fills the entire layer.)

2. **Select the Gradient tool.**

   To do it quickly, just press the G key.

3. **From the Options bar, select your desired gradient type.**

4. **If necessary, select the Foreground to Background option, the first swatch, from the Gradient Picker drop-down palette in your Options bar.**

   It creates a gradient that begins with the Foreground color and ends with the Background color.

Figure 15-4:
The
vegetables
inside the
jar have
been
replaced
with a
black-to-
white
gradient.

Gradient Picker drop-down palette

5. **Set the Foreground and Background colors the way you want them.**

   This step is up to you. You can use black and white or select new colors with the Eyedropper tool or Color Picker. For the purposes of Figure 15-4, the colors are set to black and white.

6. **Begin dragging at the point where you want to set the Foreground color.**

   In Figure 15-4, the drag began at the bottom of the jar.

7. **Release where you want to position the Background color.**

   In this case, it was the top of the jar. The result is a black-to-white gradation.

 If you Shift+drag with the Gradient tool, Elements constrains the direction of your drag to a horizontal, vertical, or 45° diagonal angle.

Changing the way of the gradient

You can mess around with the performance of the Gradient tool by accessing the settings in the Options bar (refer to Figure 15-4).

 Like the Opacity settings and Modes available inside the Fill dialog box, the Opacity and Mode options inside the Options bar for each of the gradients are best ignored. If you want to mix a gradation with the existing colors in a selection, create the gradation on a layer and select options inside the Layers palette, as discussed in Chapter 13.

Choosing among the five gradient tools

As stated at the beginning of this section, Elements gives you five gradient tools (see Figure 15-5):

- ✔ **Linear:** Creates a gradient in which colors blend in a straight line.

- ✔ **Radial:** The colors blend in concentric circles, from the center outward.

  Note: In every example in Figure 15-5, the Foreground color is black and the Background color is white. You almost always want to set the lighter color to the Foreground color when using the Radial option because doing that creates a glowing effect. If the Foreground color is darker than its Background compatriot, the gradation looks like a bottomless pit as you can see from the radial gradient shown in Figure 15-5.

- ✔ **Angle:** Creates a conical gradation with the colors appearing counter-clockwise.

- ✔ **Reflected:** If dragged from edge to edge of your selection, a reflected gradient acts like a linear gradient. However, if dragged from the interior to an edge of the selection, the gradient reflects back on itself.

- ✔ **Diamond:** Like the radial gradient, this tool creates concentric shapes — in this case, diamonds or squares, depending on the angle you drag.

Linear   Radial

Figure 15-5:
Jar filled
with five
different
gradient
types —
Linear,
Radial,
Angle,
Reflected,
and
Diamond.

Angle   Reflected   Diamond

Choosing gradient options

You find three check boxes in the Options bar: Dither, Transparency, and Reverse.

- ✔ **Dither:** The Dither check box is easy. When turned on, it helps eliminate banding. *Banding* is a problem in which you can see distinct bands of color in a printed gradient — that's a bad thing in 9 out of 10 households. Leave the check box turned on unless you're feeling especially contrary and want to create a banding effect.

- ✔ **Transparency:** The Transparency check box is a little more complicated. Here's the scoop: Gradients can include areas that are partially or fully transparent. In other words, they fade from a solid color to a more transparent color. When the Transparency check box is turned off, Elements creates the gradient by using all opaque colors, ignoring the transparency information.

  The best way to get a grip on what the Transparency check box does is to try a little experiment. First, turn on the check box and press D to get the default Foreground and Background colors. Then, choose the Transparent Rainbow option, the next to last swatch, from the Gradient Picker drop-down palette and draw a gradient. You get a fill pattern that consists of a multicolored rainbow with your background peeking out at the beginning and end of the gradient. Next, draw the gradient with the Transparency check box turned off. You now get a fill of a multicolored rainbow with no background peeking out because Elements is ignoring the transparency at either end of the gradient. In most cases, you don't need to bother with the check box — just leave it turned on.

- ✔ **Reverse:** When the Reverse check box is checked, the gradient will start with the Background color and end with the Foreground color. This option is useful for creating radial gradients while keeping the default colors intact.

Selecting your colors

The Gradient Picker drop-down palette lets you change the way colors blend inside the gradation and select from a variety of prefab gradients. Here's a description of those gradients:

- ✔ **Foreground to Background:** Normally, this option is selected. It does just what it sounds like it does: It blends between the Foreground and Background colors, as in the examples in Figure 15-5.

- ✔ **Foreground to Transparent:** If you select this option, the gradient tool blends the Foreground color into the original colors in the selection. The examples in Figure 15-6 were created with this option selected.

Figure 15-6:
Here's the
jar filled
with a linear
and radial
gradient and
with the
Foreground
to
Transparent
option
selected.

Linear

Radial

Foreground to Transparent

- ✔ **Remaining options:** The rest of the options in the Gradient Picker drop-down palette create a variety of factory-made gradients, some involving just a few colors and others blending a whole rainbow of colors.

- ✔ **Gradient libraries:** You also have at your disposal a vast array of gradient libraries, which have preset gradients that you can easily load for your painting pleasure. Simply click on the Gradient Picker arrow to access the drop-down palette. Click on the palette drop-down menu and scroll down to the bottom where you find the various gradient libraries. Select one and either replace or append to your current gradient set.

When you select a gradient from the drop-down palette, Elements displays the gradient in the Gradient Preview in the Options bar, as labeled earlier in Figure 15-4.

If none of the existing gradients suits your taste, you can create your own custom gradient, as in Color Plate 15-1. The next section explains the ins and outs of building your own gradients.

Like with the Color Swatches menu, you can view your gradients by thumbnails, text only, or a combination of both text and thumbnails.

Becoming a gradient wizard

It's pretty easy to design your own custom gradient if you just spend a few moments to dissect and understand the various parts of the Gradient Editor dialog box. Start out by clicking on the Edit button to the right of the Gradient Preview in the Options bar. The Gradient Editor dialog box, shown in Figure 15-7, appears. Uh-oh. Looks like you've ventured too far into geek space, doesn't it?

Gradient palette   Gradient preview bar

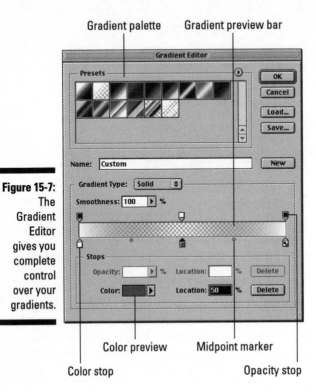

Figure 15-7:
The
Gradient
Editor
gives you
complete
control
over your
gradients.

Color preview   Midpoint marker

Color stop   Opacity stop

The Gradient Editor dialog box is a bit complex, and chances are you won't use it much. But the following list gives you a brief introduction to the dialog box and starts you off on creating your own gradient:

- **Presets:** The palette at the top of the dialog box lists all the preset gradients — the same ones in the Gradient Picker drop-down palette in the Options bar. Select the gradient you want to use as a starting point for your custom gradient from this palette. It doesn't much matter which you choose; you can change it to your heart's content.

- **Gradient Type:** You can choose between gradients made with Solid colors or those created with Noise. Noise gradients add noise that randomizes the colors of selected pixels and produces some interesting, yet unpredictable results.

- **Smoothness:** Drag the slider or enter a value to determine how smoothly you blend one color into another color. The Smoothness slider changes to a Roughness slider when you select a Noise gradient type.

- **Roughness:** This option is only available if you choose a Noise gradient. Roughness affects how smoothly or sharply one color transitions into another.

The following options are only available when the Noise gradient type is selected:

- ✔ **Color Model and Color Sliders:** Enable you to change the color model and or limit the color range by moving the sliders.

- ✔ **Restrict Colors:** Keeps colors from becoming too saturated.

- ✔ **Add Transparency:** Enables you to incorporate transparency in your noise gradient.

- ✔ **Randomize:** Changes the colors in a noise gradient. Remember, it is *random* and every time you click, you get a new set of colors. Better than watching reruns on T.V.

- ✔ **Stops:** The little house-shaped boxes on either side of the fade bar are called *stops*. There are color stops on the bottom and opacity stops on the top. You use these stops to change the colors, opacity, and location of colors in the gradient, as explained in the upcoming two sections.

- ✔ **Gradient Preview bar:** Displays both the colors and transparent areas of your gradient. Traditional gray-and-white checkerboard pattern represent transparent areas.

Gradients can be managed just like Swatches, as discussed in Chapter 5. It's important to save your gradient to disk if you want to be able to use it again later.

To remove a gradient from the list, press Alt+Shift (Option+Shift on a Mac) and click on the gradient. Note that the scissors icon signifies "delete."

Changing, adding, and deleting colors

To change one of the colors in the gradient, first check to see whether the roof on that color's color stop is black. The black *roof* indicates the active color stop — the color that is to be affected by your changes. If the roof isn't black, click on the color stop to make it active.

After you activate the color stop, you have one of three choices. You can click on the Color Preview, which brings up the Color Picker. Or you can access the Foreground or Background color from the Color pop-up menu. You also have the Eyedropper at your disposal so you can click on a color in your image or a color in the Swatches palette.

If you select the color via the Foreground or Background color options, you change the color marked by the color stop to the Foreground or Background color, respectively. Keep in mind that if you change the Foreground or Background color, the color in the gradient changes automatically. The change doesn't affect gradients that you've already drawn, but it does affect any future gradients you create. However, you can always select the color stop and choose User Color from the Color pop-up menu, which leaves the Foreground or Background color but untags it as such so no changes can occur.

Here's some more stuff you need to know about playing with the colors in your gradient:

- ✔ To add a color to the gradient, click just below the Gradient Preview bar at the point where you want the color to appear. You get a new color stop icon representing the color.

- ✔ To remove a color from the gradient, drag its color stop down and away from the Gradient Preview bar.

- ✔ If you drag a color stop to the right or left, you can change the position of the color in the gradient. Suppose that you have a gradient that fades from black to white. If you want more black and less white, drag the black color stop toward the white stop.

- ✔ The little diamonds on top or underneath the Gradient Preview bar represent the midpoint between two colors or two opacity settings. Using the example of a black-to-white gradient again, the midpoint marks the spot at which the gradient contains equal amounts of black and white. To move a midpoint, just drag the diamond.

- ✔ The Location option box shows the placement of the active color stop or midpoint marker. If you want to be terribly precise, you can enter a value into the Location box to position a color stop or midpoint marker instead of dragging the icons.

   When a color stop is active, a value of 0% represents the very beginning of the gradient; 100% represents the very end. Midpoint values are always relative to the two color stops on either side of the midpoint. A value of 50% places the midpoint an equal distance from both color stops. For reasons unknown, the minimum and maximum Midpoint values are 5% and 95%.

Changing the transparency

Hold on to your beanies — now we're really veering into the land of the propeller heads. Elements lets you adjust the amount of opacity in a gradient. You can make a portion of the gradient fully opaque, completely transparent, or somewhere in between the two.

Suppose that you want to create a gradient that starts out white, gradually fades to completely transparent, and then becomes completely white again. In other words, you want to create a variation of the effect shown back in Figure 15-6. Here's how to create such a gradient:

1. **Make the Foreground color white.**

2. **Click on the Edit button in the Options bar to bring up the Gradient Editor dialog box.**

3. **Inside the Gradient Editor dialog box, choose the Foreground to Transparent (the second swatch) gradient from the Gradient palette.**

4. **Take the opacity stop on the right and move it to the center of the Gradient Preview bar. Leave the Opacity setting at 0% (completely transparent).**

5. **Add another opacity stop at the far right. Change the Opacity setting to 100% (completely opaque).**

   The Gradient Preview bar now shows your gradient in terms of transparent and opaque areas. Black stops represent opaque areas; white stops represent transparent areas; gray areas represent everything in between. The Gradient Preview bar also shows you the opaque areas in their actual colors and transparent areas in the gray-and-white checkerboard pattern.

6. **Name your gradient.**

7. **Click on New.**

   Your gradient, with its new name, is added to the palette of gradients above. You now have a gradient that fades from fully opaque white to transparent and back to fully opaque white. Apply the gradient to an image to get a better idea of what you just created. Wow, that's exciting, huh?

   It's tempting to press Enter (Return on a Mac) after you change the Opacity value, but don't — pressing Enter (Return on a Mac) closes the dialog box. The value you enter into the Opacity setting takes effect without a press of the Enter (Return on a Mac) key. To switch to another option, press Tab.

You can also add as many opacity stops as you want and set different Opacity values for each. To move an opacity stop, just drag it right or left. To delete a stop, drag it off the bar. To move a midpoint, drag it right or left.

The Transparency check box in the Options bar determines whether transparency settings are ignored when you apply a gradient. If the check box is turned off, your gradient is completely opaque. For example, if you turn off the check box when applying the gradient created by the preceding steps, you get a completely white gradient instead of one that fades from white to transparent and back again.

Taking on Borders with the Stroke command

The last item on today's agenda is Edit➪Stroke, a command that traces borders around a selection. When you choose this command, Elements displays the Stroke dialog box, shown in Figure 15-8. Enter the thickness of the border you want into the Width option box. This value is measured in pixels, and the range is 1 to 250 pixels.

You can, however, enter units other than pixels. For example, if you type in **"2 in"** Elements accepts it and converts the value in inches to an equivalent number of pixels.

Figure 15-8:
Use the
Stroke
dialog box
to draw a
border
around a
selection.

In Figure 15-9, for example, a 16-pixel wide black stroke was placed around the jar. Then using the same selection, an 8-pixel wide white stroke was placed on top of that. Slick, huh? (Oh, come on, say it is, even if it's just to make us feel better.)

You can also pick a color from within the Stroke dialog box. Simply click on the color swatch, and you are transported to the Color Picker. No more slapping yourself on the head for not picking the right color beforehand. Note that changing the color in the Stroke dialog box changes the Foreground color as well.

Figure 15-9:
The classic double-border effect so demand at today's finer jar emporiums.

How the border rides the track

The Location options in the Stroke dialog box determine how the border rides the selection outline. The border can cruise around fully inside or fully outside the selection, or it can sit astride (centered on) the selection. Why might you want to change this setting? Well, take another look at Figure 15-9. Suppose that instead of the white border being flanked on either side by black (which was created using the Center option), you want the borders to sit beside each other. If you select the Inside option, the white border appears inside the selection, and the black border inside the white border. If you select Outside, the white border traces the outside of the jar, and the black border extends even farther.

Actually, using the Outside option isn't recommended. It has a nasty habit of flattening the edges of curves. For the best results, stick with Inside or Center.

Mix your stroke after you press Enter (Return)

Like the Blending and Opacity options in other dialog boxes, the ones in the Stroke dialog box don't provide you with a preview of how the effect will look when applied to your image. So, if you want to play with the blend modes or opacity of your stroke, ignore the options in the dialog box. Instead, create a new layer (as explained in Chapter 9) and do your selecting and stroking on that layer. You can then adjust the blend mode and opacity via the Layers palette (as discussed in Chapter 13).

On the off chance that you're curious about the Preserve Transparency check box, it affects only images with layers. If you don't have any layers going, don't worry about it. (Again, we explain layers in Chapter 9.) Even if your image does contain layers, don't worry about this option. It just ensures that the transparent portions of layers remain transparent.

We explore the Stroke command more in the next chapter, where we cast a penetrating gaze at the world of type inside Elements. So keep reading if you're curious, or go ahead and take a breather if you need it. We promise not to go ahead without you.

Chapter 16

Type Righter

Chapter 8 leads you on a merry tour of the various tools and commands for selecting a part of your image. But that chapter skips one other type of selection outline that you can create in Photoshop Elements, and you'll never guess what it is. Not in a million years. Give up? The answer is *text*. That's right, Elements lets you build a selection outline out of numbers, vowels, consonants, and any other characters you can tap in from your keyboard.

The Elements approach to text makes it an ideal program for subjecting large letters to special effects. The bigger your text, the better it looks. On the other hand, you shouldn't mistake Elements for a word processor. Even though Elements deals with text admirably, don't attempt to use it to create large chunks of text; instead, use a desktop publishing program like PageMaker, InDesign, or QuarkXPress.

Working with the Type Tool

Elements actually gives you two Type tools in the Toolbox: one for Horizontal Type and one for Vertical Type. The Vertical Type tool is great for Asian fonts, but for Roman letters it probably won't be very valuable to you. And anyway, after creating horizontal letters it's a snap to switch them to vertical letters if you need to.

You select the Type tool by pressing the T key on your keyboard. (The icon for the tool even looks like the letter T, making this the only tool that serves as its own tool tip.) Here's a briefing on the Type tool:

Figure 16-1:
The Type tool and its changing array of options.

✔ **Create a Text Layer:** When using this option (see Figure 16-1), the Type tool creates text on a new text layer (Chapter 9 explains layers in excruciating detail), which enables you to work with the text without worrying about touching the underlying image.

You can edit the text contents and attributes by simply highlighting the text with the Type tool. Although you can't use painting or editing tools on a text layer, you can make the text more or less translucent by adjusting the Opacity percentage in the Layers palette, and you can blend the text with the underlying layers using the Blend Modes drop-down menu.

✔ **Create a Selection:** This option (see Figure 16-1) enables you to create your text as a selection outline. You can manipulate, edit, paint, and otherwise play with the selection outline as you can with any other selection outline. And because the Type tool with the selection option works like any other selection tool, you can use it to add to or subtract from an existing selection outline (see Chapter 8). Note that you can't edit selection type like you can regular type created with the Type tool.

So, which option do you use when? If you want to retain true editability, obviously, use the Create a Text Layer option. Otherwise, it depends on what sort of effect you're trying to create. If you simply want opaque type, again use the Create a Text Layer option. If, on the other hand, you want to create character outlines, such as those shown in Figure 16-4, use the Create a Selection option and then stroke the selection outline using Edit⇨Stroke.

Just remember that the basic difference between the two options is that one creates editable type on a new text layer and the other gives you a selection outline in the shape of your characters. Pick the option that gives you the quickest route to the effect you're trying to achieve.

The biggest disadvantage of the Type tool with the Create a Selection option is that when you deselect the text selection, the text becomes permanently fused to the underlying image. But you can get around this problem by creating a new layer in the Layers palette before you click with the Type tool with the Create a Selection option. Now, any text you create exists on its own layer so that you can easily move, rotate, paint, and so on. Remember, however, that a regular layer is not the same as a text layer. A text layer provides for editability of contents and attributes. Read on!

Putting Your Words Onscreen

To type a few letters in Elements, select the Type tool and click inside the image. It doesn't really matter where you click, by the way. Elements positions your text at the spot you click. However, you can always move the text after you create it. You get a little blinking cursor (called an *insertion marker*) that you may be familiar with from working in other programs. After the insertion marker appears, you're free to enter your text.

Typing what must be typed

After you "commit" your text by pressing Enter (Return on a Mac) or by clicking the Commit button in the Options bar, you've created a text layer. In the Layers palette you'll notice a layer with a capital letter T icon indicating that it is indeed a text layer. The name of the text layer corresponds to the text you typed.

Here are a few more things you may need to know while inputting text on your canvas. We'll look at formatting a little later in the section "Changing how the type looks."

 ✔ After entering your text, you may find that you've made a mistake or two. To delete a letter, click after it and press the Backspace key (Delete key on a Mac). To add text, click at the point where you want to insert it and enter the new text from the keyboard. To delete more than one letter, highlight the letters and press the Backspace key (Delete key on a Mac).

✔ To replace text, drag over it with the cursor to highlight it and then start whacking those keys.

✔ Elements places all words on a single line in the image unless you insert a hard return by pressing the Enter key (Return key on a Mac). To achieve the effect shown in Figure 16-1, for example, press the Enter key (Return key on the Mac) between "Poems" and "by Slim."

While typing and editing your text, you can use the Cut, Copy, Paste, and Undo commands under the Edit menu, as well as the Cut, Copy, and Paste buttons in the Shortcuts bar. This enables you to fix mistakes in case you typed some letters or words out of order. For example, to move some letters from one place to another, follow these steps:

1. **Highlight the text you want to move.**

   Drag over the text with the I-beam cursor.

2. **Press Ctrl+X (⌘+X on a Mac) or click the Cut button in the Shortcuts bar.**

   Elements removes the text and puts it in a special location in your computer's memory called the *clipboard*. Ctrl+X (⌘+X on a Mac), by the way, is the shortcut for the Edit⇨Cut command.

3. **Click at the point where you want to move the text.**

   Your click repositions the insertion marker.

4. **Press Ctrl+V (⌘+V on a Mac) or click the Paste button in the Shortcuts bar.**

   Ctrl+V (⌘ +V) is the shortcut for the Edit⇨Paste command. Elements retrieves the text from the clipboard and inserts it at the desired spot.

If you want to duplicate a word, highlight it; then click the Copy button in the Shortcuts bar, choose Edit⇨Copy, or press or Ctrl+C (⌘+C on a Mac); reposition the insertion marker; and choose Paste. You can also undo the last edit by choosing Edit⇨Undo or by pressing Ctrl+Alt+Z (⌘+Option+Z).

Changing how the type looks

The Options bar provides all the typographic options needed to format your text. These options control the typeface, the type size, the type color, alignment, and all that other rigmarole. When all these characteristics get together in the same room, they're usually called *formatting attributes*. You can, of course, make additional enhancements to the appearance of your text after you return to the image window, but the formatting options let you set up the fundamental stuff.

Here are some things to keep in mind when exploring the Type tool options:

- ✔ In order to change the attributes of your text, the Type tool must be active. If you want to change only a portion of your text, highlight it with your Type tool. If you want to select all the text, either highlight all of it or simply have that particular text layer selected in the Layers palette.

- ✔ If you know what you want, you can always establish your formatting attributes *before* you create your type. Who knows, you may get it exactly right the first time around with no need for further editing.

- ✔ Select a typeface from the Font drop-down menu. Select a style from the Font Style drop-down menu. Assuming that you installed Elements correctly, type styles such as bold and italic (sometimes referred to as "oblique") appear in their own submenus.

- ✔ In order to successfully use PostScript fonts in Elements, you must be using ATM (that's Adobe Type Manager, not Automatic Teller Machine or Arbitrary Toaster Molester). If your text comes up smooth and beautiful, not to worry. If your text is so jagged that it looks like you drew it on an Etch A Sketch — as in the case of "Bad type" in Figure 16-2 — something's wrong. Either use a different font or consult with your local computer know-it-all to figure out the problem. You may also see jagged type if your image is of low resolution (details on resolution in Chapter 4) and you have your Anti-aliasing option turned off. Fortunately, you can remedy this by increasing the resolution of your image (again consult Chapter 4 on how to do this correctly) and by turning on Anti-aliasing in the Options bar.

- ✔ Enter the size of the text into the Font Size option box. The Size value is measured in points (one point equals $\frac{1}{72}$ inch), pixels, or millimeters, depending on the setting in your Preferences dialog box (Edit⇨Preferences⇨Units & Rulers).

Figure 16-2:
If your text looks smooth (top), super. If not (bottom), try a different font or ask your local computer guru for help.

Good type
Bad type

✔ If you want to squash or stretch your text, switch over to the Move tool and drag one of the squares on the bounding box. You can then switch back to the Type tool and, amazingly enough, the text is still editable. It's best, however, to use this option sparingly or else you run the risk of totally destroying the appealing proportions of a typeface. Most typefaces have been designed by trained artists who spend their lives perfecting the shape and form of each letter. Not that you should feel guilty or anything.

✔ In case your font doesn't have a built-in bold or italic state, the Text Options give you access to Faux Bold and Faux Italic. You can also choose to underline your text, or strike through it for that "pretend you can't read this" look.

✔ By default, the color that first appears in the Character palette is the current foreground color. To change the color before you create the text, you can use the Swatches palette or the Color Picker, which you can access by clicking on either the Foreground swatch in the Toolbox or the color swatch in the Options bar. (If you need a basic color refresher, see Chapter 5.)

✔ Select an alignment option to determine whether multiple lines of text are aligned by their left edges, right edges, or centers.

✔ You can mix most formatting attributes within the same text layer, but alignment is one attribute that cannot be mixed.

There are a couple of options that can be found not only in the Options bar, but also in the Type submenu of the Layer menu:

✔ **Horizontal/Vertical:** This text orientation option lets you switch horizontal text to vertical text, and vice versa.

✔ **Anti-aliasing:** You almost always want to select Anti-aliasing because if you don't, your text will have tiny jagged edges, and you probably don't want that.

✔ **Warp Text:** This feature is so neat it deserves its own section. So read on.

Warping type into strange and unusual shapes

Warping text in Elements is a little bit like the feature of path text found in drawing programs, such as Illustrator, Freehand, and CorelDraw. You can twist, push, and pull to create a variety of cool and crazy effects. Take a glance at Figure 16-3 to see a small sampling of these effects.

Arch   Flag

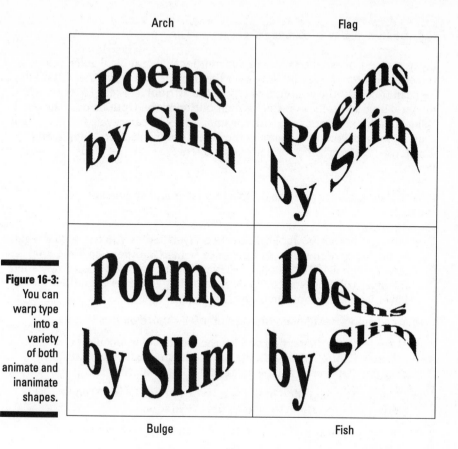

Figure 16-3:
You can
warp type
into a
variety
of both
animate and
inanimate
shapes.

Bulge   Fish

Follow these easy steps to warp your very own text:

1. **Select the text layer in the Layers palette.**

2. **Select the Type tool in the Toolbox and click on the Warp Text icon in the Options bar. Or choose Layer⇨Type⇨Warp Text (any tool can be active to choose this).**

3. **In the Warp Text dialog box, select a Style from the drop-down menu.**

4. **Play with the options.**

   Choose either Horizontal or Vertical orientation. Adjust the Bend to apply more or less warping. Use the Distortion sliders to apply perspective to the warp.

5. **If you're happy with your warp, click on OK.**

   Simple instructions, but in truth the secret to warping text is just playing around with the options. And luckily, it's such a fun command that you'll enjoy learning (imagine that).

Editing the Text Layer

If you notice a misspelled word or some other typographical gaffe, select the offending text layer and drag over the text with the Type tool to edit it. You can then edit the contents or any of the attributes. Press Enter on the numeric keypad or click on the Commit button in the Options bar. The great thing is that text layers save with the image, so you can revise the text at any time, as long as you don't simplify the layer (see the section "Simplifying a Text Layer" for more info) or flatten the layers (see Chapter 9 for more on layers).

Here are some things you can do to a text layer and still be able to edit the text:

✔ You can reorder or duplicate the text layer, just as you can with a regular layer. To move the layer in front of or behind another one, drag it up or down in the list of layers in the Layers palette. A black line shows where the layer will be inserted. To duplicate, drag the layer onto the New Layer icon at the bottom of the Layers palette.

✔ You can lock text layers (see Chapter 9 for more on this feature).

✔ Move or clone the text. Drag with the Move tool to position the text. Alt+drag (Option+drag on a Mac) to clone the text. Note that Alt+ dragging (Option+dragging on a Mac) creates another text layer.

✔ Change the orientation of the text layer. Choose Layer⇨Type⇨ Horizontal or Vertical to change the orientation.

✔ You can apply any of the blend modes and adjust the opacity of the Text layer.

✔ Perform transformation commands, such as Free Rotate, Scale, and Skew, as found in the Image menu under the Rotate, Resize, and Transform submenus. Distort and Perspective transformations aren't available to text layers.

✔ Apply Layer Styles (see details in Chapter 13) to the text layer. Even after you apply the effect, if the type changes in any way (such as a different font or even a different word), the layer style magically updates to the changes.

✔ Fill the type with the foreground or background color by using the Fill command keyboard shortcuts. Press Alt+Backspace (Option+Delete on a Mac) to fill with the foreground color. Press Ctrl+Backspace (⌘+Delete on a Mac) to fill with the background color. Note that the Edit⇨Fill menu command is grayed out — you can only utilize the keyboard shortcuts.

Here are three things you can't do to a text layer, unless you simplify the text layer and convert it to a regular layer (see more about this in the next section):

✔ You can't use any of the painting and editing tools. When you hold the painting and editing tools over the text layer, you see a slashed circle symbol indicating "No can do!"

✔ You can't apply filters from the Filters palette.

✔ You can't apply effects from the Effects palette.

A text layer can't be created for images in indexed color or bitmap modes because these modes don't support layers of any kind — text or otherwise. Type created in these modes is treated like type created with the selection option and gets applied to the Background and cannot be edited. If you want type included in GIF images you're preparing for the Web, for example, be sure and wait until you finish compositing your layers and editing your type to convert the image to indexed color.

If you decide you don't want the text layer any longer, delete it by dragging the layer to the Trash icon at the bottom of the Layers palette (for help, see Chapter 9). You can also click on the layer name and then click on the Trash icon.

Simplifying a Text Layer

In order to apply a filter, effect, or paint on a text layer, you must first do what Elements calls *simplifying* the layer. Simplifying is actually just a sort of simpler word for *rasterizing;* it means to convert the text layer into a regular layer. To simplify a type layer, choose Layer⇨Simplify Layer. The type then acts as though it was created with the Create a Selection option. After simplifying, the type looks the same; however, you can no longer edit the type. Notice that the T icon isn't there anymore! So, a word of advice — be sure the text is exactly like you want it before you simplify the text layer because editing capabilities go down the drain.

Declaring Open Season on Type Selection Outlines

The first thing you may notice when you click with the Type tool with the Create a Selection option is the appearance of a funky pink overlay. And as you type, your letters will appear white. This is Elements' way of telling you that you are creating a kind of mask, where parts of the layer are masked off and can't be affected by editing. (And when you think about it, that's exactly what you do when you make any kind of selection.) When you press Enter on the numeric keypad or click Commit in the Options bar, the overlay disappears and the familiar marching ants of the selection appear. (See Chapter 8 for more on selections.) Now that your newly created type is there selected inside your image, you can do all kinds of things with it, including the following:

- ✔ To move a text selection outline, drag with the one of the selection tools or press the arrow keys to nudge the selection outline this way or that. You can no longer drag with the Type tool, but you can still use the arrows while the Type tool is active.

- ✔ To move or clone the text selection, use the same techniques you use to move or clone any other selection (refer to Chapters 8 and 9). Drag with the Move tool to move the text; Alt+drag (Option+drag on a Mac) to clone the text.

  In other words, selections that you create with the type selection option work just like any other selection.

- ✔ You can paint inside the text. After you paint inside the letters, you can use the edit tools to smear the colors, blur them, lighten them, and so on.

- ✔ You can fill the text with the Foreground color by pressing Alt+Backspace (Option+Delete on a Mac). To fill the text with the Background color, press Ctrl+Backspace (⌘+Delete on a Mac). To fill the text with a blend of colors, just drag across the text with the Gradient tool. It just couldn't be easier.

- ✔ You can apply a border around your type by choosing Edit⇨Stroke.

- ✔ Before you fill or stroke a selection outline, be sure that your text is positioned where you want it. You can't move the stroked text after you create it without leaving a hole on your layer. Ditto with any other painting or editing commands you apply to a text selection outline. That's why it's a good idea to create a new layer before you create your text selection outline. It enables you to move the text without affecting the underlying image.

- ✔ If you want to delete text that was created with the Create a Selection option — and you didn't create that text on its own layer — you need to undo your steps by using the History palette (see Chapter 7) to bring your image back to its pre-text appearance.

Tracing outlines around your letters

The following steps tell you how to create genuine outline type, like the stuff shown in Figure 16-4. You can see through the interiors of the letters, and you can make the borders as thick as you please. What more could you ask from life?

1. **Create a new layer.**

   You don't have to put your text on its own layer, but doing so makes it simpler to edit the text later on if necessary. To create a layer, click on the New Layer icon in the Layers palette, as discussed in Chapter 9.

2. **Select the Type tool in the Toolbox and the Create a Selection option in the Options bar.**

3. **Set the formatting attributes in the Options bar.**

4. **Click with the Type tool on your canvas.**

   Type away and then press Enter on the numeric keypad or click on the Commit button in the Options bar. Then move the text selection outline into the desired position by dragging it or nudging it with the arrow keys.

5. **Set the Foreground color to white.**

   You can do this quickly by pressing D to get default colors and then X to swap them.

6. **Make sure that the Lock Transparent Pixels check box in the Layers palette is deselected.**

   In the next step, you apply a stroke to the center of your selection outline (that is, with half the stroke appearing on the inside of the outline and half appearing on the outside). If you don't deselect the Lock Transparent Pixels check box, Elements doesn't let you paint on the layer.

7. **Choose Edit⇨Stroke, select the Center radio button, and enter 12 as the Width value.**

   After making your selections in the Stroke dialog box, press Enter (Return on a Mac). You now have a 12-pixel thick, white outline around your type. Depending on the size of your type, you may need to enter a value other than 12.

8. **Make black or some other dark color the Foreground color.**

9. **Choose Edit⇨Stroke and enter 4 as the Width value. Leave the Location at Center.**

   Then press Enter (Return on a Mac). Congratulations! You get the effect shown in Figure 16-4. If you created your text on a layer, as recommended back in Step 1, you can use the Move tool to reposition the text if needed. You can also play with the blend modes and Opacity slider in the Layers palette to change how the text blends with the underlying image.

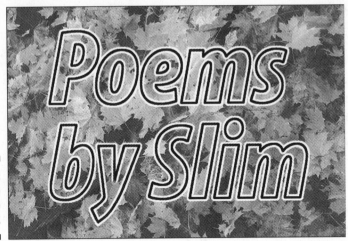

Figure 16-4:
Outline type
created the
correct way.

Text layers and layer styles go hand in hand. Once you've applied an inner bevel and drop shadow to a text layer, you probably won't ever be satisfied with plain ordinary flat text again. And don't forget that even with a layer style applied, text is still completely editable. Although why anyone would need to go back and edit his or her text is a compleet mistery.

Chapter 17

Can Photoshop Elements Do That?

· ·

· ·

*O*rganizing the many different functions of Photoshop Elements into the chapters of this book was like trying to herd a couple thousand weasels into 16 different pens, making sure they were all correctly sorted by gender, birth weight, IQ, religious persuasion, cholesterol level, and batting average. After a prolonged tussle, a great deal of squirming and wriggling, and much yanking from one pen and plopping down into another, things looked pretty good. Panting, exhausted, we turned around — and saw a few more danged weasels in the corner. These guys seemed to defy any classification. They were rebels. They refused to be pigeonholed — *weaselholed* — by The Man.

And so this, the 17th chapter, contains the weasels that wouldn't go into the 16 other pens.

On reflection though, it became clear that these seven weasels all had something in common: They all dealt with *automation*. The automation in six of these weasels — okay, these *features* — works just like you'd expect: You tell Elements what to do, say "Go!," and then sit back while Elements does it. And with the seventh feature, animated GIFs, the automation comes after the fact: Once the animated GIF is loaded in a Web user's browser, the animation plays back automatically.

Another thing these seven functions have in common: They're probably the most amazing stuff that Elements has to offer. Up to now, Elements has been a hands-on application, and necessarily so. Now it's time to sit back and watch. Prop your feet up. Take off your shoes. And put a pillow on your chest so you won't bruise your chin when your jaw drops open in amazement. This is the stuff that makes you say: "Can Photoshop Elements do *that?*"

Taking on the Effects Palette

That wacky Elements. It just can't help being a useful, educational application. Take the Effects palette, for instance. Not only does it contain 50 different options for creating frames, textures, and other special effects for your images — it's actually a mini Elements tutor in itself!

What's an effect?

An *effect,* in Elements' terminology, is a series of commands — combining filters with more mundane stuff like Filling and Image Sizing — that are pre-built and pre-recorded for your use. Like the Blur More and Sharpen More filters, effects are one-shot wonders — you just apply them, and if you don't like the end result, too bad. There's no tweaking allowed (at least, not until after the fact). Once the effect has played out and you can see the results, you are presented with a last chance "Do you wish to keep this Effect?" dialog box. You can chicken out and click No, or go ahead and click Yes. If you do click Yes, and then change your mind, be warned that you can't just click the Step Backward button once to get rid of the effect. You might have to click Step Backward literally dozens of times to completely eradicate the effect. Why? Because each individual step of an effect is recorded as a state in the History palette.

And that's where the educational aspect of the Effects palette comes in. After applying an effect, you can look in the History palette and get a general idea of how the effect was created. You won't know the precise settings of each filter used, but it can be very helpful to know that a particular effect was accomplished, for instance, with a combination of the Add Noise, Colored Pencil, and Emboss filters.

Here are a couple of caveats:

- ✔ You will need to increase the number of History States in the General panel of the Preferences in order to see all the steps for some effects. The Wild Frame effect, for example, goes through a staggering 34 steps to achieve the final result.

- ✔ Some of the states won't sound very familiar to you. This is proof positive that lurking under the hood of Photoshop Elements is none other than Adobe Photoshop itself. Some effects use steps like "Save Selection" and "Duplicate Channel," things that you can't do for yourself within Elements, but that are possible in Photoshop.

To apply effects

Applying effects from the Effects palette is almost identical to applying filters from the Filters palette. You have three options:

✔ Click the desired effect to select it, and then click the Apply button at the top of the palette.

✔ Double-click the desired effect.

✔ Drag the desired effect from the Effects palette into the image window.

Okay, we lied — there is one other way to apply an effect, and it goes for the Filters palette too. Instead of clicking the Apply button, you can also choose the Apply command from the palette menu located in the upper-right corner of the palette. Although why anyone would bypass the Apply button to go for the palette menu is completely beyond us.

There are four different categories of effects (or five if you count All):

✔ **Frames:** As you might expect, these effects can create a frame around your image. Some Frame effects will only operate if a pre-existing selection is active. As noted in Chapter 8, the Vignette effect is quite popular and attractive. Drop Shadow Frame would be a great choice for creating Web images where the Web page's background color was white. And Photo Corners is nice for that retro look.

✔ **Image Effects:** These are sort of a mixed bag. They perform a variety of different creative processes on your image, and work with either selected parts of images or entire layers. Fluorescent Chalk and Quadrant Colors perform their magic on the entire layer, regardless of whether there's an active selection. If you want the color in your image to gradually fade out to black and white, Horizontal Color Fade and Vertical Color Fade were made for you.

✔ **Text Effects:** Probably the most useful of the effects. They require a live text layer in order to work, so first create your text with the Create New Layer option in the Type tool's Options bar (see Chapter 16 for more information). While the three Outline effects can be a bit blocky, the other eight options are quite attractive. Use Brushed Metal to give your text a shiny look or Water Reflection to reflect your text in a photo of a body of water, as seen in Figure 17-1. Note that these effects automatically simplify your layer (see Chapter 16), so make sure you're through editing your text before you apply one of the Text Effects.

✔ **Textures:** You can create solid fields of different surfaces, from Bricks to Molten Lead to Sandpaper. The Ink Blots, Marbled Glass, Sunset, and Wood-Pine effects can only work on the entire layer, regardless of whether there's an active selection or not. To see the Textures effects in action, turn back to the color pages in the book. All the backgrounds behind the color plates are rendered out effects.

Figure 17-1:
Applying
Water
Reflection
from the
Effects
palette (left)
makes
Elements
perform
a pre-
recorded
series of
steps (as
detailed in
the History
palette,
center) to
create the
effect of text
reflecting in
the water
(right).

Batch Processing

If you've got a whole bunch of different images that you need to make con-
form in terms of file format and image size, the Batch command is just the
ticket. All you have to do is tell Elements where the files are, what you want
the common file format to be, whether you want it to make changes in image
size, and where to save the files. Click OK, and Batch does the rest.

Here's the step-by-step game plan:

1. **Choose File⇨Automate⇨Batch.**

   The Batch dialog box appears, as shown in Figure 17-2.

2. **Use the Files to Convert drop-down list to locate the images that you
   want to batch process.**

   Choose Folder if the images are already grouped together in a folder
   somewhere on your hard drive. Then click the Source button, navigate
   to the correct folder, select it, and click Choose. If you have other folders
   containing images inside your Source folder and you want to batch
   process those too, click the Include All Subfolders check box.

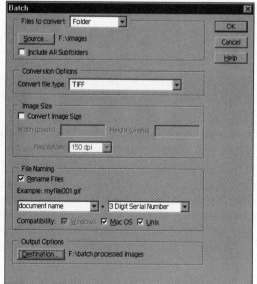

Batch

Figure 17-2:
The Batch
dialog box
lets you tell
Elements
everything it
needs to
know in
order to
process
your files.

Choose Import if you want to get the pictures from a scanner, a digital camera, or a PDF file. Pick your source on the From pop-up menu. When you click OK after choosing your other settings, Elements will take you to another dialog box, depending on the type of device and plug-ins you have installed. If you've chosen PDF file, you'll be asked to locate the file and then be given a chance to preview the images to be extracted from the PDF.

Choose Opened Files if you want to batch process all the currently opened files in Elements.

3. **Choose your desired file format from the Convert File Type drop-down menu.**

   You have Elements' usual long list of possibilities.

If you choose JPEG, the compression will be the same as if you were saving the files using the Save As command with JPEG compression set to Medium. (This might not be high enough for you, but there's no way to specify a different setting with the Batch command.) If you choose GIF, the settings will be as follows: Local (Selective) palette, 256 colors, forced Black and White, transparency on, Diffusion dither with an amount of 75 percent. This makes for relatively high-quality files, but you might be able to do fine with lower settings. Again, there's no way to specify other settings with Batch.

If you want to save your images as JPEGs, it's really better to use the Web Photo Gallery command covered later in this chapter to batch process the images, even if you have no intention of putting them on the Web. You can specify the amount of JPEG compression, and you can avoid the risk of resizing your images disproportionately. Once the Web Photo Gallery has run, look inside the "images" folder that has been created, and you'll see your newly compressed JPEGs, along with some GIF files that you can discard.

4. **Choose whether you want to change the image size or resolution.**

This can be a dangerous decision. Unless all your images have exactly the same aspect ratio (the width and height proportions of all the images are identical), clicking the Convert Image Size check box and entering specific Width and Height values will result in at least some of your images being stretched or squashed. If you are importing images from a digital camera, and you know that all the images are at the same ratio (say, 4 by 3), then it's okay to go ahead and specify proportional Width and Height values — for instance, 320 by 240, respectively.

The Resolution setting is safe to use, as it doesn't cause resampling of your image. See Chapter 4 for details.

5. **Specify a File Naming convention.**

If you want the files you're saving to have different names from the source files, click the Rename Files check box. It's necessary to have at least one of the document name, serial number, or serial letter options chosen, so that Elements doesn't overwrite each file in turn by giving it the same name as the last file. You can choose from the long lists of options, or type a name into one of the two fields. If these images are destined for the Web, it's a good idea to make sure you have all three Compatibility check boxes checked.

6. **Specify where you want the files to be saved.**

After clicking the Destination button in the Output Options section and navigating to the appropriate place on your hard drive, you might want to take the opportunity to click the Create New Folder button and save the batch-processed images into their own folder.

7. **Click the OK button, and sit back while Elements automatically processes the images according to your guidelines.**

Creating and Printing a Contact Sheet

Elements has the capability of creating a digital version of a traditional contact sheet. This feature takes a folder of images, creates thumbnails, and arranges them on a single page. It's good for record-keeping purposes because it enables you to catalog large quantities of files. It's also useful for merely checking out a big batch of images.

Here are the steps for creating and printing a contact sheet:

1. **Choose File⇨Automate⇨Contact Sheet II.**

   "So where's Contact Sheet I?" you may be wondering. Well, it's a sad, sordid story that you're better off not knowing. Trust us on this one.

2. **Click on the Choose button in the Contact Sheet II dialog box (see Figure 17-3).**

   Locate the folder containing the images you want to print. Count the number of images in your folder.

3. **Specify the size and resolution of the contact sheet.**

   Make sure to set the width and height large enough to accommodate all your images. If you are unsure about resolution, see Chapter 4 for details.

4. **Specify a color mode — RGB Color or Grayscale.**

   For information on color modes, see Chapter 5.

5. **Specify the order and the number of columns and rows for your layout in the Thumbnails section.**

   Again, be sure that the number of thumbnails you create can accommodate (or exceeds) the number of images in your folder.

6. **Choose whether you want to use the Filename As a Caption for your images.**

7. **Specify the Font and Font Size.**

8. **Press Enter (Return on a Mac) or click OK.**

   An automated process opens, copies, pastes, and positions each file. When the process is complete, you should see a file similar to the one in Figure 17-4.

Figure 17-3:
The Contact
Sheet
dialog box
presents
options for
size and
layout of
your
thumbnails.

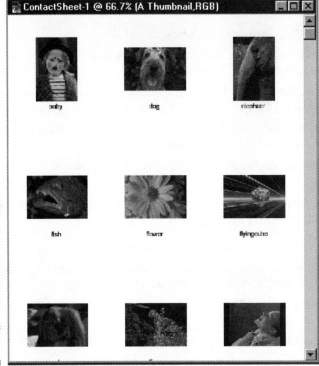

Figure 17-4:
Contact
sheets can
provide
a good
method for
cataloging
a large
quantity of
images.

Creating and Printing a Picture Package

Another Automate feature that may come in handy is Picture Package. This command fills a page with multiple copies of a single image, scaled to common print sizes, such as 5 x 7, 4 x 5, and wallet snapshots. Whether you're a professional photographer or just want to print some pictures of the kids for Grandma, this command does it all.

1. **Choose File➪Automate➪Picture Package.**

2. **Click on the Choose button in the Picture Package dialog box.**

   Locate your image.

3. **Choose your desired template from the Layout pop-up menu.**

   The preview gives you an idea of what the layout will look like.

4. **Specify a resolution and color mode.**

   Check out Chapter 4 for more information on resolution. For information on color modes, see Chapter 5.

5. **Press Enter (Return on a Mac) or click on OK.**

An automated process opens, copies, pastes, and positions each file. When the process is complete, you should see a file similar to the one in Figure 17-5.

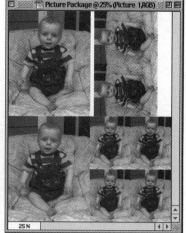

Figure 17-5: The Picture Package command can give you instant octuplets.

Creating a Web Photo Gallery

Elements offers one more command under the File⇨Automate submenu called Web Photo Gallery, which assembles a folder of images into a Web site, complete with HTML pages and JPEG images. You specify the name of your page, the size of the thumbnails, and the size and compression of the larger gallery images. As shown in Figure 17-6, your Web page isn't going to win any design awards, but it's easy to navigate and it gets the job done. And if you know a little HTML, you can use the pages as a jumping off point for a more sophisticated site.

Here are the various options involved in creating a gallery:

✔ Choose a style: You can display the various styles — Simple, Table, Horizontal Frame, and Vertical Frame — via the preview thumbnail in the dialog box.

✔ Choose settings under the various options:

• **Banner:** This is the title that appears at the top of the Web page and in the title bar. You can also specify photo credits and a date to appear on the page.

Figure 17-6:
The Web
Photo
Gallery
assembles
your images
into an
index of
thumbnails
(rear) and a
series of
pages for
the larger
gallery
images
(front).

- **Gallery Images:** This option establishes the settings for the individual image pages (the page that loads when the user clicks on a thumbnail). Specify the size of the border around each image if you wish. Choose whether to resize the images, and choose where to set the JPEG compression quality. If you choose one of the preset Resize Images options or enter a custom pixel amount, the number of pixels specified will be used as the largest dimension for the image. In other words, if an image is taller than it is wide and it is resized at 250 pixels, then the height will become 250 pixels and the width will be adjusted proportionally.

- **Gallery Thumbnails:** This option establishes the settings for the thumbnail index page. Specify the size of the thumbnails and the border around those images. You can also specify whether you want the file name to appear as a caption. If you've entered information for the file by choosing File⇨File Info and entering text into the Caption field, you can also have this text displayed as a caption.

  You can also specify how you want your thumbnails laid out in terms of rows and columns. (This pertains only to the Simple and Table Styles.) If you don't specify an adequate number of rows and columns for all your thumbnails to appear on one page, the index page will be broken down over multiple Web pages.

- **Custom Colors:** This option enables you to choose colors for all the various components of your Web page. Note that if the Table Style is used, Elements will use an attractive textured background for the site, and the Background and Banner color options won't apply.

✔ Specify your Source and Destination folders: Dump the images you want to appear in one Source folder and designate a new, empty folder for the Destination folder.

✔ After you click on OK, Elements does a little work on its own and then displays the Web page in your Web browser. Elements saves the HTML file and the JPEG images in your Destination folder.

Creating an Animated GIF

So you're tired of still, static images. You want excitement. Life. Movement. You're in luck, because Elements is not only an amazing tool for creating still images, but it's also not too shabby at animation either! Animated GIFs have been enlivening Web pages for quite a few years now, and Elements' Save for Web command makes creating them a breeze.

Chapter 9 mentions that the Layers palette works similarly to a multiplane camera, which is used in traditional cel animation. Indeed, the Layers palette holds the key for creating animated GIFs as well. Elements programs an animated GIF to display the different layers of the Layers palette in sequence, from bottom to top. If you plan your file correctly, so that each layer represents a point in time immediately after the layer below it, it's easy to build an animation in this way.

We're going to explain this feature by walking you through the creation of an actual animated GIF. We're going to create the effect of the word "motion" moving across the frame and stopping in the center. While we'll actually move the word across the frame progressively layer by layer, we'll also add the Motion Blur filter to heighten the effect.

1. **Create a new document.**

   We set ours to 600 pixels Width, 100 pixels Height, and Contents White.

2. **Type the word "motion" in the image with the Type tool.**

   Choose a highly contrasting color, like black.

3. **Simplify the layer.**

   Choose Layer➪Simplify Layer. This is necessary for when we apply the Motion Blur filter.

4. Duplicate the layer seven times.

We dragged the motion layer onto the Create New Layer icon seven times, as shown in the top-left image in Figure 17-7.

5. Apply the Motion Blur filter to the bottom motion layer.

The Motion Blur filter is in the Blur section of the Filters palette. Keep the Angle set to 0 degrees, and set the Distance to 70 pixels.

6. Apply the Motion Blur filter to each of the motion layers except the top copy, decreasing the Distance setting as you move up the layer stack.

We gave the first copy a Distance setting of 60, the next copy up a Distance of 50, and so on. You can hit Ctrl+Alt+F (@cmd+Opt+F on the Mac) to reapply the filter with access to the dialog box. Don't apply the filter to the top copy.

7. Select the Move tool and move the bottom motion layer to the left until only the very rightmost portion of the blurred text is showing. Move the layer above it to the left, but not quite as far. Keep moving up the stack, moving the layers progressively less far to the left, so that the next-to-the-top layer is barely moved at all. Leave the top layer where it is.

After you select the Move tool, use the left arrow key to nudge the layer to the left without moving it vertically. You can add the Shift key to the left arrow key to move the layer in ten-pixel increments. You'll probably need to turn on and off the visibility of layers to better see what you're doing.

8. Choose File⇨Save for Web.

The Save for Web dialog box appears. Adjust your GIF settings as desired (see Chapter 6 for details). To fill the transparent areas in the motion layers with white, set the Matte color to White. Click the Animate check box.

If you want the animation to play over and over, click the Loop check box. The Frame Delay setting determines how long in seconds each frame displays onscreen before it's replaced by the next frame. For this animation, 0.1 or 0.2 is a good setting.

You can view the frames by clicking the VCR-style buttons in the Animation section of the dialog box (see the bottom-left image in Figure 17-7). The far-left and far-right buttons take you to the beginning and end of the animation, respectively. The second button takes you back one frame, and the third button takes you forward one frame.

If you want to preview the animation in real time, click the Preview In box and select a browser. The browser will open up and play the animation. If you didn't set the animation to loop, you can click the Refresh or Reload button in the browser to watch it again.

9. **Click OK in the Save for Web dialog box.**

   You'll be asked where to save the GIF file. You can also save an HTML file to use in displaying the animation on the Web if you wish.

The image on the right in Figure 17-7 shows the nine frames that make up the final animation.

Figure 17-7: A carefully built file consisting of many layers (top left) is converted to an animated GIF using Elements' Save for Web command (bottom left). The frames from the final animation appear on the right.

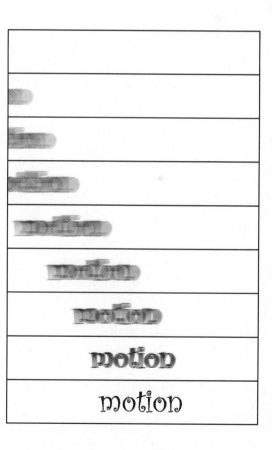

Creating Panoramic Pictures with Photomerge

And last, but certainly not least, we come to the one feature that just might make long-time Photoshop users want to plunk down a hundred bucks to buy Elements: the Photomerge command. Photomerge is an exclusive feature of Elements. What Photomerge does is simple in premise: If you shoot a group of photos, each capturing a section of a larger scene, Photomerge can automatically stitch them together into one big panoramic shot. And we do mean automatic; if the images are ideally framed, there's almost no work necessary on your part.

The effectiveness of Photomerge depends hugely on the suitability of the photos you're trying to unite. Images need to overlap, but not too much; Adobe recommends an overlap of between 30 to 50 percent. However, too much overlap can cause just as many problems. The best advice is to overshoot, taking more photos than you'll need, with large areas of overlap, and then removing the unnecessary ones once you're inside the Photomerge dialog box. While Photomerge can correct for rotational problems between images, photo sequences shot with a tripod yield the best results. Photomerge compositions don't have to be exclusively horizontal in nature; vertical shots of tall objects like buildings work well too.

Here's how to use the Photomerge command:

1. **Choose File➪Photomerge.**

   The first Photomerge dialog box appears.

2. **Click the Add button to select the photos you want to merge.**

   You can Shift+click images to select a group. When you've selected all the images you need, click Open. The images are added to the list. If you made any mistakes in selecting images, you can click on an image's name in the list and click the Remove button.

3. **Choose from the check boxes in the bottom of the dialog box.**

   By all means, check the Attempt to Automatically Arrange Source Images check box. At its best, Photomerge does an amazingly good job of analyzing the images and assembling them automatically. If there are problems, you'll get an error message telling you so — and that's usually a good sign that you'll also encounter difficulties in trying to assemble the panorama manually.

   It doesn't matter whether you check Apply Perspective, as you'll get a chance to apply it within the main Photomerge dialog box anyway. But we recommend not checking this option here, as it will give you a chance to see what your image looks like without perspective correction applied — and it might look just fine without it.

Applying some sort of Image size reduction is probably a good idea. Photomerge is a memory-intensive command, and it can encounter problems when dealing with large images. Remember that if you're trying to merge six photos taken in a horizontal line, and each image is 1,000 pixels wide, then your final panorama will be somewhere in the neighborhood of 4,000 pixels wide if you don't apply any Image size reduction. Using 50 percent usually yields good results, but if you're afraid that's too much reduction, at least give 75 percent a try.

4. When you've selected your images and chosen your options, click OK.

The magic begins. You can watch Photomerge opening up each of your images, shrinking it down, and then apparently pasting them all into a very long document. What's it doing? Who knows? But it's fun to watch.

You may have to wait a few minutes, depending on the number of images involved, but eventually the main Photomerge dialog box opens, as seen in Figure 17-8. You'll see Elements' best effort at assembling the photos in the large window. If it's encountered problems placing some of the images, those will be in the long horizontal box at the top of the window.

Figure 17-8:
The workspace of the Photomerge command gives you lots of ways to tweak the construction of your panoramic shot.

Photomerge has a Navigator window very similar to Elements' Navigator palette, which lets you zoom in and out on your image by clicking the buttons on either side of the slider or by dragging the slider itself. You can also reposition the view box to center in on the portion of the composition you need to see. The Move Image tool (in the upper-left grouping of tools) doesn't need to be fingerprinted for us to know that it's our old buddy the Hand tool in disguise; you can even hold down the spacebar to temporarily select it, and use it to drag the composition within the large window.

5. **If there are images in the top portion of the dialog box that you want to try to place into the composition, click on them with the default Select Image tool and drag them into the large window.**

   As you drag, by default the image will turn translucent so that it's easier to see how it might overlap with the other images. This "ghosting" can be turned off by switching the Dragging drop-down menu in the Tool Settings section from Ghost to Blend. The Snap to Image check box can also be deselected if you don't want Photomerge to try to help you place the image by "snapping" it to areas of similar pixel content. If an image you're trying to place needs to be rotated, click the Rotate Image tool (second from the top in the upper-left grouping of tools) and drag to rotate the image.

6. **Adjust the perspective of the composition if desired.**

   Adjusting perspective can help solve distortion problems within your composition. The wider your composition is, the more dramatic these problems can be. However, the composition can also be too wide for perspective correction to be effective.

   To adjust the perspective, first check the Use Perspective check box in the Tool Settings section of the dialog box. Then select the Set Vanishing Point tool (third from the top in the upper-left grouping of tools), and click an image in your composition. You will typically want to click the centermost image. If you're having trouble telling where one image stops and the next one starts, hold down the Alt key (the Option key on the Mac). A red outline will appear around the border of each image as you pass over it with the tool. Once you've clicked to set the vanishing point for your image, the image containing the vanishing point will have a light blue border instead of a red one.

7. **Adjust the Composition Settings.**

   One problem that perspective can introduce to your composition is the "bow tie" effect, where the overall composition is stretched tall on the edges and squeezed in the middle. Turning on Cylindrical Mapping can help untie the "bow tie" effect. Advanced Blending helps correct problems resulting from different exposures in adjacent images. The effects of the Composition Settings are only visible in Preview mode; click the Preview button to see the Cylindrical Mapping and Advanced Blending. Click Exit Preview to leave the preview.

If you want to go ahead and render your panorama but think you might want to come back to Photomerge for further tweaking, you can save the settings for your composition. Click the Save As button, give a name to your composition work area, and click OK. It's a good idea to save the composition file in the same folder with the source images. To load it again, choose File⇨Photomerge and click Open.

8. **When you're satisfied with your settings, click OK.**

Elements will work a little more magic, and then your finished panorama will appear onscreen. You'll probably need to crop the image to eliminate areas where the background shows behind the stitched photos.

While it's neat that Elements can automatically construct a panoramic image from a series of individual images, with almost no work on your part whatsoever, why can't it also perform the necessary cropping automatically? Gee, what a slacker.

Part V
The Part of Tens

The 5th Wave — By Rich Tennant

"THAT'S A LOVELY SCANNED IMAGE OF YOUR SISTER'S PORTRAIT. NOW TAKE IT OFF THE BODY OF THAT PIT VIPER BEFORE SHE COMES IN THE ROOM."

In this part . . .

◄ ◄ ◄ **W**e say goodbye, but not before we take a last, loving look at Photoshop Elements from a different angle. You've made it this far with us, as we've painstakingly sifted through the enormous mountain of Elements features and functions. You've gone from "What's a pixel?" to creating animated GIFs to liven up your Web site. Just getting through each tool and command has taken us a few hundred pages (eight of them in color), but we've done it. So what's left?

We start this final part with a chapter on ten important techniques to remember, all of them centering on easily forgotten keyboard shortcuts. From there, we look at ten ways to digitally screw up a person's face using Elements. And finally, we look at ten things you *can't* do with Elements, but you can do with Elements' almighty ancestor, Adobe Photoshop.

Catch the common thread? All three of the following chapters center around the number ten. Hence the title of this part of the book: The Part of Tens. Why tens? Well, we could tell you tales of Little Indians, fingers and toes, or Woodmen (okay, we guess that last one doesn't really count), but those would be nothing more than tales. The Part of Tens is the Part of Tens because it's a *Dummies* tradition, that's why. And to break with tradition, we'd have to be Dummies indeed.

Chapter 18

Ten Shortcuts to Commit to Long-Term Memory

*P*rofessor, politician, and Pulitzer Prize-winning author Odell Shepard once said, "Memory is what makes you wonder what you've forgotten." No doubt Odell — or Odie, as his friends called him — was talking about that feeling you get (usually when you're in bed, trying to sleep, or when you're on the way home from work and it's too late to turn back) that you've forgotten something that's pretty much going to send your life spinning into a state of absolute chaos. This feeling is commonly known as the Odie Syndrome.

Well, we can't help you with every aspect of your life, but we can help you with Photoshop Elements. Suppose, for example, that you wake up at 2 a.m. with the dreaded suspicion that you've forgotten an important Elements shortcut. You'd just have to give up on your technological pursuits and take up beet farming. But thanks to this chapter, people like you can live happy and productive lives again because these pages contain all of the most important Elements shortcuts. A few minutes of reading restores order in your life.

The following tips don't begin to address all of the many Elements shortcuts. For some additional time-savers, be sure to check out (or rip out) the Cheat Sheet at the front of this book.

Displaying and Hiding the Toolbox and Palettes

Tab

Just press the Tab key. The Toolbox, the Options bar, the Shortcuts bar, all the palettes, and the Status bar on the PC disappear, leaving just you and the image. To bring everything back, press Tab again. To make the Toolbox, Options bar, Shortcuts bar, Status bar, and palettes flash crazily onscreen and off, press Tab over and over again until your finger gets numb. It's not clear why you'd want to do this, but we like to spell out all the options.

If you want to hide the palettes but keep everything else visible, by the way, press Shift+Tab. Press Shift+Tab again to bring the palettes back.

If you have a dialog box open or an option in the Options bar active, Tab and Shift+Tab take you to the next option box or move you back one option box, respectively. But after you close the dialog box or deactivate the option, Tab and Shift+Tab control your palettes and Toolbox once again.

The F keys

Press F5 to display the File Browser, F6 for the Recipes palette, F7 for the Filters palette, F8 for the Effects palette, F9 for the Layer Styles palette, F10 for the History palette, F11 for the Layers palette, and F12 for the Hints palette. Press the key again to send the palette back into the palette well.

Changing an Option Box Value

Up arrow, down arrow

Activate the option box and use the up or down arrow key to raise or lower the value by 1. Press Shift+↑ or Shift+↓ to raise or lower the value by 10, respectively. Then press Enter (Return on a Mac) again to accept the new value.

Scrolling and Zooming

Spacebar

Press the spacebar to temporarily access the Hand tool. As long as the spacebar is down, the Hand tool is available. Spacebar+drag to scroll the image.

Ctrl+spacebar and Alt+spacebar (⌘+spacebar and Option+spacebar on a Mac)

To get to the Zoom In cursor, press Ctrl+spacebar (⌘+spacebar on a Mac). Pressing Alt+spacebar (Option+spacebar on a Mac) gets you the Zoom Out cursor. This means that you can magnify the image at any time by Ctrl+spacebar+clicking (⌘+spacebar+clicking on a Mac). To zoom out, Alt+spacebar+click (Option+spacebar+click on a Mac). You can also Ctrl+spacebar+drag (⌘+spacebar+drag on a Mac) to marquee an area and magnify it so that it takes up the entire image window.

Ctrl++ (plus) and Ctrl+– (minus) (⌘++ and ⌘+– on a Mac)

Another way to magnify or reduce the image is to press Ctrl++ (plus sign) (⌘++ (plus sign) on a Mac) to zoom in or Ctrl+– (minus sign) (⌘+– (minus sign) on a Mac) to zoom out.

Double-click on the Hand tool icon

To zoom the image so that you can see the whole thing on your monitor, double-click on the Hand tool icon in the Toolbox or press Ctrl+0 (zero) (⌘+0 on a Mac).

Double-click on the Zoom tool icon

To restore the image to the 100% (Actual Pixels) zoom factor, double-click on the Zoom tool icon or press Ctrl+Alt+0 (zero) (⌘+Option+0 on a Mac).

Shift+Enter (Shift+Return on a Mac)

When you change the zoom factor by using the Magnification box in the Status bar, press Shift+Enter (Shift+Return on a Mac) instead of Enter (Return on a Mac) after you enter a new zoom value. That way, the option box remains active after Elements zooms your image. If you need to further magnify or reduce your image, just enter a new zoom value from the keyboard. When you have the image at the magnification you want, press Enter (Return on a Mac) to finalize things.

This trick also works when you're using the Magnification box in the Navigator palette.

Changing the Brush Size

Left bracket ([)

For the round and fuzzy round brushes, press [(left bracket) to reduce the brush size in the following increments: 1 pixel increments to a size 10 pixel brush, 10 pixel increments to a size 100 pixel brush, 25 pixels to a size 200 pixel brush, 50 pixels to a size 300 pixel brush, 100 pixels to a size 900 pixel brush, and finally it jumps to the maximum of a 999 pixel brush.

Right bracket (])

For the round and fuzzy round brushes, press] (right bracket) to increase the brush size by the same increments listed in the preceding "Left bracket ([)" section.

Shift+[and Shift+]

Shift+[(left bracket) reduces the hardness of a brush in 25 percent increments. Shift+] (right bracket) increases the hardness in 25 percent increments.

Creating Straight Lines

Shift+click

To create a straight line with any of the painting or editing tools, click at one end of the line and Shift+click at the other. Elements connects the two points with a straight line.

Click with Polygonal Lasso and Alt+click (Option+click on a Mac) with regular Lasso and Magnetic Lasso

The Polygonal Lasso creates straight-sided selections; you just click to set the first point in your selection and keep clicking to create additional points.

When working with the regular Lasso tool, you can temporarily switch to the Polygonal Lasso by Alt+clicking (Option+clicking on a Mac). Alt+click (Option+click on a Mac) to set the first point in the selection and keep Alt+clicking (Option+clicking on a Mac) until you finish drawing the desired outline.

When working with the Magnetic Lasso, press Alt (Option on a Mac) and click with the mouse to get the Polygonal Lasso. Release the Alt key (Option key on a Mac) and drag momentarily to reset to the Magnetic Lasso.

However, don't use this approach when you want to add to or subtract from an existing selection. When you have an active selection, pressing Alt (Option on a Mac) subtracts from the selection instead of switching you between lasso tools. So use the Polygonal tool to add or subtract straight-sided areas from a selection.

Adding to, Subtracting from, and Reselecting Selection Outlines

Shift+drag and Shift+click

To select an additional area of your image without deselecting the part that is currently selected, Shift+drag around the new area with a lasso or marquee tool or Shift+click with the Magic Wand.

Alt+drag and Alt+click (Option+drag and Option+click on a Mac)

To deselect an area of the selection, Alt+drag (Option+drag on a Mac) around it with a lasso or marquee tool or Alt+click (Option+click on a Mac) with the Magic Wand.

Shift+Alt+drag and Shift+Alt+click (Shift+Option+drag and Shift+Option+click on a Mac)

To retain the intersection of the existing selection and the new outline you draw with a lasso or marquee tool, Shift+Alt+drag (Shift+Option+drag on a Mac) with the tool. To retain an area of continuous color inside a selection, Shift+Alt+click (Shift+Option+click on a Mac) with the Magic Wand.

Ctrl+Shift+D (⌘+Shift+D on a Mac)

To reselect your last selection, press Ctrl+Shift+D (⌘+Shift+D on a Mac).

Moving, Nudging, and Cloning

Ctrl (⌘ on a Mac)

To move selections and layers, use the Move tool. To temporarily access the Move tool when any tool is active, press and hold Ctrl (⌘ on a Mac). This shortcut doesn't work with the Hand tool or any of the Shape tools.

Arrow

To nudge a selection one pixel, press one of the arrow keys with the Move tool selected or press Ctrl (⌘ on a Mac) and an arrow key with any tool except the Hand or Shape tools.

Shift+arrow

To nudge a selection 10 pixels, select the Move tool and press Shift with an arrow key. Or select any tool but the Hand or Shape tools and press Ctrl+Shift (⌘+Shift on a Mac) with an arrow key.

Alt+drag, Alt+arrow, and Shift+Alt+arrow (Option+drag, Option+arrow, and Shift+Option+arrow on a Mac)

To clone a selection and move the clone, Alt+drag (Option+drag on a Mac) the selection with the Move tool. You can also press Alt (Option on a Mac) with an arrow key to clone a selection and nudge it one pixel. Press Shift+Alt+arrow key (Shift+Option+arrow key on a Mac) to clone and nudge 10 pixels.

With any tool other than — yes, you guessed it — the Hand or Shape tools, you can accomplish the same cloning feats by pressing and holding the Ctrl key (⌘ on a Mac) with the other keys. Pressing Ctrl (⌘ on a Mac) temporarily accesses the Move tool, remember?

Drag with a selection tool

To move a selection outline without moving anything inside the selection, just drag it with a marquee tool, lasso tool, or the Magic Wand. You can also press the arrow key or Shift+arrow key to nudge the selection outline in 1-pixel and 10-pixel increments, respectively. This works with any tool except the Move and Crop tools.

Ctrl (⌘) with a Shape tool

Pressing Ctrl (⌘ on a Mac) with any of the Shape tools brings up the Shape Selection tool, letting you quickly move shapes and lines.

Filling a Selection

Ctrl+Backspace (⌘+Delete on a Mac)

To fill a selection with the background color, press Ctrl+Backspace (⌘+Delete on a Mac). If the selection exists on the background layer, you can also press Backspace (Delete on a Mac) to accomplish the same thing. However, if the selection is on a layer or is floating on the background layer, pressing Backspace (Delete on a Mac) wipes out the selection instead of filling it. So, pressing Ctrl+Backspace (⌘+Delete on a Mac) instead of Backspace (Delete on a Mac) to fill your selections is a good idea.

Alt+Backspace (Option+Delete on a Mac)

To fill any selection with the foreground color, press Alt+Backspace (Option+Delete on a Mac).

Shift+Backspace (Shift+Delete on a Mac)

Press Shift+Backspace (Shift+Delete on a Mac) to bring up the Fill dialog box, which lets you fill a selection with all kinds of stuff.

Making, Switching, and Selecting Layers

Ctrl+J and Ctrl+Shift+J (⌘+J and ⌘+Shift+J on a Mac)

To clone a selection and place the clone on a new layer, press Ctrl+J (⌘+J on a Mac). To cut a selection and place the selection on a new layer, press Ctrl+Shift+J (⌘+Shift+J on a Mac).

Alt+[and Alt+] (Option +[and Option+] on a Mac)

To activate the layer below the one that's currently active, press Alt+[(left bracket) (Option+[on a Mac). To activate the next layer up, press Alt+] (right bracket) (Option+] on a Mac).

Alt+right-click and Ctrl+Alt+right-click (Option+Control-click and ⌘ +Option+Control-click on a Mac)

To activate the layer belonging to a certain image, Alt+right-click (Option+Control-click on a Mac) on that image with the Move tool. Or Ctrl+Alt+right-click (⌘+ Option+Control-click on a Mac) with any tool other than the Hand or Shape tools.

Ctrl+click (⌘+click on a Mac) on layer name

To generate a selection outline from the contents of a layer, Ctrl+click (⌘+click on a Mac) the layer name in the Layers palette. You can use any tool to do the job.

Stepping through the History Palette

Ctrl+ Z and Ctrl+Y (⌘+ Z and ⌘+Y on a Mac)

To step backward one History state at a time, press Ctrl+Z (⌘+Z on a Mac). To step forward one state at a time, press Ctrl+Y (⌘+Y on a Mac). You can change these keyboard equivalents via the Edit➪Preferences➪General menu.

Chapter 19

Ten Digital Facelift Techniques

• •

• •

*N*ormally, we're all pretty fond of our loved ones. But on that one day when a loved one gets kind of pesky — or two days during leap years — it's nice to have Photoshop Elements within easy reach. So, are you mad at your boyfriend for going to Paris with a childhood sweetheart? Just scan his face and while away the hours modifying it in a way he won't soon forget. Peeved at your sister for snagging all of Aunt Rowena's multimillion-dollar inheritance? Open Sis in Elements and distort her as you please. No need to get angry. Just warp your loved one's face and e-mail them the results or tack it on neighborhood telephone poles.

Rather than singling anybody out here, we're going to give digital facelifts to the perfect strangers shown in Figure 19-1. These ladies are from stock photos, making them stock people whom we can feel free to twist and tweak without fear of retribution. If you know one of these ladies — or perhaps worse, if one of these ladies is *you* — we apologize.

Figure 19-1:
Two faces
that cry
out "Muck
me up in
Elements!"

Creating the Movie Starlet Glow

Here's how to create that soft face-flaw-forgiving glow that the movie stars of yesteryear were so fond of. Check out the magic in Figure 19-2:

1. **Select Layer⇨New⇨Layer via Copy or press Ctrl+J (⌘+J on a Mac).**

   This creates a layer that looks just like the background.

2. **Choose the Gaussian Blur filter from the Blur category of the Filters palette.**

   Select a pretty high radius. Try 5.0 pixels.

3. **Lower the Opacity in the Layers palette to 70%.**

   This enables the original image to show through a bit to lessen the blurry effect.

4. **In the Layers palette, change the blend mode to lighten.**

   Doing this applies the glowy, blurry effect only to areas in the layer that are lighter than the underlying original image.

Figure 19-2:
Applying the soft glow in Elements is a lot less messy than smearing petroleum jelly on the camera lens — or your monitor.

Turning the Face into a Button

Find out how to really push someone's buttons (see Figure 19-3) by following these easy steps:

1. **Choose Layer⇨New⇨Layer via Copy or press Ctrl+J (⌘+J on a Mac).**

   You have a layer that is a duplicate of the background image.

2. **From the Bevels category of the Layer Styles palette, double-click on the Simple Sharp Inner Layer Style.**

3. **From there, double-click on the little *f* icon on Layer 1 in the Layers palette, and tweak the Lighting Angle and Bevel Size to taste.**

By the way, you can use the same method to create buttons for Web pages — a tad more practical use of this technique. Create buttons from selections made from images, patterns, gradients, or solid color.

Figure 19-3:
Here's a
button just
begging to
be pushed.

Creating a Painted Masterpiece

So you say you're not artistic? Well, people won't believe you when you show them a work of art like Figure 19-4.

1. **Choose Layer⇨New⇨Layer via Copy or press Ctrl+J (⌘+J on a Mac).**

   You're getting to be quite the pro at this command.

2. **Choose Gaussian Blur from the Blur category of the Filters palette.**

   Set the radius to approximately 6.0 pixels.

3. **Set the Layer Opacity to 80% and the Mode to Darken.**

   This enables the original image to peek through and applies the blurry effect only to areas in the layer that are darker than the underlying background image.

4. **Choose Texturizer from the Texture category of the Filters palette.**

   Select your desired texture, scaling, relief, and light source direction. Figure 19-4 shows the texture set to Canvas, with a scaling of 150%, a relief of 4, and the light from the top left.

In addition to pictures of loved ones, this technique also works especially nicely with color landscape photos. So dust off the old travel snapshots and go to town. And if you think your masterpiece is deserving, add a frame around it by using the technique described in "Framing the Goofy Pose" later in this chapter.

Figure 19-4:
Just think
of what
Leonardo
could have
done with
some
Elements
filters.

Giving the Face a Bath

If you're only slightly piqued at your loved one, you may want to make his or her face appear under water, as shown in Figure 19-5. Here's how to submerge the image:

1. **From the Distort category of the Filters palette, choose Ripple.**

   There are lots of great face-mucking features in the Distort category. Check them out when you have a spare moment or two.

2. **Select Medium from the Size pop-up menu in the Ripple dialog box.**

   The Small option isn't enough, and the Large option is too much. As with the baby bear in the famous story (Snow White and the Three Pigs, wasn't it?), Medium is just right.

3. **Enter any old Amount value you want and press Enter (Return on a Mac).**

   Figure 19-5 shows an Amount value of 300 in the first image and 999 — the maximum setting — in the second image.

Figure 19-5:
This is what
happens
when you
apply the
Ripple filter
with an
Amount
value of 300
(left) and
999 (right).

Stretching the Face This Way and That

Next, let's try out some manual distortion techniques. Figure 19-6 shows how to distort an image using Transform and Free Transform commands. The following steps tell you what the figure leaves out:

1. **Press Ctrl+A (⌘+A on the Mac) to select the image.**

2. **Choose View➪Selection Edges.**

   Elements hides the selection outline. Otherwise, the outline just gets in your way.

3. **Choose Image➪Transform➪Free Transform or press Ctrl+T (⌘+T on a Mac).**

   The Free Transform command surrounds the image with a box and displays square handles on the sides and at the corners. With the Free Transform command, you can resize, rotate, skew, distort, and apply perspective effects to your selection.

Figure 19-6:
The Free
Transform
command
lets you
bend, pull,
rotate, and
otherwise
stretch a
selection in
whatever
way you
please.

To scale (resize) the selection, drag any handle. Shift+drag to scale proportionately, and Alt+drag (Option+drag on a Mac) to scale symmetrically around the center of the selection. To rotate the selection, move the cursor outside the marquee until you see a curved, double-headed arrow and then drag. To move the selection, drag inside the marquee.

But to really have some fun, use the following techniques: Ctrl+drag (⌘+drag on a Mac) any handle to distort the image freely. Ctrl+Shift+drag (⌘+Shift+drag on a Mac) a side handle to skew the image. And Ctrl+Shift+Alt+drag (⌘+Shift+Option+drag on a Mac) a corner handle to apply perspective effects.

If you don't like the outcome of a drag, just press the Esc key or press Ctrl+Z (⌘+Z on a Mac) to undo it. You can also click the Cancel button (the X icon) in the Options bar.

4. **After you've distorted the image to your satisfaction, press Enter (Return on a Mac).**

    You can also click the Commit button (the check icon) in the Options bar.

Figure 19-6 shows two lovely effects created by tugging this way and that on the crying woman. The left example shows the image skewed and distorted, giving Miss Crocodile Tears shoulders that a linebacker would envy. The right example was Ctrl+Shift+Alt+dragged (⌘+Shift+Option+dragged on a Mac) to create an infant-looking-up-from-a-crib view.

The Image⇨Transform submenu contains individual commands for distorting, skewing, and adding perspective to the image. When you choose one of these Transform commands, you get the Transform box as you do when using Free Transform. Just drag the handles to apply the effect — no Alt, Ctrl, Shift key (Option, ⌘, Shift key on a Mac) combinations required. If you want to apply a different effect, you can choose the desired effect from the Image⇨Transform submenu. Or, just think of Free Transform as one-stop shopping for transforming.

Applying the Atomic Sunburn Effect

Phew, that's enough of that manual stuff. You're entitled to automation, and automation is exactly what you're going to get. This next effect takes a different approach. Rather than moving the pixels around, the Atomic Sunburn effect relies on commands that change the pixels' colors. As you can see in Figure 19-7, the face takes on a kind of eerie luminescence.

1. **Select an image.**

   Make your selection as detailed or as imprecise as you like.

2. **Choose Solarize from the Stylize category of the Filters palette.**

   Sounds like an exciting command, huh? Actually, by itself, Solarize is pretty dull. It makes the black pixels black, the medium pixels medium, and the white pixels black again. Big whoop. But have no fear; we're going to spruce things up a little.

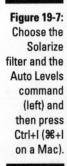

Figure 19-7: Choose the Solarize filter and the Auto Levels command (left) and then press Ctrl+I (⌘+I on a Mac).

3. **Choose Enhance⇨Auto Levels, or press Ctrl+Shift+L (⌘+Shift+L on the Mac).**

   Elements lightens the gray pixels and makes them white, as shown in the first example in Figure 19-7. The areas that were previously either dark or light are now dark; the medium areas are now light.

4. **Choose Image⇨Adjustments⇨Invert or just press Ctrl+I (⌘+I on a Mac).**

   This command inverts the image, turning the black pixels white and the white pixels black, as in a photo negative. The finished result is shown in the second example of Figure 19-7.

Applying the Cubist Look

We created this effect with the 3D Transform filter. This filter isn't the greatest; for example, it doesn't map all sides of the shape. But, hey, Elements isn't a 3D drawing program either! Take it for whatever it's worth. You can check it out in Figure 19-8.

Figure 19-8: The 3D Transform filter gives a new meaning to the saying, "She's kind of square."

1. **Select an image.**

   In this case, the Lasso was used (see Chapter 8) to select the face and hand, which now looks like it was surgically attached to her face. Ah, the wonders of digital plastic surgery.

2. **Double-click the Background in the Layers palette to convert it to a layer.**

3. **Choose Select⇨Inverse and then press Backspace (Delete on a Mac).**

   This gets rid of the background and leaves the area around the selection transparent.

4. **Choose Select⇨Deselect.**

5. **Apply 3D Transform from the Render category of the Filters palette.**

   A dialog box containing a small Toolbox appears, enabling you to choose various mapping types — sphere, cube, or cylinder.

6. **Select the Cube tool in the Toolbox and drag a cube around the whole image.**

   You can resize the cube by dragging on the cube's handles with the white arrow. To move the cube itself, drag on a side of the cube.

7. **When you have the cube positioned the way you want, select the Trackball tool (black circle with a curved arrow) in the Toolbox and drag the cube to rotate it.**

8. **Use the Pan Camera tool (to the left of the Trackball) to move the image if needed.**

   You can also use the Field of View and Dolly sliders on the right side of the dialog box to adjust how large the image appears against the background.

9. **Press Enter (Return on a Mac).**

   Elements may take a couple of minutes to render the image, so be patient.

Stamping the Face in a Marble Haze

A fairly weak name for a wonderful effect. The following steps alternatively lighten and darken the image, utilizing a cloud pattern that ends up looking a lot like marble, as you can see in Figure 19-9.

1. **Select an image.**

2. **Apply the Difference Clouds filter from the Render category of the Filters palette.**

   Of the two Clouds filters, this one is the more exciting. It blends Elements-generated clouds with the selected image using the Difference mode. The first example in Figure 19-9 shows the result of this single-shot filter.

3. **Press Ctrl+F (⌘+F on a Mac) to reapply the Difference Clouds filter.**

   Elements blends the clouds with the image. Things are getting more mottled.

4. **Repeat Step 3 three times.**

5. **Choose Enhance➪Auto Levels.**

   Looking a little dark? Auto Levels brings the colors back to life.

6. **From the Sharpen category in the Filters palette, apply the Unsharp Mask filter.**

   An Amount value of 50% and a Radius of 0.5 should bring back some of the detail. The second example of Figure 19-9 shows how the face now appears emblazoned on a dense, marble wall. At least, that's what the image looks like to us. Feel free to draw your own conclusions.

Figure 19-9: The result of choosing the Difference Clouds command once (left) and five times (right).

Effecting a Total Molecular Breakdown

This technique reduces your image to a bunch of colored shapes and then blends them with the original image to form something truly otherworldly, as shown in Figure 19-10.

1. **Select Layer➪New➪Layer via Copy or press Ctrl+J (⌘+J on a Mac).**

   This creates a layer that looks just like the background.

2. **Apply the Crystallize filter from the Pixelate category of the Filters palette, enter 30, and press Enter (Return on a Mac).**

   Nice words, Crystallize and Pixelate, but what do they mean? Like most of the commands in the Pixelate category, Crystallize subdivides the image into blocks of color. In this case, the blocks resemble little particles of stained glass, as in the first example in Figure 19-10.

3. **Choose the Difference option from the Mode pop-up menu in the Layers palette.**

   Elements uses the stained-glass pattern to invert the face.

Figure 19-10: After applying the Crystallize command to my image, the Difference blending mode was used to mix the new image with the original (right).

4. **Press Ctrl+L (⌘+L on a Mac) and use the options in the Levels dialog box to lighten the image.**

   As things stand now, the image is way too dark to print. The image on the right side of Figure 19-10 was lightened by setting the three Input Levels values to 0, 2.30, and 170, respectively. Press Enter (Return on a Mac) to apply the changes.

5. **Apply the Unsharp Mask filter.**

   The image on the right side of Figure 19-10 uses an Amount value of 100% and a Radius of 0.5, but feel free to sharpen according to your personal tastes.

Framing the Goofy Pose

Sometimes, you're lucky enough to dig up a photograph of your unruly loved one that's embarrassing all on its own — no special effects required. In that case, all you need to do is add a little finishing touch, such as the wood frame or vignette effect shown in Figure 19-11.

The Effects palette contains many nice framing effects in its Frames category, such as the two shown in Figure 19-11. Here's how to create the wood frame effect by using the Effects palette:

1. **Make sure your image is at least 100 pixels wide and tall.**

   If you aren't sure, choose Image⇨Image Size and check the dimensions. (For more info on sizing, see Chapter 4.)

2. **Double-click the Wood Frame effect in the Frames category of the Effects palette.**

   Elements works its magic.

3. **When asked if you wish to keep the Effect, answer truthfully.**

   Our feelings won't be affected either way.

Well, that was easy! To create a rectangular vignette, as shown in the right-hand example in Figure 19-11, follow similar steps:

Figure 19-11: You can easily create a wood frame or vignette effect using the Effects palette.

1. **Select the face with the Rectangular Marquee tool.**

2. **Double-click the Vignette effect from the Frames category of the Effects palette.**

3. **Once again, answer whether or not you wish to keep the Effect.**

Again, what a snap, huh? Bear in mind that you can't just hit the Step Backward icon to get rid of the wood frame or vignette because Elements has actually applied a series of commands to create the effect. You can, however, easily undo the Vignette effect with the aid of the History palette. To undo the Wood Frame effect, you need to have increased your maximum number of History States beforehand from the General panel of the Preferences.

Well, that should do it. If you don't have the anger worked out of your system by now, maybe you should try counseling. Why not dig deep down in your soul and try to be a more forgiving, understanding person?

Then again, the Liquify filter has some terrific face-stretching capabilities. . . .

Chapter 20

Ten Reasons You Might Possibly Want to Upgrade to Photoshop One Day

*B*y this late stage in the book, we'd certainly like to think you're so pleased with Photoshop Elements — and your newfound skills in using it — that the thought of all other image editing applications has completely faded from your memory. But there is one image editor that can probably never be driven from your mind by Photoshop Elements — and that's Photoshop itself. We've already told you that in Elements, you've got the majority of Photoshop's power for a tiny fraction of its price. But still, you could be wondering . . . "What exactly am I missing?"

That's the purpose of this chapter: to give you a good idea of how the power of Elements is extended in Photoshop. This chapter is by no means designed to make you want to spend hundreds of dollars on new software. You've got a great thing in Elements, and unless you plan on making a living creating graphics, Elements is probably the only program you'll ever need. But Photoshop does have some amazing and useful features, and we thought you might be curious about them. So after a good deal of deliberation, we've singled out ten interesting, cool Photoshop features that are missing in Elements.

Now, you'll notice that the word "upgrade" appears in the title of this chapter. It's not a well-known fact, but you can, in fact, upgrade from Elements to Photoshop. The upgrade costs $499 (roughly the price of Photoshop minus the price of Elements), and it's available directly from Adobe only. You can call (800) 492-3623 for details if you're interested.

So, without further palaver, here are the Ten Reasons You Might Possibly Want to Upgrade to Photoshop One Day.

Ctrl+H (⌘+H on the Mac)

What . . . a keyboard command? You should spend hundreds of dollars for a keyboard command?

Well, the absence of this keyboard command is probably the number-one complaint Photoshop users have when using Elements. Pressing Ctrl+H (⌘+H on the Mac) in Photoshop hides the "marching ants" of active selections. The selection is still active and behaves exactly like a normal selection, but the distracting ants don't get in the way of you seeing what you're doing.

True, you can hide the ants in Elements by choosing View➪Selection Edges, but there's no keyboard equivalent. And for diehard Photoshop users, hitting Ctrl+H (⌘+H on the Mac) is like an immediate nervous twitch that happens every time they make a selection. It's a total drag to have to choose a command from the menus instead.

Actually, Ctrl+H (⌘+H on the Mac) can hide other Photoshop features aside from selection outlines, including guides (sort of like individual grid lines you can drag to wherever you want) and annotations (see later in this chapter).

Ctrl+H (⌘+H on the Mac): To know it is to love it. To not have it is to miss it.

The Channels Palette

We've talked about color channels in this book, but when using Photoshop Elements, you have to more or less take our word that they exist. Channels do pop up in a couple of different commands like Levels and Histogram, but by and large they are a phantom presence. Not so in Photoshop; there's actually a Channels palette in Photoshop, which lets you view and edit each color channel individually. You also can directly edit *alpha channels,* which control transparency in images. The fact that channels are a tangible, easily viewable presence in Photoshop makes it much easier to be in complete control of every pixel in your images. Figure 20-1 features the Channels palette showing off another Top Ten Photoshop feature.

Figure 20-1: Photoshop's Channels palette presents conclusive evidence that color channels exist; here the Channels palette is displaying the channels for an image in CMYK color mode.

CMYK Color Mode

Just as RGB color mode rules when viewing images onscreen, CMYK color mode rules on paper. As Color Plate 5-2 illustrates, cyan (C), magenta (M), and yellow (Y) inks absorb different portions of the spectrum of light and bounce back other portions to your eyes. Black ink (K) is also added because in the imperfect real world, cyan, magenta, and yellow inks combine to produce a muddy brown, not black. Since Photoshop is a vital tool for preparing images for print, Adobe lets you work directly with your images in CMYK color mode, as shown in Figure 20-1. Combine the CMYK mode with Photoshop's advanced color management capabilities, and it becomes a lot easier to ensure that a fussy client's teal-and mauve-colored logo will be the precise shades of teal and mauve when it comes back from the printer.

Masking

Actually, Elements already gives you a tiny taste of masking with its adjustment and fill layers (see Chapter 12 for details), letting you determine which areas of an adjustment or fill layer will have an influence on the image by allowing you to paint a layer mask. Masking has a much fuller implementation in Photoshop, with a very handy means of creating a mask located right in the Toolbox (see Figure 20-2). Quick Mask mode lets you create a selection outline not with the marquee and lasso tools, but rather with the painting tools. As with Elements' layer masks, black areas aren't selected, white areas are fully selected, and in-between areas are partially selected. If you don't feel you've ever quite gotten the hang of the selection tools, but the painting tools are like old friends to you, you'll love Quick Mask mode.

Figure 20-2:
Quick Mask mode lets you paint your way to an active selection outline.

Edit in Quick Mask Mode (Q)

Following the Paths

Elements gives you a small sampling of Paths with the Shape tools (see Chapter 14). However, Photoshop gives you a host of tools for drawing your own vector-based paths, as seen in Figure 20-3. Photoshop uses *bezier* tools for drawing paths, which enable you to create shapes by clicking anchor points and dragging control handles. It takes a while to master the bezier tools, but once you do, you can draw any shape imaginable. Once you've drawn a path, you can then convert it into a selection or manage it with the Paths palette.

Figure 20-3:
Photoshop gives you a host of tools for drawing and editing paths.

Eyeing Those Curves

If you thought Levels was an intimidating command, get a load of Curves! True, the Curves command makes using Levels seem positively intuitive, but it can accomplish things that Levels simply can't. By clicking to add points to a line and dragging the points around the graph shown in Figure 20-4, you create a curve that can be used to give you unparalleled control over the brightness levels in your image.

Par for the course, Elements gives you just a tiny taste of Curves in the Adjust Backlighting and Fill Flash commands. Although these one-slider commands are models of simplicity, they do perform Curves-like image correction, letting you bring out details at one end of the brightness spectrum without completely wiping out details at the other end.

Figure 20-4: Photoshop's Curves command can take you down the winding road to improved brightness levels.

Lights . . . Camera . . . Actions

If you think Elements' Batch feature (see Chapter 17) is the coolest thing since sliced bread, then Photoshop's Actions are definitely for you. Batch lets you take a bunch of files and automatically convert them so they have the same file type, image size, and resolution. Actions let you take a bunch of files and do almost *anything* to them. Just set up a new Action, click the Record button in the Actions palette (see Figure 20-5), and then go to town on your image. You can change the image size, apply filters, make selections and fill them, create text layers — almost any operation you can perform in Photoshop, you can record with the Actions palette. And from there, you can perform that sequence of commands on another image with a click of the Play button.

Photoshop also comes with prerecorded Actions — but that's really no big deal because Elements has prerecorded Actions too. "How can Elements have prerecorded Actions when it doesn't have an Actions palette?" we hear you ask. Well, Elements' Effects are actually nothing more than a set of prerecorded Actions given a new name and a nice tidy palette to live in. Of course, you can't record your own Effects, but they should give you some idea of the awesome timesaving powers of Actions.

Figure 20-5:
The VCR-style controls at the bottom of Photoshop's Actions palette let you record and play back a sequence of image-editing operations.

Being an Art Historian

While Elements' History palette lets you travel back in time and reverse mistakes, Photoshop's History palette also gives you the option of sending only *portions* of your image backward in time. The History Brush (see Figure 20-6) lets you paint from a previous History state of your image onto the current state. You could, for instance, apply an artistic filter to your image and then paint from the previous non-filtered state of your image onto the filtered state, in effect erasing the filter from wherever you paint. Likewise, the Art History Brush (see Figure 20-6) packs the whirlin', twirlin' power of Elements' Impressionist Brush with the Art History Brush's time-traveling capabilities, making for a truly creative experience.

Figure 20-6: The History Brush and Art History Brush let you revert selected portions of your image to a previous History state.

Photoshop Speaks!

Okay, this one is truly weird. But if you're passing an image along to be reviewed by a co-worker or client, it's understandable that you might want to also give them a note about the image, saying something like "Do you like this font?" or "Should I Clone Stamp this zit off the model's nose?" The Note tool lets you click and add a virtual yellow sticky note to your image. Of course, it doesn't actually meld into the pixels in the image, but it sort of floats above the surface as a little icon viewers can click to see your comments (see Figure 20-7).

But that's nothing compared to the Audio Annotation tool. Click the Audio Annotation tool on your image, and you actually get a chance to record a spoken message that is embedded into the image. The audio message appears on the image as a little speaker icon; you can double-click the icon to play the message back. While this certainly could be a useful tool for passing comments along with an image, we'd like to propose an alternative use for this multimedia tool: recording mood music to be listened to while your work of art is viewed. Sure, you've done great job of cleaning up that spaghetti picture for the Italian restaurant's ad campaign — but wouldn't it be even more effective if the restaurant owners could listen to "That's Amore" while they're reviewing your work onscreen? We think so.

Figure 20-7:
Audio Annotations and Notes mean that your Photoshop work doesn't necessarily have to speak for itself.

A Little Help to Get Your ImageReady

And finally, one last thing you'll get if you upgrade from Elements to Photoshop is . . . an additional application! Adobe ImageReady is installed along with Photoshop on your hard drive. ImageReady bears a very strong resemblance to Photoshop (see Figure 20-8) but is tailored specifically for creating Web graphics. In fact, Elements inherits its animated GIF-making capabilities (see Chapter 17) not from Photoshop, but from ImageReady. Other Web features that ImageReady can handle include rollover Web buttons that change as a Web surfer's cursor moves over them and image maps that let you assign different Web links to various portions of a graphic.

Figure 20-8:
The
ImageReady
interface
looks
a lot like
Photoshop
— which
looks
a lot like
Elements,
come to
think of it.

Index